THE RESPONSIBILITY OF REASON IN LEADERSHIP, MANAGEMENT, AND LIFELONG LEARNING

THE RESPONSIBILITY OF REASON IN LEADERSHIP, MANAGEMENT, AND LIFELONG LEARNING

JAMEY M. LONG AND
JOSEPH A. PISANI

ANTHEM PRESS

Anthem Press
An imprint of Wimbledon Publishing Company
www.anthempress.com

This edition first published in UK and USA 2025

by ANTHEM PRESS
75–76 Blackfriars Road, London SE1 8HA, UK
or PO Box 9779, London SW19 7ZG, UK
and
244 Madison Ave #116, New York, NY 10016, USA

© Jamey M. Long and Joseph A. Pisani 2025

The author asserts the moral right to be identified as the author of this work.

British Library Cataloguing-in-Publication Data
A catalogue record for this book is available from the British Library.

Library of Congress Cataloging-in-Publication Data: 2024949070
A catalog record for this book has been requested.

ISBN-13: 978-1-83999-350-3
ISBN-10: 1-83999-350-2

Cover credit: Jamey M. Long and Joseph A. Pisani

This title is also available as an e-book.

CONTENTS

v

TABLE OF FIGURES

FOREWORD

The Responsibility of Reason in Leadership, Management, and Lifelong Learning touches on the keystones to effective and impactful leadership. Whether in the corporate realm or in education, leadership is critical to achieving the goals of an organization. What makes this book powerfully practical is that the authors, Jamey Long and Joseph Pisani, touch on the key elements to successful leadership and demonstrate through stories and anecdotes the effect poor leadership decisions have on the culture and morale of an organization. The authors also highlight the importance of ascending beyond situational leadership and truly becoming a transformational leader. They demonstrate how ethics can guide leader's decisions, but communication is the thread that connects everyone to the goals and decisions. The format of this book makes for an engaging read while offering practical applications for leaders to implement immediately.

The Responsibility of Reason is an excellent accompaniment to their prior book, *The Value of Voice in Shared Leadership and Organizational Behavior.* What makes this book an excellent resource is that the authors move the proverbial needle on how effective and impactful people can transcend management and truly emulate the essential characteristics of leadership—how leaders move from an intrinsic perspective to an extrinsic perspective; how they genuinely become servant leaders not just to the organization but to the people who work within the organization and the people served by the organization. *The Responsibility of Reason* is a must-read for anyone interested in leadership.

Dion Foxx[1]

---

1 Dion Foxx, NFL linebacker for the Miami Dolphins, Washington Redskins, and Green Bay Packers. Began his football career as a standout linebacker at Meadowbrook High School in Virginia. He continued his playing career at James Madison University, where he was a dominant linebacker for a very successful JMU program. Most recently, Mr. Foxx has taught at the middle school and high school levels and currently is serving as athletic director for a high school in Richmond, Virginia. Mr. Foxx is currently pursuing his doctorate in educational leadership.

INTRODUCTION

Does this sound familiar? You go to work like any other day as you have done so many times in the past. However, this time when you arrive at work, when you arrive at the parking lot, you find that someone has parked in your spot. Frustrated and exasperated, you lug your heavy bags for work and carry your sack lunch that has been punctured by the corner of your bag. The sack lunch that is now dripping from the juice box only to discover that you are now late for an unscheduled meeting. During the meeting, you are given new guidelines sent down from the very top of the organization. You are doing your job like every other routine day for as long as you can remember. Now you are now asked to do a new task or process. The request that was communicated by your supervisor does not make sense. You decide to ask the all-important question, "why?"

The response you received is the common one that happens in most places of business: "It has come down from the top that this is the new course of action and must get done." There is no more explanation. There is no justification. You ask the follow-up, "yeah, but [...]" and you are not allowed to finish your sentence. There is no more discussion about the topic. You are told to just do it. There is no responsibility for reason.

Too often, decisions are made within all levels of an organization to go in a different direction. Orders from the top are blindly sent out to be followed by the masses. While the organization allows people to have a voice and share what will be done, there is a lack of communication and Responsibility of Reason for what is being asked, which will directly impact both the person and the entire organization. While having communication and a shared voice is a critical component within organizational behavior, it is equally important to understand the importance of what is being said, how it is being said, and the impact the words you say will have on the individual and the company.

To be successful as a system, subsystem, or individual, there must be a value of voice and a Responsibility of Reason to create and sustain shared leadership and effective organizational behavior. Leaders rely on past philosophies based on their current leadership styles to guide them to achieve success. However, all philosophical leadership types and actions will face the same universal issue of being responsible for their actions. Others must be responsible for their reasons in sharing their voice or performing a function in the organization.

The world is broken up into three separate parts: education, management and small business, and organizational leadership. The history of education has been to provide students with the necessary skills required to support local communities. However, that focus has changed with the rapid growth and diverse demands of the communities and stakeholders that require new ways of thinking and resources to support each organization. History has demonstrated that most businesses, specifically small businesses that make up most of the market today, fail within the first five years. In most cases, this situation is due to a lack of proper education, resources, understanding, and a lack of a value of voice and no Responsibility of Reason.

For organizational leadership, there has been a failure to focus on the six major issues. First, organizations and leaders have been heavily criticized for not developing others to succeed them. As a result, large corporations are facing attrition and extinction in the dynamic environment. The second challenge is the inability to lead change. Failure to facilitate change has created static organizations instead of relying on dynamic leaders to navigate change. Third, organizational leaders must address the issue of handling different and diverse perspectives to support the inclusion of all groups. Fourth, imposter syndrome of organizational leadership can develop, causing new leaders to try to "be" the old leader instead of using their own skills and abilities that are needed in the new era of business. The fifth challenge for leaders at any level is to effectively manage resources, make hard decisions, and provide feedback.

With a limited scope and sequence based on the economy or other factors, leaders will need to plan so they can properly manage and leverage their assets. Leaders will need to make hard decisions for the greater good of the company instead of only having a narrow focus on one or a small group of people. Feedback gives an opportunity to get input to make improvements and can ultimately be the key to success. The final challenge of organizational leaders is to make hard decisions and to create feasible benchmarks that support success. In today's environment, it has become common place to blame others and to not take responsibility. Everyone in the organization plays a part in the outcome and should share in the success or failure. This comes down to taking responsibility for your actions based on reason.

While many of the issues plague education, businesses, and individuals today, they are not new. In fact, most of these issues have existed for hundreds of years. Many different theories have been tried to solve these problems. The wheel has been invented and reinvented many times to no avail. Why do they still exist today? The solution is simple. The true meaning of Responsibility of Reason has not been understood and applied. Through the course of this book, the reader will learn how to successfully structure their organization or business to combine management skills that will affect their business and use shared voice to effectively answer the "why" and to develop a Responsibility of Reason. Once you have finished reading this book, you too will be an expert at understanding the "who, what, where, when, why," and "how" of any situation and what your actions will be based on these concepts for your own Responsibility of Reason.

The structure of this book is to divide each chapter up into three relatable areas. First, we will start with a humorous story or situation that is so unbelievable that it must be truc. This small tale will be used as a tool to set up the need for each chapter to make it more meaningful to you (the reader). Following the Part 1 of each chapter there will be a summary of the information and data that was provided in the chapter content along with bulleted points to discuss what is happening in the example provided using logic and Responsibility of Reason. Finally, each chapter will contain a "Simpleton Summary" to provide a quick review of what was covered. The Simpleton Summary also serves as a quick source of information that will contain a model to help create an easy-to-reference guide when you need it most. Whether you are a teacher, administrator, employee, manager, or leader, you will find the layout of the chapters helpful and informative. Finish up what's left of your juice box, put away your cookies, and snack time is over. Now let's get started.

CHAPTER 1

ANCIENT PHILOSOPHY AND THE BLANK SLATE NEEDS MODEL OF RESPONSIBILITY OF REASON

The Situation: Sanity vs. Insanity of Olives

You go out to eat at a fancy restaurant the night before to eat like the king of the world, and you cannot finish your meal. You look at what is left on the plate and think to yourself, "This would make a great lunch tomorrow" at work. With great gusto, you ask the waiter for a doggie bag. You gingerly carry the hand-crafted swan-shaped tinfoil home, put it in your refrigerator until morning, and then go to bed. When the alarm goes off the next morning, you get up, get dressed, and get ready for work. After grabbing your car keys, you go to the refrigerator and delicately take out your swan-shaped meal made for a king.

You drive carefully to work, making sure not to hit any speed bumps that would mess up the neatly placed arrangement of your food. After a long and tedious drive, you arrive at work. You park your car and then proudly walk into the office carrying your leftovers as if they were the Heisman trophy. You carelessly throw your bag on the floor by your desk and then cautiously carry your Swan-covered leftovers to the community refrigerator. When you get close to the refrigerator, you begin to smell something strange. It is not your food as it has been sealed airtight, so it has to be something else. When you open the door to the refrigerator, there is a pungent odor that knocks your socks off. "What is that putrid smell?" you ask yourself in horror and disbelief. You stare into the abyss of the refrigerator and see it's full of stale food, leaking bottles, half-eaten food, and a jar of olives that has been there since you started working 10 years ago.

"This is insanity," you say in disbelief. "Someone, a sane person, should clean this out. No one in their right mind would want to use this refrigerator." Then you look at your perfect swan in its pristine magnificence and tinfoil beauty. Then, without another thought, you hold your breath and shove your swan in next to the nuclear olives and close the door as fast as you possibly can. You pay no attention to the fact that the long neck has now bent down, causing the swan to hold its head in shame. "I can't believe people live like that," you blame the rest of your coworkers. "Whoever is responsible really should take ownership and clean this up for the rest of us," you say to yourself. "We are all civilized human beings after all."

As you walk back to your desk to do work, your coworkers get together, look at one another, and shake their heads. "There he goes again," they say, "putting something else in the refrigerator, leaving no room for the rest of us."

"It's a sad state of affairs," said another employee.

"I agree," said yet another. "Our refrigerator could be an exhibit at Ripley's Believe It or Not."

After a long pause and a moment of silence for another lost item that went to refrigerator Heaven to die, "Do you think he will ever remember to eat those olives he brought in?" asked the new guy. "They've been here since I started working here [...]"

Philosophy in Education, Management, and Leadership

What is the Responsibility of Reason? At first glance, the question seems easy enough to answer. However, that belief would be wrong. The answer to this question is very complex. To begin to answer it, one must first understand the different theories and methods that have led to the way people think, act, and respond. The first thing to look at is responsibility and what it really means. Responsibility is when an individual or organization does something that they are supposed to do and fully accepts the results of their decisions and actions. When being responsible, one does what they say they will do and then willingly takes the rewards or punishment for what was done. This means that responsibility is more than just doing a duty or task that you are asked to do. Instead, responsibility depends on the task of dealing with and taking care of a situation for yourself along with the others that are involved in the decision or action.

Second, when answering this question, it is essential to understand reason. Reason is the cause or motive for a condition or situation, which is used to define and explain the results of a decision or action. A reason is required for any situation where a certain outcome is needed to see if the actions are plausible and appropriate. The goal is to have the actions match the words for an accurate judgment to be made on the success of the outcome based on the person's logic, perspective, and philosophy. As a result, reason relies on logic. The more powerful the logic, the better the reason for solving problems to make sense within a given environment. Finally, reason has been used in the past by ancient philosophers, in the present by managers and emergent leaders, and in the future to support the behaviors of organizations.

Now that reason and responsibility have been explained, their meaning must be traced back to their roots in ancient philosophy. Philosophy and the ancient philosophers are very important to study. However, when most people hear the term "philosophy," they begin to get that glazed look over their eyes and do not want to read any further. The philosophers and topics discussed in this chapter will be critical to understand since their theories are used today by each person, educator, manager, and leader. That's right. You are a philosopher. This chapter is not designed to just give you a history lesson about each philosopher and their theory. Instead, these philosophies will be used to help you better understand your responsibility, reason, and leadership style. Philosophy will explain why we act and respond in a certain way. It will ultimately explain the difference between sanity and insanity in how we turn decisions into actions and then take ownership of those choices.

It is necessary for us to discuss Socrates, Plato, John Locke, and other philosophies of business and education. It is through their reasoning that we have reached Maslow and other models based on human and business needs used in education, management, and organizational behavior. Through philosophy, the responsibility of the past is directly tied to the reason of the present by demonstrating the importance of communication and logic to improve the future. It is important to compare, contrast, and explain the different philosophical views that have been used across the world and why countries and different entities have a diverse application to these theories in their decisions and actions. Each of these philosophies and philosophers has been used to create educational theories, management and leadership theories, and governments and countries. Once we understand the logic of the philosopher, it can then be tied to a behavior that goes into creating a leadership and management theory or practice that is appropriate to survive in the global environment.

To begin our journey of philosophy, let's start with a "Tablu Rasa" and a fresh beginning to build our own Blank Slate Needs Model of Responsibility of Reason. When studying any philosophy, there is an ideal belief known as idealism that looks at the reality of the world compared to that of the individual. Idealism is the belief that the thoughts or ideas in everyone's mind are the central environment that defines reality. While some idealists believe that any form of the world exists outside of an individual's mind, others hold the belief that the properties or objects do not hold any fundamental value when they are free from the mind's ability to perceive them. Third, if an external world does exist, then individuals will not truly know anything about it. Instead, what people can understand about the outside world is only based on the perceptions that are created by our minds.

The next philosopher was Augustine, who believed that education was a process and required a desire to expand an individual's mind to critical thinking and new ideas. This belief is based on being skeptical and questioning anything and everything, which does not seem to support logical thinking. Like the example of asking "why" at a company to your superior when given a task, and if the response is "because I said so or that is what we were told," one should be skeptical and seek more truth to gain critical knowledge. Logical thinking is critical to gaining knowledge in education and developing a high level of reasoning to determine fact and truth. When education is gained by an individual, it can lead to happiness. While growth is needed in the learning process, everyone also comes into the learning process with an inborn nature or ability to initiate the reasoning process to improve the sight of one's mind, which we refer to as reason.

Some observers argue that the realist position makes a strong plea for facts and basic subject matter. Realism is the belief that the "view" or "reality" of material things, and possibly of vague ideas, exists in an external world independently of our minds and perceptions. Next, realism states that value, knowledge, and reality exist separate from the human mind. Regardless of whether the human mind can comprehend or perceive an object, the object still exists in the physical world. If a person chooses not to believe something is the way it is, that does not change the true nature of the subject matter. A person can choose their own perspective, but in doing so, they may accept or reject the basic facts of the subject. As a result, all matter has a specific type of matter and form.

Realists rely heavily on facts as part of their belief system. Facts refer to "the reality that makes a statement valid and true." Next, realists use an empirical approach to the learning process. Based on what can be proven with facts, a belief system is then determined and formed. Second, realists use the scientific method to study something or a certain subject. Once the results have been proven, the result becomes a fact to the realist observer. The fact is then used as a building block to lead to higher understanding, creating a new fact. Finally, realists use the gained and understood facts as part of their belief system based on observation and inductive thinking of rules that are applied to the material world.

The realist approach also has affected the teaching methods used in education today. First, some topics in schools implement both religious and scientific realism. Second, realists do not believe that the personality of the teacher influences the learning process. Regardless of personality, the facts remain the same in the transference of knowledge from teacher to student. Instead, realists focus on the method of teaching. Only through exposure to facts will students begin to learn. Schools that follow the realist approach will therefore only focus on teaching facts, and teaching in every subject is conducted using the same generic methods.

The realist approach in today's education has forced schools to focus on a fact-based instead of a faith-based approach to learning. By only limiting teaching to the believed knowledge of this world, the true understanding of the laws of the universe cannot be achieved. Only relying on old facts will eliminate any future knowledge from occurring without the implementation of faith or the belief that new facts can be discovered. As a result, realism can cause a narrow-minded belief in the learning process. If what is already learned is thought to be true, then there is no reason to continue seeking wisdom.

However, the greatest difference between classical and modern realism is the emphasis placed on human factors. Classical realism relies on human and domestic factors that relate back to ancient traditions of a culture to form a singular belief system. The belief that existed long ago is the root of all knowledge that we know today. This can result in all information being based on ideas and concepts developed from ancient history. On the other hand, modern realism relates ideas and concepts of the past with what a person knows and experiences using inductive and deductive reasoning to determine the facts of the physical world. Francis Bacon and John Locke believed that people are not born with "any inborn, natural, or preconception," but rather are a "blank slate," which is used as the foundation of modern realism.

Another difference between classic and modern realism is that classic realism only looks at past knowledge. The answer is believed to already have been solved, resulting in no new knowledge being formed. Unlike classic realism, modern realism uses new logic along with existing information to develop new knowledge to get a broader view of the universe. The understanding of individuals will manifest through new logic. By applying new thinking and logic, the people living in the modern world will develop the potential to examine the facts of the past with the help of new information to create a new understanding of reality.

One more difference between classic and modern realism manifests itself in education, particularly in the curriculum of today's schools. Classic realism relies on the teaching of established facts and does not rely heavily on a faith-based approach to learning. What was learned and understood long ago is still believed and taught today as fact. However, modern realism believes that how the facts are learned is an important part of gaining knowledge and that everything should be considered. The learning method of the teacher becomes more important in the learning process as they will guide the students through it. The method that the teacher uses will be copied by the students in how they shape their learning and form new ideas.

The method the teacher uses to communicate information can cause students to become disengaged and potentially not want to learn anything new about the subject matter. Next, the thoughts, opinions, and methods used by a teacher can be biased and not allow room for creative or new methods of seeking facts about a subject. The knowledge is expected to be accepted as fact because it was said by the teacher, without the students being able to ask or truly understand the "why." As a result, students can learn a "fact" without understanding the theory behind the result and are required to accept the answer based on "faith."

Another major philosopher was Plato. Plato was a Greek philosopher who studied under Socrates. Like Socrates, Plato believed in the universality of the inner-rational being. It is important for one to be true to oneself. Socrates also believed that a life is not worth living if it is unexamined and not studied. Next, Socrates believed that the dialectical method of inquiry was necessary to argue against the new and old beliefs of a person to find truth and fact. While Socrates taught Plato the dialectical method, he did not have his own definition of truth. Instead, Socrates believed that "real" truth and knowledge came from a person being able to learn shared or universal beliefs related to piety, virtue, and the dichotomy of good and evil.

Unlike Socrates, Plato did have a definition of truth. Plato believed that truth was based on and depended on being. With Plato's truth, there exists an eternal truth. An eternal truth is the belief that when a person interacts with another person or a thing during a period, it will eventually die or become worn out. However, the concept of the person or thing will live on within the person. The thoughts or interactions with the individual regarding the person or thing will remain relatively unchanged. As a result, the perception of the person or thing will become relatively eternal to the person as long as they exist.

Aristotle believed that each piece of matter has a meaning and purpose. Since each object of matter has different properties, everything is believed to have a particular and unique purpose. No two people or things will be the same in the world. However, objects can share similar characteristics that help establish universal properties. Understanding both the particular and universal properties enables an individual to grow in their knowledge. Next, Aristotle stated that when people learn, they maintain the characteristics of children. While the body of the individual grows, humanness remains through the developmental and learning process. This situation can cause form to remain constant while matter will change over time. Through the growth process, people can begin to gain knowledge and a better understanding that will lead to living a good life.

Based on Aristotle's belief, there is a specific order and design for the universe. Everything that occurs happens in an orderly way. When something happens, the event can be understood by studying all the events that have occurred over time, creating purpose. For humans, the main purpose is to think. If we do not think, then we are not living well. To live a good life, we must do something that is a means to living and should be done to continue living. Failure to perform an action will cause an individual to live poorly and will take away from the meaning of life.

With the two varying definitions of truth, Plato's definition of truth is both relative and absolute through his forms. The one form of the world is based on absolute truth that does not change. Things are how they have always been. Ideas were more than real things and existed universally throughout the world. However, Plato's second form of the world is based on interaction and physical things. While someone can interact with a physical thing, the idea behind it is still absolute, but the understanding of the person will be relative due to their limited interaction or unique experience. Since everyone's interaction with the physical object will be different, a relative truth will be created based on each person. As a result, Plato's idea of truth is absolute in that truth always exists but is relative to a person's potentially distorted interaction with the physical world.

The idealists have their own view of the appropriateness of contemporary life. With idealism, there is a central belief in the ideal and its interpretation through experience. Sensory interactions of a person are what make something real to the individual, so they can understand the ideal. Through consciousness, an experience is gained while laws exist in the components of thoughts and ideas. This situation can cause a relationship between universality and individuality. In contemporary life, idealists would view this time as a part of the bigger picture. While it is relevant today, modern life is only a piece of the wider perspective of eternity. While something may be relevant today, the real truths will transcend beyond this time. Next, idealists would believe that there should be internal relations and the coherence of truth. The reality of a person during modern times is a "building block" to the "wall" of truth in eternity.

Idealists react in a positive way to the emphasis on technical and specialized education in schools today. In education, students should learn the truth about all things. Modern schools have established standards of learning and methods to help scaffold various levels of understanding for all students. Idealists would most likely support the creation of universal truths and the teaching of education to help create an ideal or single belief. This strategy can be necessary to help everyone to develop a shared understanding of the eternal history of learning and knowledge.

Technical skills create specialized people; there is a required practicality to the education that supports the universality of the needs of the world. However, it is important to not let the form of the material world replace the "laws of nature" that exist universally in our laws and ideas. When the emphasis on technical and specialized education in schools today is placed on a practical approach, it will help to eliminate any narrow-minded thinking and a decreased desire for universal wisdom. When the emphasis on technical and specialized education in schools today is based on supporting ideals, then new inventions and methods of learning these truths will become more dominant in the world.

In Eastern philosophy, there are four main areas that include Chinese, Indian, Japanese, and Middle Eastern beliefs. The main beliefs of Eastern philosophy include mysticism, inner peace, and intuition of oneself. Through Eastern philosophy, there have been many different religious ideas and beliefs that include Christianity, Islam, and Judaism. Some of these Eastern philosophies were used to influence Western culture. Two of the main philosophers to borrow from Eastern philosophy to influence Western culture were Augustine and Aquinas. Augustine used Platonic philosophy along with religious beliefs. Aquinas relied on Aristotelian philosophy with Christian theories. Aquinas believed that moral philosophy is thinking about what one should or should not do based on the use of opportunity within. With the help of Augustine and Aquinas, Middle Eastern religion was combined with Christian beliefs that originated from Aristotle and Plato to help form international religious beliefs and organizations.

There is a comparison of what Dewey borrowed from Bacon and Locke in developing his philosophy of education. It can also be determined how Dewey used their insights in developing his own views on education, as well as how he differed. Dewey believed in the democracy of education. In the *Democracy of Education*, Dewey believed that education and learning of knowledge should have a naturalistic approach. The naturalistic approach to learning focused on a person interacting with their environment and gaining knowledge and understanding from those exchanges. Through these observations of the world, the individual develops their own ideas and hypotheses that relate to truth through the manipulation of the environment.

Next, John Dewey believed in pragmatism. When studying pragmatism, there are no ideas out there to just be discovered. Ideas serve as tools to help people cope in the real world. With this belief, a single individual does not create an idea. Instead, an idea is created within a social structure or group of people through their shared actions and understanding. The truth of the idea is based on the success of the application of the theory. As a result, ideas can become dependent on individuals and their current environment and experiences.

Dewey also borrowed his beliefs from philosopher Francis Bacon. Francis Bacon thought that what was once believed could now be proven wrong with science. Dewey believed in the scientific method to collect and catalog information. Based on the information gathered, reliable data would be applied to help determine the correct solution as it relates to the individual. The nature of the experience is what can help to identify and define the main idea about a situation. Based on the experience of everyone, a different idea or belief can exist in the world due to their unique experiences and the impact and result of those interactions with the material domain.

There are some advantages and disadvantages to the pragmatist view on curriculum used in education and by companies as a process rather than a mere body of subject matter. Through pragmatism, ideas that include enlightenment, the technological revolution, and humanism have evolved and become part of the world's culture in learning and education. The pragmatist point of view has helped to push education in a new direction by using science and facts to study topics that include economics, psychology, ethics, politics, and education in society. With natural growth and development from childhood through adulthood, all interactions and knowledge will be gained to help create a biological, flexible, and natural method of learning and understanding for everyone.

Pragmatists prefer flexible education and learning methods for each person. Flexible educational methods allow for a more customizable learning environment that can better meet the needs of students from different ages and cultural backgrounds. Next, pragmatists desire functional schools that provide resources that can match the needs of each child. Laboratories and facilities may be used to simulate real-world examples within the current society to help support learning. Finally, pragmatists do not believe in a single authoritarian teaching method. Instead, pragmatists use multiple avenues and resources to help children learn that include textbooks, libraries, museums, and taking field trips to historical locations so they can experience things themselves using various formats and stimuli.

Philosopher Rorty believed that global human rights in a culture were created by using sentimental education. Empathy is required in teaching children or other individuals so they can potentially better learn and understand other people's plights and sufferings. When empathy is used in teaching, people become more connected and can better put themselves in another person's shoes to understand their point of view. Language and emotion are used to support education so it can best make sense to the person being taught. Since people come from different backgrounds, cultural influences will need to be used in teaching that support the area or community of learners.

Incorporating political, cultural, and social context will support the content of the lesson while answering the "what's in it for me" question of the student so they can learn the importance of what is being taught. As a result, once a cultural context has been applied to the educational theory, the student will stay engaged in the lesson and improve their level of knowledge. This strategy can lead to improved understanding, new critical thinking skills, and an improvement in educational learning for each student.

When looking at the different philosophies and philosophers' perspectives, there are some major differences between Western and Eastern thought on education. Eastern thought of education is more collaborative and collective for students, which is different from Western education, where learning is more singular. In Western education, the focus is on the sole success of the student instead of the combined understanding of all learners within the culture. Next, Eastern philosophy and religion stress inner peace, tranquility, intuition, mysticism, and attitudinal development. Third, Eastern philosophy and religious views are a combination of four major areas of thought that include Chinese, Indian, Japanese, and Middle Eastern. The philosophical beliefs of the East have affected the West to include Christianity and Judaism.

Finally, the views of Eastern philosophy involve the individual focusing on understanding the universe and the process of endless becoming for the learner to become the teacher. As a result, the main point of life is for every individual to try and achieve nirvana so they can transcend oneself and to be reborn. Next, Eastern philosophy and religious views treat the relationship with other human beings by teaching that everyone is connected to one another. Life is not about the self but rather about the group. Individuals who believe in Eastern philosophy in education will learn to conform to their own beliefs to meet the needs of society. This situation can cause human beings to practice conformity instead of focusing on individualism.

In education, Eastern philosophy seeks to teach the individual the purpose of living. Rules and order are used in classroom teaching to help each student conform to the needs of society. Second, Easterners focus on passive learning. Passive learning occurs when students gain knowledge from the teacher and are then expected to remember and apply the given knowledge. Third, Easterners gain knowledge from their teachings of religion, which impacts the way students gain knowledge. Within the classroom, the instructor is responsible for the learning process. As a result, there is no freedom or democracy in the learning process. What does occur is that the learning structure is very rigid and structured to maintain the status quo of learning.

In contrast, Western philosophy education is centered on the teachings and beliefs of major historical figures such as Socrates. Socrates and the Socratic Method are used to find the truth and logic behind the subject matter. The main goal is to question what exists to determine and understand the beliefs, actions, and views of the subject matter instead of accepting what has been passed down through history. While there are universal truths, there is also the goal to encourage students to find truth for themselves and to use reason in their daily lives to achieve idealism.

Next, Western philosophy in education works to create and build a community and achieve solidarity among its members. Learning that occurs from all students in all subject areas should be combined to improve critical thinking and potentially lead to a more comprehensive understanding. Intelligence and knowledge are guided through educational activities and the participation of the learner. The Western philosophy of education seeks to grow and increase the educational potential of new possibilities by making connections. Existing and new perspectives and paradigms are united and combined. This situation can lead to combined perspectives so new and unified ideas can be developed and implemented to benefit everyone in a shared environment. Ideals and subject matter are constantly evaluated and then reevaluated to hopefully make new connections and improve what is known, leading to a better understanding of the truth.

Finally, Western philosophy uses advancements in technology and various learning settings to improve the engagement of students so they can have unique learning experiences to make education more accessible and shared with those around them. As a result, students will learn the importance of the connection between existing and new ideas to help make better decisions that benefit others through the investigation and analysis of human understanding.

In the past, education and schools were used to introduce individuals to new concepts, social cultures, and traditions. The belief was that schools were a place to learn and gain knowledge through exposure to different subject matter and ideas. However, technology and industrialization modified cultural traditions and how things were done. As a result of the changes brought by modern science, George Counts believed progressivism would not be successful in the future or best serve the needs of society. Instead, reconstructionism was needed to enable instructors to take a more forceful role in making political changes. Finally, George Counts criticized progressivism for its lack of ability to allow instructors to address the current and future issues of social change in the classroom. To fully engage students, Counts knew that students needed to be engaged in a curriculum that was directly tied to impending societal issues.

Reconstructionism has major strengths and weaknesses. For a society to survive, everyone must be able to contribute to combating social problems. It is a shared community of knowledge to help improve the social affairs that impact everyone in the culture. To accurately prepare students for their role in society, the education of each student should occur outside of a classroom and in society instead. This situation can enable each student to gain a real-world perspective on current issues and better understand the impact they have on the daily lives of society. With reconstructionism, learning will occur outside of the classroom in real-world situations to help show the value and importance of what is being taught. Today, Career and Technical Education (CTE) uses this strategy to fully engage students in workplace readiness and apprenticeship programs while in school to gain useful skills and resources that are based on the idea of reconstructionism.

When there is only one perspective, a narrow lens or understanding can exist, leading to the loss of new knowledge and understanding. For reconstructionism to succeed, society and educational institutions must develop a world community that is united around common goals, objectives, and shared understandings. A world community is important to connect everyone in society to each other. Next, a strong sense of brotherhood is needed so that everyone sees other people as their family instead of being separated from themselves through goodwill. Finally, reconstructionism relies on democracy. Democracy is required to enable the people in society to determine what issues need to be addressed and how society will function. While reconstructionism creates a strong framework for learning, it can lack the ability to provide truth and knowledge outside of what is decided to be taught and how that information is communicated.

According to reconstructionists, there is a certain kind of person that would make the best teacher. Reconstructionists believe that the kind of person that would make the best teacher is an advocate with a strong belief in social change. Social advocates help to bring about social change and justice that support the common community. Social advocates also promote human understanding and give voice to those around them within the entire community. Education should work to benefit everyone in the society or community around them, and students should be taught this skill in school by learning advocacy as it relates to all subject matter.

There are two practical actions teachers can take to bring about the changes that reconstructionists deem so necessary. The first practical action is innovation. During the Cold War, teachers developed new programs and materials that would help students gain a better understanding of science and math to improve technology and advancements in modern society. The potential goal of innovation is to advance society to achieve things they previously did not have or understand. For innovation to succeed, each teacher must develop new assignments and curricula that match the changing needs of society. With new knowledge, higher levels of understanding exist, which will lead to refinements of existing ideas and can generate new thoughts and advancements through innovation. The changes that are developed will impact education in the future and have a lasting effect on each student.

The second practical action for teachers to bring about change is to not only look at the needs of education for today but also to focus on the future needs of society. While it is important to understand the current needs, those needs will change, and it is critical to plan so the quality of life can be sustained. Teachers should develop workshops for elementary, middle, and high schools. These workshops would be designed to prepare students with real-life examples of problems that they will one day face, including global warming, nuclear war, and greening the environment. An example is global warming and learning how what we do today will impact the world and future generations. Events of the past and present must be studied so new innovations can be made to change negative impacts and support new growth. As a result, the practical action required is for instructors to apply the scientific method to explore new methods to prepare students for the present and future problems in society.

Society today is facing new issues that never existed before. With the development of technology, germ warfare and nuclear war are real possibility. For the first time in history, humans can annihilate themselves with their technological advancements. To prevent disaster from occurring, instructors must prepare students for the potential impact of current actions and how they will impact the entire society. Second, instructors must use a worldview or perspective to incorporate the viewpoints of minorities and all the various cultures in the world that make up a global community. Since society is made up of different races, traditional methods of learning conducted in one area are not always appropriate when trying to bring about change for everyone involved. Finally, reconstructionists use these methods to forecast the future. This strategy works to support students to think about the possible outcomes of his or her action and to determine the best course of action that not only benefits them but also those around them through reconstructionism.

To support the behaviorist belief, teachers must use conditioning techniques to reinforce desired behavior. Conditioning in behavioral psychology is a theory that is based on the direct response to a stimulus that can be modified through conditioning and learning. An example is an instructor using a computer program to teach a math lesson to a student. When the student gets the question right, he or she can move on to the next lesson. However, if the student fails to provide the right response, he or she will remain in that lesson until he or she successfully completes it or pass. When using a computer program, the teacher can reward the student for the right answer and punish the student for the wrong response. This situation can help establish the desired behavior that leads to success while reinforcing unwanted behaviors or outcomes.

As a result, the student will become conditioned to understand that they can only move on to the next lesson once the previous lesson has been successfully completed. This technique is critical to the learning process of the student because it enables independent learning for everyone while establishing the behavior of the classroom. Behaviorism also creates an environment that uses scaffolding to help students learn since new information or subject matter is not released until the previous lesson has been mastered. Consequently, the teacher can observe the behavior of each student and can then use linguistics to describe the reaction to define the pattern of behavior.

There are at least two ways that behavioristic values have been incorporated into today's teaching. Interpretations as to whether these developments are educationally sound and backing your argument can also be determined. The first behavioristic value that has been incorporated into today's teaching is conditioning. An example is when a dog being trained is introduced to meat powder and an individual enters the room; it will begin to salivate in expectation of being fed. The response of the dog is based on past stimuli that when a human comes in proximity with meat, it will be fed. As a result of this situation, the behavior of the dog can be learned by the individual to predict how it will react each time this event is repeated. If the introduction of the meat powder when the individual enters the room changes, the dog will change its behavior and will not always salivate in expectation of being fed. Behaviorism relies on consistency to reinforce a desired action or outcome.

The instructor in the classroom will also condition students. Conditioning in the classroom occurs when the bell is rung at the beginning of the day. Once the student hears the loud, familiar sound of the bell, they become aware that the class is about to start. Each student will then respond to the stimulus by putting their things away and getting ready for their school day to begin. The ringing of the bell is a catalyst and is responsible for the learned routine of the students each day during the start of class. Next, the bell rings at the end of the school day. The sound of the bell will cause the student to pack up their things to go home. As a result, each student becomes conditioned based on the external environment and will conform to the needs of society based on learned behavior. However, when there is a deviation from the behavior, new behaviors will be learned to compensate for the lack of the original or established stimuli.

The second way that behavioristic values have been incorporated into today's method of teaching students is to use control and to reject innate freedom inside of the classroom. Skinner believed that everyone has already been predetermined by his or her genetics, parental upbringing, and religious beliefs. People only know how to respond to an event based on what has been learned or observed within society. Learned behaviors begin with a child's parents, who establish the rules and beliefs, and then by others in society based on religion and other social conventions. As a result, control is a predetermining factor for the learning process that will create learned or controlled behavior within the person. To overcome control, instructors in the classroom must rely on positive reinforcement. Positive reinforcement helps to motivate the individual to achieve the desired result. With positive reinforcement, something is being added to encourage the individual to repeat the behavior. An example is when a student gets an answer right and the teacher says, "great job." The student will continue to want to give the right answers to receive verbal praise from the teacher.

Unlike positive reinforcement, most teaching relies on negative reinforcement that punishes the student for the wrong response and does not encourage learning or participation in society. Negative reinforcement is when someone takes something away in response to a certain situation or event that is unwanted. An example of positive reinforcement is for a teacher to provide an intrinsic reward or affirmation to a student for participating and providing the right answer. If a child participates but does not get the answer right, the instructor can still encourage the child to participate and help him or her find the right answer to further the learning process. However, negative reinforcement can occur in the classroom if a student does not follow the rules or talks out of turn, causing them to lose recess as punishment for the unwanted behavior. Since the student will not want to lose their recess time, he or she will not talk out of turn and will learn the consequences of the undesired behavior.

To benefit society, reconstructionism can use a curriculum that encourages new possibilities and actions through unique experiences both in and out of the classroom that provide a positive benefit. These different methods used in the classroom can include discussion board responses, verbal communication, group work, and classroom interaction. Fishbowl is another effective method for formative assessments since it involves all students and encourages participation during the class. When probing or open-ended questions are used, the student can share their knowledge freely instead of answering a checkbox on a test. This situation can enable the student to openly share his or her understanding using their learning strengths. Next, the teacher can use guided questions to engage higher-level thinking to support more open-ended responses based on each student's learning strengths.

Social groups in the classroom can be used to promote social reform through projects that study and analyze current issues that need to be addressed. Second, assignments that focus on social realization through direct interaction will be required to promote an attitude of goal orientation and bring about positive change in society. Studying government and civics is a good subject matter to teach students how civilizations were formed and governed using positive and negative examples and then encouraging students to build their own forms of currency and government structure to support the people.

Education must be founded on a specific purpose to improve society using a worldview approach instead of focusing on the micro-economy and what will only impact the small area where you are located. Third, Makarenko believed that education should be established through the collection of ideas from loyal and reliable groups with which an individual can identify and be an active member. Within the established group, everyone would learn his or her role to understand their own independence while also supporting the interests of the group. Each person would contribute to support themselves while also catering to the needs of the entire society or community.

With all these different philosophies and from an analytical perspective, the teacher is given a prominent role when instructing students to help enable them to strive to impress upon students about the relation between logic and language. Using the scientific method and logical thought is important when truly understanding a subject matter, concept, or idea. Next, the rational and logical techniques that are used to improve cognitive thinking must support the theories of modern science that study nature, society, and formal science to help support known rules and laws. Third, analytic philosophy uses language as the primary tool to communicate the results. Challenges of using common or ordinary languages arise not only from word-for-word translation, but also the literal translation and the linguistics of the language that must be properly understood, such as tone and syntax. This situation can cause the beliefs and ideals of society to be incorrect and ultimately misunderstood. Only when using logic and mathematics that rely on rules can someone accurately articulate and communicate an idea or thought.

From the analytic perspective, the main role of the teacher is to focus on logical positivism. First, teachers must be able to clearly communicate and clarify the topic to the students. The more logically the teacher can present the material, the more useful the material will become to the students, enabling them to potentially apply what they have learned in the real world. This situation can help students within society to understand the logic of the current ideologies that are used within the culture to help it maintain its stability or make advancements for the future. As a result, the teacher will use logic to help students gain a better understanding of the material and to gain more meaning from their education that not only supports themselves but also the collective community.

The role of the teacher is to emphasize the relationship between logic and language. Teachers must be aware of how complex language can be based on its diverse usages and meanings. Based on the words used to describe a topic, the teacher can influence the thoughts and beliefs of the students. The teacher must try to remember to only communicate facts using clear and concise language so that it is easier to understand and less subject to misinterpretation. To communicate topics, teachers can use different methods of teaching, as well as various forms of media to express the right meaning of the subject matter. Finally, teachers must focus on pragmatic and practical research instead of personal beliefs to teach students to keep the learning factual instead of based on opinion.

Based on these factors, the demographic of the classroom will be more diverse than at any time prior in history. In the past, the demographic was made up of Anglo-Saxons. The population in schools will increase to include different cultures, new institutions and definitions of what constitutes a family, changing family norms, and language diversity. The teaching field is also being filled with younger teachers. Within the next 20 years, schools will continue to become even more diverse. Minorities will make up more of the population of students and account for significant growth in the number of students who will graduate from public schools. Schools will continue to become more inclusive and serve students from across the globe, those with special needs, and those students who speak different languages. Schools and teachers will need to continue to rethink how schools teach and how children learn. This situation will require the philosophy of modernism, where rational thought and ideas rely on science and technology to support individualism in learning. Technology will play an important role in this transformation to provide an equal and fair education to each student in the future, which is a major issue facing schools as they address the sociological factors surrounding cultural diversity and need, stratification, school board curriculum regulations, and other newly proposed curricula within their school districts.

This point is demonstrated in Figure 1. With every great decision or action, there must be a core concept that it is centered around. The core is responsibility and reason. The individual or organization must take that seed and plant it firmly within the organizational culture and shared leadership. The education that was used to make each employee the most valuable resource will flourish and spread its roots throughout the entire hierarchy of the business. The philosophy, knowledge, and education that are learned will then be combined with the management and leadership objectives and goals to produce long-term shared value and voice within the business.

FIGURE 1 Seed for reason of responsibility.

Simpleton Solution

There has been a lot of information thrown at you in this chapter. If you are like us, writing it made us feel like we were back in college with our heads spinning, trying to understand all the different philosophers and their theories in philosophy class. We used to ask, "Why do managers or leaders need to know this stuff?" My professor responded with the generic answer: one day there will come a time when you need this information again. As much as it pains me to say, they were right. We must admit it since it helped us to write this book. Here are the key takeaway points from the chapter to remember:

- There are many different philosophies that come from the Eastern and Western cultures of the world.
- Each philosopher developed their own theories based on their current situation and environment.
- Unique experiences within a given environment help form the thoughts and beliefs of each person when making decisions.
- The world is a diverse place that requires people to understand different cultures and their backgrounds when making a decision or performing an action.
- There are different analytical perspectives that can lead to different decision-making choices using logic and scientific methods.
- All philosophies strive to answer the "who, what, where, when, why," and "how."
- Education is important since it is the foundation where information is learned based on philosophical methods to teach individuals how to acquire and perceive data.
- Management relies on what it learned through education to make more informed decisions in current and future environments based on its unique perspective.
- Leaders rely on philosophy to develop a mission and vision statement that will be used to determine how the company will operate and the Responsibility of Reason that is needed to make top-down and bottom-up decisions in both the internal and external environments through both shared leadership and voice.

The main takeaway from this chapter is to recognize and understand sanity vs. insanity for the reason of responsibility. Insanity happens when the same process is repeated while expecting a different result when no factors are being changed. However, sanity is having a healthy state of mind. Decisions are made based on facts and quantitative data using logic to come up with an expected outcome. The best decisions are those that rely on logic and relate back to one of the ancient philosophies to support the decision-making process. No matter what your philosophy is, it must answer the "who, what, where, when, why" and "how" of the situation and work toward a positive solution. If you have not done so already, figure out which philosopher you most relate to when making decisions. Share this information in the classroom or with your staff at work so everyone can understand the logic in your process. This will flip the switch between sanity vs. insanity for the reason of responsibility. Like the moral of the story about the nuclear olives, one person may think they know what is going on while someone else has a different point of view, leading to misperceptions of the truth and how decisions and actions are carried out in everyday life.

CHAPTER 2

INTRODUCTION TO THE RESPONSIBILITY OF REASON

The Situation: Rollin' with the Punches

The sounds of summer had faded, and the new school year was rolling in. I drove into the parking lot with Kid Rock's "All Summer Long" blasting one last time out of my windows in a last-ditch effort to hold on to my suntan of freedom. Administrators and teachers were going back to school to begin plans for the students who would be arriving the following week. With only a week left, there was too much to do with too little time. On the first day back, administrators at every school called a meeting to welcome the teaching staff back and to set the tone for the new year. The content of the meeting at each school was the same: to set the tone, objectives, and goals for the year. Since the morale at the school was at an all-time low, the administration wanted to try something new. At this school, the message was delivered through a uniquely themed presentation to try to boost morale and to give a purpose for their annual meeting.

Each administrator came into the auditorium in a costume from their favorite movie with the theme music playing in the background. Favorite characters from the movies *Top Gun*, *Barbie*, *Indiana Jones*, and *Heavy Metal*, were present and applause was given as the teachers appreciated the humor of the situation. As the administrators lined up, there was one missing. "Where is Delilah?" asked one of the teachers.

"You know her," replied another teacher under their breath. "She is never around when she is needed. We probably will not see her until the end of the school year. She always skates by."

Just then, the room went dark. Strobe lights colored the ceiling and walls. Then a loud rumbling sound could be heard from behind the door. The doors swung open, and in she rolled. Delilah was wearing a fluorescent tank top and athletic wear as she sped into the auditorium on her shiny roller skates. She did a few laps around the room, weaving in between the aisles, until she came to an abrupt stop at the microphone at the front of the auditorium. She obviously was showing her love for the roller-skating cult movie hit, Whip It.

While on her roller skates, she curtsied to the crowd of teachers. "Welcome back, everyone," said Delilah. "I cannot wait to get things started off right this year."

"That would be the first," said Ted, who was a veteran teacher at the school and had heard all this before. "Sometimes I think there is a better chance of her solving a 10-year-old cold case file than the administration taking more responsibility for their actions this year than before."

Sitting next to Ted was a new teacher. Her name was Tilda. Tilda was not as disillusioned as Ted and wanted to believe that good things were coming from Delilah.

"Are you ready to have fun this year?" shouted Delilah.

A few teachers halfheartedly responded, "Sure, why not."

Delilah did a few crossovers and then the moonwalk on her roller skates to Michael Jackson's "Thriller." "I can't hear you!" shouted Delilah as she moved backward. "I said, Are you ready to have fun this year?"

This got the crowd excited. They saw the dedication she put into learning to roller skate and hoped the same passion would be used to support them this year. Everyone burst out with, "Yes, we are!"

The crowd began to chat and enjoy themselves as they let their guards down to enjoy the show. The teachers began to mingle and work collectively to have fun, something that they had not experienced since teaching online. It was a refreshing start to the school year, and the teachers were having fun being in a mandatory meeting. However, Delilah was growing impatient that they were not paying attention to her as she continued to do her tricks on roller skates. "Everyone needs to pay attention to me," said Delilah.

The crowd of teachers continued to talk to one another. The principal listened as they were talking and realized that they were having a positive bonding experience. He was happy since he had long wanted his teachers to support one another. Before he knew it, Delilah began to yell into the microphone. "Now everyone," she said in a different tone from before, "do I have to use my mommy voice like I do with my children with you, as if you were toddlers? You know that meetings are not for having fun. They are for me to deliver important information to you."

Ted, Tilda, and the other teachers instantly paused and stopped talking with one another. Tilda could not believe what they had just heard. The principal watched as the smiles turned to frowns, and the joy and excitement about being back at school quickly faded off into the sunset. Ted just looked at her with a sad, supportive look of understanding. Without having to say it, he knew she now experienced the mixed messages that were constantly being provided by Delilah as part of the administrative team. This put a damper on the mood, and the tone was set for the year, echoing the same as that of past school years.

"I thought she was genuine when she wanted us to have fun in our jobs," said Tilda. "Does she not take any responsibility for getting us excited and then changing what she wanted? What is the reason for that?"

"No one knows," replied Tom. "If you are going to work here, you just have to learn to roll with the punches."

When the meeting was over, everyone left the auditorium dejected and no longer excited to have returned to work. They got in their cars and drove away faster than Delilah could roller skate.

As for me, I got back in my car. Counting Crows' "A Long December" began to play through the speakers. *That's exactly how I think this school year will be,* I thought to myself as I began to sing along. "And the feeling that it's a lot of oysters but no pearls" summed up how we all felt about returning to school this year.

Planting the Seed of Reason for Responsibility to Grow

The Responsibility of Reason and the value of voice in shared leadership are important to all organizations. Together, the Responsibility of Reason and the value of voice ultimately seek to answer the "why" of a decision and the shared voice that was used in the process to ensure that the proper action is taken. When making decisions, the leader will need to relate back to their education and learning theories that were provided in the previous chapter. Leaders will need to show the use of the Responsibility of Reason in the chronological process of decision-making, through implementation, and then shared support to develop a sound process in achieving an inclusive model for organizational behavior.

When applying these theories, we are all students of learning, no matter our age or position within an organization. Each leader needs to compare the cognitive and constructivist theories of learning when making the right decision in the given environment. Cognitive theory focuses on learning that is based on the individual academic needs or requirement of each student. Next, cognitive learning theories work to explain how all internal and external factors or stimuli experienced by an individual will influence his or her mental processes to supplement and enhance the learning experience. Since the levels of development and comprehension are different for each learner, teachers must provide a variety of learning experiences using scaffolding techniques and social interaction to support the learning process of each student. This strategy is based on social cognitive theory. As a result, leaders must build upon the structure that their employees learned in school and incorporate the same logic and structure into their organizational behavior. We will now look at some of the different theories that have impacted individuals since they were young and have come to structure how they learn and operate today.

The main belief of social cognitive theory is that an individual is born with skills that are intrinsic to themselves. First, self-efficacy is required, which enables the individual to have control and execute their behavioral outcomes. Second, behavior capability is needed to understand the skills required to perform the desired or expected behavior. Third, expectations are needed to determine the outcome of the change in behavior. Expectancies are also needed to place a value on the outcome of the changed behavior based on the internal skills of the child. Fourth, self-control is required to monitor and regulate the individual behavior of a child. Fifth, observed learning by watching the outcomes of other individuals is important to model a child's behavior through modeling. Finally, reinforcements using rewards or punishments are necessary to direct the desired change in behavior.

Cognitive theories of learning enable individuals and learners to group information, allowing for the assimilation or integration of material to be developed and understood. Once the information is understood, the student is then able to build a connection or make a direct link between one concept and another to further their learning development about the topic. This strategy is based primarily on Piaget. There are different concepts from Piaget's theory that apply to cognitive theories of learning and the abilities of each student to process and comprehend information. First is equilibrium. Equilibrium occurs when there is a balance between assimilation and accommodation. The more development that occurs, the better an individual can understand and process what they are doing based on their mental schema. The second part of Piaget's theory is organization. Organization explains how experiences are related to each other. Information and experiences are combined to make the individual thinking process more effective and efficient.

Adaptation is the ability of a child to meet situational demands. As a result, adaptation relies on assimilation and accommodation. When a child can recognize an object as similar to another similar object, like a whale to a fish, then they have shown assimilation. Accommodation then must occur when the child is able to recognize new information. While recognizing the whale as similar to a fish, the child would then be able to state that the whale is a mammal. With this process, the child has created a balance between themselves and the world. Adaptive functioning is matched to the situations of the event.

In cognitive theories of learning, learning is described in terms of information processing. The first way to process information is with dual coding theory. Dual coding theory is the belief that when a teacher uses different types of stimuli or senses of learning, the student will be able to encode the information more effectively so it can be recalled more accurately at a later point in time. The second method of processing information is cognitive load theory. Cognitive load theory focuses on sensory memory, working memory, and long-term memory. The human memory model is based on the belief that because you have had an actual experience, you now have a memory of how to act in that situation. Your action is based on firsthand knowledge that is relevant to the experience that you had through your working memory.

Working memory is the capacity to hold small amounts of information in an active and easily accessible state for short periods of time. The main idea behind this model is that information is stored and then recalled for short- and long-term purposes. Through experiences, sensory information is gained, and reactions and thought processes become "hardwired" actions based on given responses. Cognitive theory of multimedia assumes that the human brain or mind is dual channeled instead of a single or linear channel. This situation means that the brain must have multiple methods of stimuli to make the information being processed relevant. A dual channel is necessary to increase the learning capabilities of a student since the brain has a limited capacity for storage and requires an active processing system for understanding information and stimuli from the environment.

Constructivist theories focus on how learners construct their knowledge instead of just relying on passively taking in information. When learners experience new concepts and skills, he or she will reflect on those unique experiences to create and establish their own representations and incorporate new information into their preexisting knowledge stored in their memory recall. The Social Constructivism teaching strategy allows for a range of consortiums and interactive methods of learning. Examples of interactive teaching methods under Social Constructivism methods include total class discussions, fishbowl conversations, think-pair-share, small group discussions, or students working in pairs on given projects or assignments to learn a topic or lesson objective.

This strategy is also useful for leaders by having meetings and informal observations by management walking around to gain information before making decisions.

Knowledge and experience are not necessarily a result of observing the world but rather result from many social processes and interactions. The goal under Social Constructivism is to enable students to attach meaning to their learning experiences through a direct and unique relationship to the material. It is not so much about the result but the journey that was created during the learning experience. Instead of a traditional lecture format, teachers will need to find ways to enable students to come up with their own questions and reasons for learning, which will lead to the desire for future learning. Classrooms must become more integrated with technology and learning material that extends beyond a textbook and the limits of the classroom walls. The use of technology and new resources will challenge students to learn in new ways and to consistently participate in self-organized and other creative activities. Dialogue and communication will be an important part of the learning process. Students will be able to directly communicate in class with the teacher or each other while having virtual communications, such as Zoom meetings with working professionals or going on virtual field trips with tour guides providing real-world perspectives.

Learners are directly involved in the journey of learning, as all barriers to communication and the subject matter will be removed. Another Social Constructivism technique revolving around communication tools is virtual and blended learning. Virtual and blended learning are important parts of education. Virtual learning allows students to learn from a remote location. In the past, students used to only go to school and did not have to work. In today's world, many students go to school while working or have other obligations that limit their time to attend school. With virtual learning, the way students learn and access material becomes more readily available. Next, more students can attend school and have access to information and resources they once did not. Third, virtual learning has replaced traditional learning methods that enable students to work at their own pace and to complete work around their schedules. As a result, students can do more things at one time instead of having to choose what needs to be done and when.

Blended learning is also known as hybrid learning. Blended learning is a mixture of traditional methods mixed with technology and online resources. Essentially, the student gets the best of both worlds by having some onsite instruction mixed with virtual methods of completing work and modules in a remote location that is more conducive to his or her environment. For blended learning to be effective, it must be based on a well-thought-out plan and course design. This method is very important since it uses various modes of teaching methodologies. The benefits of virtual and blended learning are an increase in student engagement, time management, flexible scheduling, autonomy of learning, improved accessibility, advanced learning outcomes and goals, and courses tailored to the individual preferences of the learner.

Based on the prominent theorists that include Dewey, Bandura, Vygotsky, Piaget, Bruner, and Freire, the goal is to create a learning experience that is familiar and meaningful to all students. Data is then gathered to show the successes or areas of improvement in the classroom. New and improved insights into technology and learning management are developed for future learners based on the immersion of learners in the lesson unit or objective. Hands-on learning will take place in the use of computers, student devices, virtual field trips, virtual meetings and lectures, and presentations. Next, the learning environment becomes more dynamic and engaging for the student. Third, work is completed in both an individual and a group dynamic.

Exploration and empowerment of the student also play an important part in the classroom. The time constraints on learning are eliminated with flipped classroom capabilities, providing more opportunities to learn, which increases the motivation and desire to learn. All social constructivist integration strategies work to provide deeper learning skills, cooperative group skills, increase the relevancy of the lesson to the lives of each student, and promote different critical thinking skills that enable students to solve problems on their own as they occur or develop based on the lower and higher levels of pedagogy (methods of instruction) using educational technology as the backbone to learn. As a result, the social constructivist integration strategies will integrate creative problem-solving skills into each lesson or subject, establish mental models to improve the transfer of knowledge, establish cooperation between groups of students, and provide a diverse and culturally responsive approach to all situations based on the current social change and environment.

Assimilation is a necessary component in the theories of learning. Assimilation refers to the process of taking in new information. Once new information is gained, the individual will take the new information and fit it into an existing paradigm or set of learned and established processes. However, when focusing on accommodation, the individual will use the newly learned or acquired information to revise and redevelop an existing knowledge or idea from their stored memory using memory recall. As a result, cognitive theory's primary focus is on how information is gained, stored, and then recalled, while constructivist theory focuses on taking the knowledge and finding unique ways to create a new learning experience based on the interpretation and connection with the learner.

The school is described as a complex social system. First, a school is composed of many different departments, activities, and people. Within the confines of the educational institution, the school must reconstruct and create a new society through fields of study with higher levels of educational objectives and goals. The learning process is done through learning new material and through forming patterns of relationships with other students, teachers, and administrators, all working toward the same common goal. Through this process, both formal and informal relationships and structures will emerge to help everyone contribute to the learning process and establish a school culture and diverse society. As a result, a school is a complex social system.

Today, there are more pressures placed on students and teachers while they are in school. Students come from many diverse backgrounds and socoeconomic structures. As a result, the norms and rules established within the educational system must meet the changing demands of the population of students it serves. First, there is a change from a national to a global perspective of education based on the current needs of the economy and the desire to produce students who can be successful worldwide in various industries instead of helping a local economy.

The main goal of teaching is to address contemporary issues. The only way to benefit students fairly is for schools to address the issue of cultural diversity by reconstructing the curriculum that includes the interests and beliefs of each culture. It is necessary for teachers to take such actions to bring about changes that reconstructionists deem necessary. Cultural diversity and community factors look at the area where the school is located. The three types of areas for schools are suburban, urban, and rural. Each type of school district area will be impacted by economic factors. Economics can also create a barrier to learning within schools set in suburban, rural, and urban locations. Students from different backgrounds will not learn at the same level or have access to the same learning resources. The instructional methods of the teacher and school must match the needs of the community. The community factors are based on the socioeconomic status of the community.

Socioeconomic status is a major factor for at-risk students or communities. The types or styles of teaching will be based on the available resources and skills required to keep students in school. Diversity is an important factor. Classroom diversity is used to benefit a school and its teachers by utilizing the unique characteristics and traits from a diverse population. This strategy will enable a teacher to improve their effectiveness and efficiency by forming an assorted classroom strategy from different cultures and viewpoints. As a result, the teacher can meet the needs of diverse students and market segments. The language, lingo, or slang that is used must match the language and diversity of the student body within the classroom. Using diverse language is important to provide an all-inclusive classroom learning environment for all learners.

When teachers take community factors into account when planning lessons, they should also use colloquialisms and idioms that make the most sense to the community of students. When giving examples to support the lesson content, it should relate directly to the students. In southern states, teachers would use the example of sweet potato pie, whereas in northern states, using the example of pumpkin pie would be more appropriate. To make an impact on students, teachers need to develop a frame of reference for all students, which helps to increase the desire and motivation to learn. If these factors are incorporated into the lesson plan, teachers will be able to engage more students in the classroom and increase their learning potential.

Schools address issues outside of the material taught within a classroom. Schools focus on the social and emotional processes that exist within the school culture. Third, schools have complex and established formal cultures as well as complex informal social cultures that learners must navigate to thrive and succeed in school. The formal culture is one that the adults, including the principal, administrators, and teachers, have shaped to govern the interactions of the staff with students. This process also applies to the relationships between students and students.

The behavioral expectations that have been established are then shared and communicated among all members of the school society. The informal socio-emotional culture is how learners engage and interact with each other in a social dynamic. Finally, how people choose friends and which circles of students an individual chooses to associate with will be based on societal standards, group norms, and different cultural structures. Physical and visual norms and cues that include clothes, hair, and style will be followed based on the need to fit in and be accepted by other students, helping create different groups within a social culture, making the school a complex social system.

There are several critical aspects of the teaching-learning process. The main job of a teacher is to help support the needs of individuals and learners within the classroom. Next, teachers work to understand and create a unique environment for learning so a direct connection and relationship can occur between the student and the material. The goal is to create a special learning environment that fosters and supports higher learning based on individual experiences and feelings. As a result, the overall goal is to create a process where learning and education become meaningful and beneficial to each student.

For teaching to occur, one person must share knowledge with another. The person who learns the knowledge will then share the information or process of learning with someone else. This situation results in the interchange of information between different people, causing people to become both students and teachers. The goal of teaching or imparting knowledge is for one individual to advise or guide another person to a higher level of understanding. The teaching-learning process is based on three different models. The second aspect of the teaching-learning process is experiential learning. Experiential learning involves the unique experiences of the individual in the learning process that help to enhance the overall understanding of the topic. The third process is cognitive learning.

There are different types of cognitive learning that include concept learning, problem-solving, and cognitive strategies. First, concept learning describes the "process by which experience allows us to partition items in the environment into classes for the purpose of generalization and recall." Second, problem-solving is the ability to develop a search process for a solution to a given problem based on a desired outcome and any possible alternative paths or strategies. Third, cognitive strategies are the specific methods or ways that learners use to solve given problems and to find new opportunities for future situations. Skills included in this process are critical thinking, planning, utilization, and rational reasoning.

With the use of the teaching-learning process, there are seven different components. The first is to engage, where the student completes an activity that creates a connection between the student and the material. The second step is to explore, where the teacher encourages the student to closely study a topic and then gain higher learning by diving deeper into the subject. Third, students must explain the topics they have been learning about through the activity and be able to communicate their level of understanding. The fourth process is to elaborate, which is done when the teacher has the student work directly on an assignment. The fifth process is to evaluate, where the teacher determines the level of understanding and comprehension of the learning process gained by each student through their submission of work and assessments. Sixth, the teacher will extend additional help and resources to enforce the learning process of the student so he or she can apply their knowledge to new situations. The final step in the teaching-learning process is to develop standards. Standards are part of a lesson or educational plan that is established by the school board or department of education to determine a standardized result and level of understanding.

The teacher-learner process is where the teacher assesses the needs of the students or learners by establishing learning objectives. Next, this process creates teaching strategies, develops a learning plan, and assesses the outcomes and success levels of each student. Overall, teaching is the process of connecting needs, learner experiences, and feelings to create new learning opportunities. Next, the main purpose of education is to make learning and the process of gaining new knowledge useful and meaningful to the learner. This situation creates a process of understanding, demonstration, and facilitation for individual intellectual growth. The teaching-learning process is the creation of a safe environment where all learners can interact with one another and exchange ideas on how to learn and gain knowledge. Finally, the focus of the teaching-learning process is to establish a technique that focuses on the sharing of information and fosters the collaboration of knowledge, skills, attitudes, beliefs, values, and a shared community. Classroom diversity is used to benefit a school and its teachers by utilizing the unique characteristics and traits of a diverse population. This strategy will enable a teacher to improve their effectiveness and efficiency by forming an assorted classroom strategy from different cultures and viewpoints. As a result, the teacher can meet the needs of diverse students and market segments. The classroom will become more successful, and the teacher will be able to make better decisions in the future to help benefit their student population.

One can achieve the right balance of teaching facts and teaching for discovery and understanding by successfully integrating the correct perspectives for learning. First, facts must be given for learning to begin to occur. All necessary information must be provided to the students, so they have all the resources to succeed in the learning objective or goal. The best way to communicate facts and the commitment of that information to memory is through rote memory. Rote learning is the process and ability to memorize information based on duplication and repetition. Rote learning assists learners in understanding a concept by repeating the process repeatedly until it becomes firmly implanted in their stored memory for easy recall. This situation relics on lower-level thinking skills.

There are aspects of the human memory model view of memory and learning that have the most important implications for instruction. A model of human memory is based on the information processing theory. For data to become information, it must first be relevant and applicable to the learner. The information given should be directly related to the individual so they can develop a response to the situation. The understanding and development of a response are done using three main processes involved in human memory.

The first process is encoding. Encoding is the input of information into the memory system based on internal and external factors. Once sensory information is received from the external environment, the brain then labels and codes the information related to the situation. This situation leads to the automatic processing of the data by analyzing factors such as the time, frequency, and meaning of the event.

The second process is storing. Storing is the process of taking newly acquired information into your memory and then modifying it for easier storage and retrieval when it is needed. Information can be stored in short-term memory for temporary use or long-term memory for processes that will become hardwired into our thinking and actions. The third process in human memory is the retrieval of information. Retrieving allows a person to reaccess information from the past that has been stored in their brain. The previously stored information has already been encoded and stored for either short-term or long-term access based on the needs of the individual.

There are several content factors within the three processes of human memory. The first factor is the volume of material. The greater the volume of material, the harder it can be to encode the information for future use. Second, the degree of organization of the material is important. The more organized the material is, the easier it will be to encode and then retrieve. Third, a high level of familiarity is required to better encode and access the saved information. Fourth, the structure of the content is important to understand the beginning, middle, and end of the material so it can become easy to access. Finally, the nature of the material must be understood. The material must be directly linked to the individual, so they know where and how to encode, store, and then retrieve the data for all relevant future responses.

The human memory model view of memory and learning have the most important implications for instruction since it applies prior experience to new settings. Training your brain will help learners in the classroom remember more information and make it relevant and applicable to the lesson. Working memory is required cognitive or mental skill for both the student and the teacher. The human memory model is also used to help strengthen the students' conscious processing of material and information. Teachers must use different techniques that include repetition, visualization, relevance, games and activities, and peer teaching to help improve the learning process so all information can be properly encoded, stored, and then retrieved. The human memory model and learning are important applications for instruction because they cause creative tension. Creative tension is necessary to help force students to think outside of their comfort zone. Teaching students new and unfamiliar topics will help to expand their learning process and foster a more culturally diverse understanding of their metacognition of the situation.

Next, students will use this model to help process new information and solve a problem within an unknown scenario. While younger students rely on cognitive processes to improve their development, older learners will use the human model to develop strategies in the learning process to make the material more meaningful to them on an internal level using expressive encoding. Finally, social interaction facilitates learning by encouraging students to expand their knowledge and see things from a broader perspective. Once the broader perspective has been established, a better method of encoding the material can be achieved based on the perspective and input of other students, creating a more desirable learning activity within the learning process of the classroom.

The cognitive learning theory posits that both implicit and explicit learning will occur for the student in the classroom environment. Implicit learning refers to what happens or develops with the learner without a mindful effort using memory recall. Explicit learning focuses on what happens to the learner when he or she makes a conscious effort to remember. This situation means that learning will develop with both internal and external factors within the classroom. Coursework and social relationships will combine to create a unique learning experience for the student or learner. Classroom material and social interaction will work together to create a unique learning experience that will be stored in the student's memory based on his or her interaction and real-world experience. As a result, collaborative learning becomes prominent in the classroom.

Collaborative classrooms encourage students to work together on an assignment or project that they helped design. Throughout the school year, students will be given the chance and opportunity to work with other students on a variety of tasks and objectives that become part of the greater group goal. Second, collaboration within the classroom focuses on collaborative teaching and learning methods that work to help empower female students to think for themselves and to become equal partners in the learning process within the group dynamic.

Collaborative classrooms enable parents, teachers, and others from outside the classroom to come into the learning environment to share their knowledge. Based on the success and expertise of the outside individual or classroom visitor, students get to see how learning is used in the "real world" and become encouraged to learn and then apply the material to their own lives so he or she can develop their own unique experiences. Fourth, collaborative classrooms provide an environment that combines and shares the knowledge of various teachers teaching the same class. A free exchange of ideas is provided and then integrated into the different classrooms that share the same subject area.

Motivational strategies can be used when promoting student learning and understanding. When a student is motivated to learn, he or she will try harder and work longer to learn. Next, motivation yields higher-quality results and helps students perform better on both formative and summative assessments. Student motivation is directly tied to the internal desire to learn and grow, based on the student being directly tied to the lesson and developing their own experience with the subject matter.

The motivational strategy that is the most motivating for students is to personalize their objectives. Personalizing objectives enables us to motivate students with many different methods. First, students are given a voice and choice in the tasks they are required to finish. Second, students' culture is taken into consideration since each person is valued and heard. Third, differentiation is an important component of personalizing the objectives. Differentiation tailors the material in the lesson to meet the specific needs of students considering different learning styles, cultures, and learning abilities among general ed, ELs, gifted, and special needs students. Fourth, adaptive learning occurs in the learning process. Adaptive learning is the delivery of custom learning experiences that address the unique needs of an individual through just-in-time feedback, pathways, and resources instead of a canned or one-size-fits-all learning approach within the classroom environment.

Next, pacing becomes important. Pacing is used to help motivate students and to personalize the objective by enabling each learner to learn at their own pace based on their individual skill level and learning strengths. Objectives and goal setting are created based on the time requirements of the learner to keep them measurable and attainable for the student. As a result, the motivation of the student increases and promotes learning instead of decreasing and leading to disengagement.

With motivational techniques directly tied to instruction, the learner is able to use any branch from the main topic to personalize the learning experience by focusing on their area of interest, which will then lead to the learning of other modules or categories. Next, this strategy allows students to be flexible in their learning and to have a choice in how the knowledge is gained. Learning then becomes fun and interactive for the student, creating positive motivation to learn more. Third, personalizing objectives will connect the learner to the lesson so they can directly identify with the learning through personalized experiences.

This situation makes learning relevant and valuable to the student. Additional learning goals and objectives are then sought by the learner on their own cognition instead of being explicitly told to learn the subject. Finally, personalizing the objectives matches the strengths of each student throughout the entire learning process to help promote direct knowledge, memory recall and storage, personal connection, and new experiences that will continue to motivate the learner to want to learn new subjects.

Finally, motivation helps to create and lead to thoughtful learning by putting the student directly into the learning process. Students become the center of teaching and learning when instructional materials use techniques that include scaffolding and self-efficacy. Both situations create environments that release the learning to the student and create a student-centered learning environment instead of a teacher-centered environment. The teacher must use a combination of internal and external motivational strategies that celebrate learning milestones and benchmarks to encourage higher-level learning for all students within the classroom.

To make good decisions, information is required before any action can be taken. All changes must be based on data and the impact of the results on the students. The first step in "preparing students for knowledge base" that is needed to enable student learning is to use inference and predictions. The process of inference relies on the knowledge that comes from a conclusion that is based on existing data or facts. The students' prediction is important since it will further the learning process by generating curiosity to see if they were right or wrong based on what happens next.

Next, the principal, teachers, parents, and students must understand the three frames of reference to be considered when determining student grades and results using direct or indirect instructional methods, and the achievement levels of each student. The different types of reference are pre-assessment, formative, and summative assessments. A pre-assessment is used as a pretest to judge the prior knowledge of a student. Using this strategy can be useful for a teacher when gauging the learning strengths of the students. Based on the pre-assessments, the teacher can structure and scaffold the learning objectives to meet the current needs of the class. Pre-assessments also help to assess the learning potential of the student. The student will get an early "preview" of what will be covered in class. Pre-assessments also help students become more comfortable and set the culture and rules for the objectives and goals for the subject.

As a result, the main challenge for a teacher is to effectively use direct and indirect instructional methods to promote student engagement and to establish different effective ways to introduce lesson objectives. The first effective way to introduce lesson objectives is through lectures. Lectures enable the teacher to provide the background information that is needed for student learning to begin. Next, lectures provide the academic vocabulary that will be needed to complete the work in the lesson. Finally, lectures provide direct focus to establish the rubric and parameters of the learning process. Next, a flipped classroom can be used. A flipped classroom is used to provide the material for learning before the students arrive in class. This strategy enables the foundation to be understood so instructional time can be used to have the learning released to the students. The third effective way to introduce lesson objectives is through the academic vocabulary.

When teachers take community factors into account when planning lessons, they should also use colloquialisms and idioms that make the most sense to the community of students. When giving examples to support the lesson content, it should relate directly to the students. In southern states, teachers would use the example of sweet potato pie, whereas in northern states, using the example of pumpkin pie would be more appropriate. To make an impact on students, teachers need to develop a frame of reference for all students, which helps to increase the desire and motivation to learn. If these factors are incorporated into the lesson plan, teachers will be able to engage more students in the classroom and increase their learning potential.

Technology will play an important role in this transformation to provide an equal and fair education to each student in the future, always making classroom policies and rules easily accessible during the school year. Finally, the impact of student diversity on the development of classroom policies and rules will need to be understood to help create and organize a learning environment that is all-inclusive. Next, diversity must be considered when supporting the self-development and self-management of students based on their culture, customs, and background. Third, establishing teaching rules and procedures for classroom use will need to be culturally diverse to avoid one group being given priority over another. Next, diversity will be implemented with technology to help translate the rules and policies so they are easily understood.

In Figure 2, we can see how the same seed for reason of responsibility can either grow to its full potential or wilt away. If the seed of reason of responsibility is not based on a combination of education, management, and leadership, it will be ineffective. This seed will create a "me" instead of "we" organizational culture, causing a poor foundation within the organization. However, when the seed of reason of responsibility is planted in rich soil, a solid foundation will

FIGURE 2 Good soil for the seed of reason of responsibility to grow effectively or ineffectively.

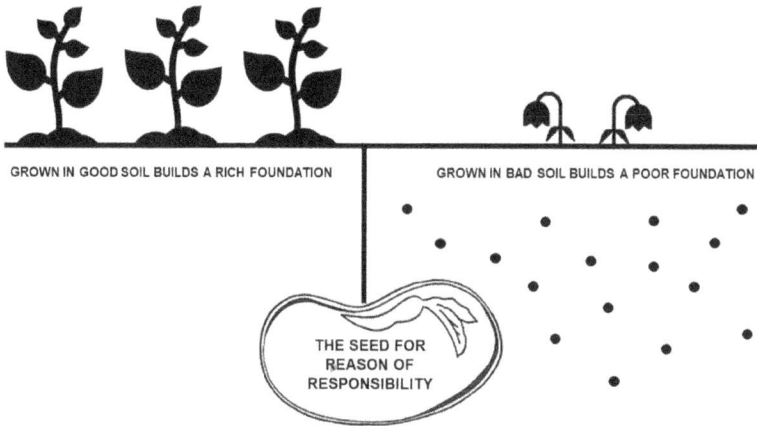

support organizational growth so it can continue to grow and flourish by supporting common objectives and goals. As a result, there will be a Responsibility of Reason in leadership, management, and lifelong learning.

Simpleton Solution

It is important to remember that for Responsibility of Reason to exist, there must be a seed planted firmly in the ground. When the seed is grown in good soil, a rich foundation will begin to grow. Each plant, or entity, will take root and expand the development of the seed. However, if the responsibility seed is planted in poor soil, then there will be inner turmoil, causing the seed not to take root and eventually shrivel up and die.

To be successful, it is important to always remember:

- That a shared voice is important to all organizations.
- To always answer the "why" question.
- To explain the internal and external factors of the reason.
- To rely on cognitive theories to help provide the framework for the journey.
- To base the Responsibility of Reason on supported learning theories with direct and indirect instruction and learning methodologies.

CHAPTER 3

THE REASON FOR THE SEASON OF RESPONSIBILITY

The Situation: Ethics Can You Hear Me Now—Riding the Lightning in Telecom

Jamison J. Matthews was a recent college graduate. He had earned his bachelor's degree in business management and administration. With all that he had learned over the last four years, Jamison was ready to take on the world with his newfound sense of pride and dedication for an employer in his respective field. While his friends were enjoying their summer freedom, he spent his time applying to various jobs in technology and telecommunications. Jamison went on several interviews. He received offers from these companies but ultimately decided that none of them were the right fit.

Finally, he received a request for an interview with East Quick Communications. East Quick was an up-and-coming telecommunications company. Jamison was excited for the interview. He rehearsed his answers and interview skills that he had learned so he would be sure to make a good impression. On this big day, Jamison woke up early. He put on his new suit, shirt, and tied his tie with the perfect knot and length. He was ready. He got into his car and drove to East Quick's corporate headquarters. He patiently rode the elevator to the 13th floor of the large glass building. When the elevator dinged, the doors opened, and he walked over to the reception desk. "I am here for my interview," said Jamison.

"Welcome," replied the front desk. "The director will be with you in a moment."

Jamison waited until the director came out from his double-doored office. "Jamison," said the director, "come on in. Let's get started. The telecom industry is all about speed and efficiency. It does not wait for anyone. We ride the light of technology to the future."

He followed the director into the office where they conducted the interview. During the interview, the director stressed the company's dedication to ethics and doing the right thing. "Many companies in this industry cut corners and do things that are illegal to get big contracts or to get their products to market before their competition," said the director. "Here at East Quick, we believe in doing things right. Ethics is our top priority, and we only hire the best people we know we can count on, and we want you."

"Thank you," replied Jamison. "From what I have heard, I believe that East Quick is the place for me."

"See you on Monday," replied the director.

Monday could not come soon enough. Jamison showed up to work with high expectations and the belief that he was working for a company that would do some good in the world through their strong beliefs in ethics and its people. He walked in 15 minutes early and made his way to the orientation room, where he would be joined by the other new hires. When he entered the room, he saw that there were over 50 people with varying levels of experience and degrees. Jamison wondered if the company was growing that quickly and why there were so many people there. If they only wanted the best, wouldn't they be more selective in their hiring process?

As he sat there, the manager came in. "My name is Stephano," he said. "I will be your manager. Let's get right to it. You will work hard at East Quick. You will work every day, night, during weekends, or whatever it takes to get the job done. No exceptions. Look around the room and you will see that there are many new employees. This is because we think of you as cattle, and you are our new herd. Fail to perform and you will be turned into beef. Welcome aboard."

Jamison and the other recruits looked at one another. He had never worked a "real" job before, so he thought this might be what a company does to motivate its new hires to be hard workers. He was skeptical but had given the company his word that he would work hard for them and did not want to break the loyalty that he had pledged during his interview.

Jamison found a vacant cubicle and tried to go right to work. He sat there with the other new hires, waiting for someone to train them in their job duties and requirements. Hours passed, and no one came. Jamison found an old manual from the person who used to work there and began to try to figure things out on his own. He had some success during his first year there but was never sure if he was doing things right. Since the manager never complained about his performance, he assumed that he was doing things ethically and efficiently. One day, the manager called Jamison into his office. "I am impressed with your work," said Stephano. "I am too busy to manage everyone, so I am making you the new team lead."

"Thank you," replied Jamison. "I will do my best to follow the code of conduct and be a good manager."

Jamison then saw Stephano go back to work on his computer. At first, he thought that Stephano was working hard on a project. In a way, he was. He was writing a letter to one of the team members that Jamison would now be managing. Later that day, Tina came over to Jamison. "Are you our new team leader?" asked Tina.

"Yes," said Jamison, turning to give Tina his full attention.

"I have an issue I am supposed to report to my manager to follow the chain of command."

"I am here for you," replied Jamison.

"Stephano just sent me a letter," said Tina.

"Yes," said Jamison, "I saw him working on it while I was in his office."

"So, you knew about this?" replied Tina with a shocked expression.

"I knew he was writing you some kind of correspondence," replied Jamison. "But I did not know what it was about."

"Read this for yourself," said Tina, and she handed him the email she received from Stephano.

As Jamison read it, his face became redder than his hair. The email was filled with inappropriate comments and sexual harassment statements that would make anyone uncomfortable. *In a company that supports ethics, how could this happen?* Jamison wondered, but he had been here long enough to see many other things he could not explain and knew did not match the ethical code that they claimed to support.

"Is this the first one you have received?" asked Jamison.

"No," replied Tina. "This is the seventh. I tried to gently get out of the situation by saying that it was wrong to be involved with your direct supervisor. His solution was to make you my team leader so there would be no direct conflict in his mind."

"This is still a violation of the company's ethical code of conduct," said Jamison. "I will do something about it."

"Thank you," said Tina. "You will be the first person here I can count on and trust if you do."

Jamison wasted no time. He took the email up to the director of human resources (HR). When he went to tell the HR director about the situation, Miss Carol said she would take care of it immediately. Jamison left thinking that everything was under control. What he did not know was that not only was

Stephano sexually harassing Tina, but he was also having an affair with Miss Carol. Miss Carol punished Stephano by transferring him back to California. Later that week, the company announced they would be doing layoffs due to poor performance. However, the layoffs only occurred with the staff that was supervised by Stephano on the order of Miss Carol.

That Friday, Jamison went to lunch. When he came back, he found himself locked out of his machine. Five minutes later, he was called into Miss Carol's office. "Due to layoffs and other circumstances you have been involved in," said Miss Carol with an evil smile, "you are being laid off and your employment terminated."

A security guard then escorted Jamison to his desk. Once his desk was cleared, the security guard walked Jamison out of the building, where he had to sit on the curb. Jamison looked at the others he had worked with. They were all sad and crying; they lost their jobs while Jamison was sitting there smiling. He was finally happy to be free from the company that violated its ethical policy and did not value its employees. He would miss the paycheck, but money was not everything. He was finally free from their tyranny and able to find a better company to work for that valued ethics and its employees.

Eventually, Jamison found a new job and was happy in his new career. One day, he was reading the news during his lunch break. He saw an article that caught his attention. The chief executive officer (CEO) of East Quick had been arrested on federal charges for corruption and unethical company practices. "It is what they say," said Jamison, "ethical leadership starts at the top, and East Quick never had a chance. They were riding the light to their own execution from the top-down."

Components of Responsibility

The ability to define responsibility within the context of your organization and/or environment is critical to building the foundations of successful leadership. Leaders need to be collaborative, inviting, and transparent in their leadership matrix while maintaining their adherence to the organization's goals. How can leaders be accountable to their organization, as well as the stakeholders within the organization and those engaged with the organization? How can leaders maintain integrity and dependability so that there is trust in the organization? The discipline a leader must possess to remain focused on the objectives of the organization and to support the stakeholders is critical to their success. Discipline is a crucial component of responsibility. Disciplined individuals can exercise control over their impulses and emotions and make responsible choices that align with their long-term goals and values. They demonstrate a strong sense of self-control and motivation and can resist distractions that may hinder their progress. Discipline is essential for achieving success and personal growth, as it enables individuals to prioritize their responsibilities and stay focused on their objectives.

Part of being a disciplined leader is to have and enact a strong system of ethical behaviors and choices. Ethical behavior is a fundamental component of responsibility. Ethics involves adhering to a set of moral standards and principles that guide one's behavior and decision-making. Ethical individuals act with integrity, honesty, and fairness in their interactions with others and strive to do what is right, even in challenging situations. They consider the impact of their actions on others and make choices that are consistent with their values and beliefs. Ethical behavior is essential for creating a positive and inclusive work environment, as it fosters a culture of trust and respect among colleagues and ensures that individuals uphold high standards of conduct and professionalism. Trust is central to establishing a dynamic organization. Trust is developed through actions; those actions must have a strong root in the ethical values of the leader. Even among the most trusted members of the leadership team, the leader must exhibit ethical values and choices. The consistency of these ethical values and decisions will create the foundation for trust.

How does a leader create the stakeholder lens of being an ethical leader? How can the leader demonstrate their core values and beliefs so that the members of the organization have a clear understanding of the expectations and the end goals of the organization? The leader must establish a pattern of behaviors that demonstrate integrity. Integrity is also a key component of responsibility. Individuals with integrity adhere to a set of moral and ethical principles and consistently uphold these values in their actions and decisions. They demonstrate honesty, fairness, and transparency in their interactions with others and strive to do what is right, even when faced with difficult choices. Integrity is essential for building trust and credibility, as it establishes a foundation of respect and ethical behavior in one's personal and professional relationships.

The building of trust within the organization and the creation of an environment that allows for the collaboration of ideas and thoughts to better meet the goals of the organization must be rooted in integrity. The willingness to be open and transparent with how decisions are made and how action plans are developed creates a stronger sense of inclusion and buy-in by the stakeholders. The shared process of leadership is not just among the few members of the leadership team but among all the stakeholders. Each person in an organization has a unique lens on the issues and functions of the organization. Their role within the organization affords them a perspective on not just how the systems of the organization function but also how the people within those systems function. The demonstration of integrity in leadership and the ethical choices that are made shape how the systems within an organization function and how those same systems allow the people within the organization to function. Not all decisions that are made have 100 percent agreement of all stakeholders; no system creates an outcome matrix that requires 100 percent agreement. However, the clarity and transparency of how the decision was made and what factors were central to the final decision create an opportunity for understanding. The understanding of the underlying factors that were central to the decision and the eventual outcome goals is essential.

Another ethical idea that should be included in a shared voice within an organization is integrity. Integrity involves acting with honesty, transparency, and ethical behavior in all interactions and communications. In an educational setting, integrity is vital for upholding academic standards, research ethics, and intellectual integrity among students, teachers, and researchers. By demonstrating integrity in their work, individuals can build trust, credibility, and respect within the academic community and uphold high standards of academic excellence and professionalism. Collaboration is another key ethical idea that should be included in a shared voice within an organization. Collaboration involves working together toward common goals, sharing ideas, resources, and expertise, and seeking input and feedback from others in decision-making processes. In an educational setting, collaboration is essential for promoting teamwork, knowledge sharing, and interdisciplinary research among students, teachers, and scholars. By collaborating with peers, individuals can leverage their diverse expertise, skills, and perspectives to achieve common objectives, create innovative solutions, and drive academic excellence and intellectual growth.

Transparency is another ethical idea that should be included in a shared voice within an organization. Transparency involves being open, honest, and accountable in all communications and interactions. In an educational setting, transparency is essential for creating a culture of trust, openness, and ethical conduct among students, teachers, and administrators. By being transparent in their actions and decisions, individuals can build credibility, trust, and confidence within the academic community and demonstrate their commitment to academic integrity and ethical behavior.

Accountability is central to creating an environment of responsibility. Leading is not an exact science; there are times when leaders make poor decisions. The catalyst for these decisions may be the lack of information or misreading the plan to reach the stated goals. Leaders need to take responsibility for their choices and be accountable to those who work with them and for them. When leaders are accountable for their actions and are transparent with stakeholders within the organization, they strengthen the connection between themselves and the members of the organization. Part of being accountable is the acceptance of consequences that happen due to the choices made. Leaders need to "pull" blame from their teams and "push" the blame on themselves. By centering the consequences on themselves and being the person who is accountable for the failures of the plan, stakeholders see how the leader demonstrates their loyalty to the team. When the leader asks for loyalty from the team, there is an established expectation modeled by the leader. When individuals are accountable, they demonstrate a sense of maturity and self-awareness, as they can acknowledge their mistakes and learn from them. Accountability also involves being transparent in one's actions and being willing to provide explanations or justifications for one's behavior when necessary. One aspect of accountability is being dependable. Dependability is another crucial component of responsibility. Dependable leaders are reliable and trustworthy, as they consistently fulfill their obligations and commitments. Leaders demonstrate a strong work ethic and a dedication to completing tasks in a timely and efficient manner. Dependability is essential in both personal and professional relationships, as it establishes a sense of trust and confidence in one's ability to follow through on promises and responsibilities.

Ethics in Education and Business Models

Ethical leadership is a complex endeavor of blending the application of leadership theory and the values of the leader in the decision-making process. Ethics are influenced by the environment, past experiences of the leader, and the current moral structure of the leader. How these conditions work collectively to shape the decisions and actions of the leader becomes the matrix that will guide how the leader interacts with stakeholders and organizational demands. Ethics play a critical role in the concept of a shared voice, which refers to the idea of ensuring that all individuals have a platform to express their thoughts, ideas, and perspectives in a fair and inclusive manner. In both education and business environments, the ethics of a shared voice are essential for promoting open communication, diversity of viewpoints, and collaboration among individuals. In promoting a shared voice within an organization, ethical considerations are paramount in fostering a culture of openness, inclusivity, and respect among individuals. By upholding key ethical ideas, organizations can create an environment where all voices are valued, heard, and integrated into decision-making processes. When comparing the ethical ideas that should be included in a shared voice in education and business environments, several key principles emerge that are essential for promoting transparency, collaboration, and mutual respect.

In education, ethics have increased importance for leaders. Many of the decisions that are made have a direct impact on students. Students are considered a vulnerable population that has a limited voice in the decision-making process and the outcomes that become part of the operational environment. Additionally, many of the choices that leaders in education make have impacts on the instructional staff. The ethics of a shared voice are closely tied to the principles of academic freedom, intellectual diversity, and inclusive dialogue. In a school system, students, teachers, and administrators are encouraged to engage in open and respectful discussions and exchanges of ideas. The ethical considerations in this context revolve around creating a safe and welcoming environment where all voices are heard, respected, and valued. This not only fosters a culture of mutual understanding and respect but also promotes critical thinking, creativity, and innovation among individuals. In education, the ethics of a shared voice are vital for promoting academic freedom, intellectual diversity, and critical thinking among students, teachers, and researchers. By encouraging open dialogue, debate, and exchange of ideas, educational institutions can create a dynamic and intellectually stimulating environment where individuals are empowered to express their thoughts, challenge conventional wisdom, and engage in meaningful discussions. This not only cultivates a culture of innovation and discovery but also fosters a sense of intellectual curiosity and lifelong learning among individuals.

In business, the process of implementing ethics and shared voice is equally important for creating a culture of transparency, collaboration, and mutual respect among employees, stakeholders, and customers. The business environment expects individuals to contribute their unique perspectives, insights, and expertise to drive organizational success and growth. The ethical considerations in this context involve ensuring that all voices are given equal opportunities to be heard, acknowledged, and integrated into decision-making processes. This not only enhances employee engagement and morale but also fosters a sense of belonging and community within the organization. By valuing each voice and conducting operational ethics, leaders' decisions have greater buy-in and understanding of how and why the decision was made. Ethics is the benchmarking value structure that gives organizations transparency of method and process.

In a business environment, respect is equally crucial for promoting a culture of collaboration, teamwork, and mutual understanding among employees, stakeholders, and customers. By respecting the diverse expertise, skills, and perspectives of individuals, organizations can leverage the collective wisdom and creativity of their workforce to drive innovation, solve complex problems, and achieve common goals. This not only enhances employee engagement and job satisfaction but also contributes to creating a positive and inclusive work environment where differences of opinion are welcomed and valued.

When comparing the ethics of a shared voice in education and business environments, some key similarities emerge. In both settings, the ethical considerations revolve around promoting inclusivity, diversity, and collaboration among individuals. Ethics in both environments is a method that rests on values and morals. By having a shared sense of the norms that are rooted in the values of the organization and its members, leaders can create a working environment that supports all stakeholders. In both education and business environments, the ethics of a shared voice are essential for promoting transparency, accountability, and ethical decision-making. By fostering open communication, collaboration, and diversity of perspectives among stakeholders, organizations can enhance the creativity, innovation, and problem-solving capabilities of their members. This not only leads to improved employee engagement and job satisfaction but also drives organizational success.

Despite these similarities, there are also notable differences in how the ethics of a shared voice are applied and valued in education versus business environments. In education, the emphasis is often placed on academic freedom, intellectual exploration, and the pursuit of knowledge for its own sake. This is especially true at the university level. The primary goal is to create a learning environment where individuals are free to express their thoughts, question existing paradigms, and engage in critical inquiry without fear of censorship or reprisal. This helps to nurture a culture of independent thinking, academic integrity, and intellectual growth among students and scholars. In business environments, the emphasis is often placed on achieving organizational goals, driving innovation, and enhancing financial performance. The primary goal is to leverage the diverse expertise, skills, and perspectives of employees to solve complex problems, make informed decisions, and achieve sustainable growth and success. This requires a focus on creating a culture of collaboration, teamwork, and shared accountability among individuals, where all voices are valued for their contributions to achieving common objectives.

In both education and business environments, the ethics of a shared voice require a commitment to upholding principles of respect, integrity, and inclusivity in all interactions and communications. This involves creating a culture of open communication, active listening, and mutual understanding among individuals, where differences of opinion are welcomed and constructive feedback is encouraged. By promoting a culture of shared voice, organizations can foster a sense of belonging, empowerment, and collective ownership among individuals, which, in turn, leads to increased engagement, productivity, and overall well-being.

Loyalty in Reason and Decision-Making

When addressing the constructs of reason and decision-making, the concept of loyalty plays a significant role in shaping individuals' perspectives, actions, and choices. Loyalty can influence how individuals prioritize their values, beliefs, and relationships when making decisions and can have a profound impact on the outcomes of those decisions. By examining the role of loyalty in reason and decision-making, we can gain insight into how it shapes ethical considerations, interpersonal relationships, and individual identity. Loyalty, as a fundamental human trait, often involves a sense of commitment, trust, and dedication to a person, group, or organization. Loyalty takes many forms, such as loyalty to family, friends, colleagues, employers, or even to one's own principles and beliefs. Loyalty in reason and decision-making can influence individuals in different ways, prompting them to consider the interests, needs, and values of those to whom they are loyal when making choices. In ethical reasoning and decision-making, loyalty can present both challenges and opportunities. On one hand, loyalty to a particular person or group may influence individuals to prioritize their interests over others, leading to biased or unfair decisions.

Loyalty can be a positive force in ethical reasoning and decision-making when it is grounded in values such as honesty, trust, and mutual respect. Loyalty to an organization's mission, vision, or core values can guide stakeholders to make decisions that align with the organization's ethical standards and social responsibility. This type of loyalty promotes a sense of cohesion, unity, and shared purpose among individuals, facilitating collaboration, teamwork, and collective decision-making in the pursuit of common goals and objectives.

Loyalty plays a crucial role in shaping how individuals interact, communicate, and collaborate with others. Loyalty to friends, family members, or colleagues can foster trust, empathy, and understanding in relationships, strengthening social bonds and creating a sense of belonging and support. Loyalty in reason and decision-making can influence individuals to consider the impact of their choices on others and act in ways that are supportive, caring, and respectful of their relationships. In an organization, loyalty to employers, colleagues, or other stakeholders can also impact how individuals make decisions and navigate ethical dilemmas. Loyalty can enhance teamwork, collaboration, and organizational outcomes, as individuals work together toward common goals and objectives, prioritizing the success and well-being of the group over individual interests.

Loyalty can shape how individuals perceive themselves, their values, and their relationships with others. Loyalty to one's principles, beliefs, or values can provide a sense of purpose, integrity, and authenticity in decision-making, guiding individuals to act in ways that are consistent with their moral compass and ethical standards. This type of loyalty can help individuals navigate complex ethical dilemmas, make difficult choices, and stay true to themselves, even in the face of challenges, pressures, or conflicts. Moreover, loyalty can also influence how individuals construct their identity and roles in different contexts, such as work, family, or society. For example, a person who is loyal to their profession may prioritize their career goals, development, and growth over personal relationships or leisure activities, dedicating time, energy, and resources to advancing their professional aspirations. This type of loyalty can shape one's sense of identity, purpose, and fulfillment as individuals align their actions and decisions with their professional goals and values.

When comparing loyalty in reason and decision-making between personal and professional contexts, some key similarities and differences emerge. In personal relationships, loyalty is often based on emotional connections, trust, and shared experiences, guiding individuals to act in ways that nurture and sustain their bonds with others. Loyalty in personal contexts can lead individuals to prioritize the well-being, happiness, and interests of their loved ones, demonstrating care, support, and commitment in their interactions and decisions. In professional settings, loyalty is often based on organizational values, goals, and responsibilities, guiding individuals to act in ways that uphold the interests, reputation, and success of the company or team. Loyalty in professional contexts can lead individuals to prioritize teamwork, collaboration, and organizational objectives, demonstrating dedication, accountability, and loyalty to their colleagues, superiors, and clients in the pursuit of shared goals and outcomes.

Responsibility and Reason in Educational Administration

Responsibility is a fundamental concept that plays a crucial role in demonstrating leadership and excellence in educational administration. Defined as the state of being accountable for one's actions, decisions, and obligations, responsibility encompasses a range of values, behaviors, and qualities that are essential for effective leadership and management in educational settings. By combining responsibility with reason, educational leaders can exemplify integrity, accountability, and ethical conduct in their roles, guiding their organizations toward success and excellence. Reason, as the ability to think, understand, and make sound judgments based on logic and evidence, is a key component of responsible leadership in educational administration. Educational leaders must employ reason to analyze complex situations, evaluate options, and make informed decisions that are in the best interest of their students, staff, and stakeholders. By combining responsibility with reason, leaders can demonstrate ethical leadership, critical thinking, and effective problem-solving skills in addressing challenges and opportunities in the field of education.

Responsibility in educational administration involves a commitment to upholding ethical standards, promoting organizational values, and fostering a culture of accountability and integrity within the institution. Educational leaders must take responsibility for their actions, decisions, and behaviors and act in ways that align with the mission, vision, and goals of the organization. This includes demonstrating transparency, honesty, and ethical conduct in all interactions and communications and holding oneself and others accountable for upholding the highest standards of professionalism and excellence in education. When combined with reason, responsibility in educational administration can lead to effective leadership practices that prioritize ethical considerations, stakeholder interests, and organizational sustainability. Educational leaders who employ reason in their decision-making processes can analyze complex issues, consider multiple perspectives, and assess the potential impact of their choices on students, staff, and the broader community. By using reason to guide responsible actions and decisions, leaders can ensure that their institutions operate with integrity, transparency, and accountability, promoting a culture of trust, respect, and excellence in educational administration.

Leadership in educational administration requires a deep sense of responsibility toward ensuring the success, well-being, and development of students, staff, and the broader educational community. Responsible leaders must demonstrate a commitment to ethical conduct, integrity, and accountability in all aspects of their role, including decision-making, resource allocation, and strategic planning. By combining responsibility with reason, leaders can make informed, ethical decisions that reflect the values, priorities, and goals of the institution and lead to positive outcomes for all stakeholders involved. Leaders who demonstrate responsible leadership in educational administration prioritize the interests of their students, staff, and community and act with integrity, transparency, and ethical conduct in their decision-making processes. They take ownership of their actions, decisions, and outcomes and hold themselves and others accountable for upholding ethical standards, promoting diversity and inclusion, and fostering a culture of collaboration and respect within the institution.

Through responsible leadership and reason, educational administrators can inspire trust, confidence, and engagement among their stakeholders and drive positive change and transformation within their organizations. By demonstrating a commitment to ethical leadership, critical thinking, and strategic decision-making, leaders can shape the future of education, promote excellence and innovation, and create a culture of continuous improvement and learning within their institutions.

Logic, Responsibility, Reason, and Ethics

In the process of decision-making, a commitment to logic and reason through responsibility is essential for ensuring that choices are well-considered, ethical, and aligned with the goals and values of an organization. When decisions are made based on sound reasoning and a sense of responsibility, ethical considerations come to the forefront, guiding individuals toward choices that lead to positive outcomes and shared benefits. Ethics plays a crucial role in this process by providing a framework for evaluating the impact of decisions on stakeholders, promoting fairness, transparency, and integrity, and fostering a culture of respect and trust within an organization. Ethics, as a branch of philosophy that deals with moral principles, values, and codes of conduct, provides individuals with a set of guidelines for making decisions that are morally right, just, and ethical. In the context of decision-making, ethics serves as a compass that helps individuals navigate complex moral dilemmas, weigh competing interests, and determine the best course of action that upholds ethical standards and promotes the well-being of all stakeholders involved. When decisions are made with a commitment to logic and reason through responsibility, ethical considerations play a central role in shaping the outcomes and events that result from those decisions. By adhering to ethical principles such as honesty, fairness, respect, and accountability, individuals can ensure that their choices are in line with the values and goals of the organization and lead to positive and ethical outcomes that benefit all stakeholders.

Ethical decision-making involves a process of reflection, analysis, and evaluation where individuals consider the potential consequences of their actions, assess the impact on others, and weigh the ethical implications of their choices. By integrating ethics into the decision-making process, individuals can ensure that their decisions are guided by values such as integrity, justice, and empathy and contribute to a culture of ethical behavior, mutual respect, and social responsibility within the organization. Ethics also plays a crucial role in promoting shared events and outcomes that are aligned with the values and goals of the organization. When decisions are made ethically, based on a commitment to logic and reason through responsibility, individuals can avoid conflicts of interest, biases, and unethical practices that may harm stakeholders and erode trust within the organization. Instead, ethical decision-making fosters a culture of transparency, accountability, and integrity, where individuals are empowered to act in ways that uphold ethical standards and promote the common good.

By considering ethics in decision-making processes, individuals can create shared events and outcomes that are fair, equitable, and respectful of the rights and interests of all stakeholders involved. Ethical decisions contribute to a positive organizational culture that values honesty, trust, and integrity and fosters collaboration, teamwork, and mutual respect among individuals. This leads to the creation of shared events and outcomes that reflect the organization's commitment to ethical conduct, social responsibility, and sustainability and contribute to building a positive reputation, credibility, and trust with stakeholders and the broader community. Ethics in decision-making helps organizations navigate complex challenges, uncertainties, and dilemmas by providing a framework for assessing the moral, legal, and social implications of choices. By considering ethical considerations in decision-making processes, individuals can minimize risks, prevent conflicts, and promote ethical conduct that aligns with the organization's values and goals. This ensures that decisions are made with a broader perspective in mind, considering the interests and well-being of all stakeholders and leading to outcomes that are just, fair, and socially responsible.

Ethical decision-making also contributes to the development of a transparent, accountable, and ethical organizational culture, where individuals are empowered to act with honesty, integrity, and respect in all their interactions and decisions. By promoting ethical behavior and values, organizations can create an environment where employees feel valued, respected, and trusted and are motivated to uphold ethical standards, contribute to the common good, and work toward shared goals and outcomes that benefit the organization and society.

Sustainability of Reason and Shared Voice

Achieving sustainability within an organization is crucial for its long-term success, growth, and relevance in a rapidly changing and competitive business environment. Sustainability, defined as the ability to meet present needs without compromising the ability of future generations to meet their own needs, encompasses various dimensions, including economic, environmental, and social aspects. Failure to achieve sustainability can lead to negative consequences that impact the organization's performance, reputation, and overall viability. By examining the implications of failing to achieve sustainability and implementing a shared voice to guide everyone toward success, organizations can mitigate risks, enhance resilience, and position themselves for long-term growth and sustainability. When sustainability is not achieved within an organization, the organizational processes are at risk of failing, leading to a range of negative outcomes that can impact its operations, stakeholders, and performance.

One key reason for this is the lack of alignment between the organization's strategies, actions, and goals and the broader principles of sustainability. Organizations that ignore or neglect sustainability considerations may face challenges such as resource depletion, environmental degradation, social unrest, and regulatory non-compliance, which can hinder their ability to operate efficiently, innovate effectively, and adapt to changing market conditions. The failure of organizational processes due to a lack of sustainability is the erosion of trust, credibility, and stakeholder relationships. In today's interconnected and transparent business landscape, organizations are increasingly held accountable for their environmental, social, and ethical practices and are expected to uphold high standards of corporate responsibility and sustainability. Failure to demonstrate a commitment to sustainability can result in reputational damage, loss of customer loyalty, and investor skepticism as stakeholders question the organization's values, integrity, and long-term viability.

The absence of sustainability within organizational processes can lead to inefficiencies, waste, and missed opportunities for innovation and growth. Sustainable practices such as resource conservation, waste reduction, and stakeholder engagement not only contribute to cost savings and operational efficiencies but also drive innovation, differentiation, and competitive advantage in the marketplace. Organizations that fail to embrace sustainability may struggle to adapt to changing consumer preferences, regulatory requirements, and market trends, putting them at a disadvantage compared to more sustainable and forward-thinking competitors. To address the challenges and risks associated with failing to achieve sustainability, organizations can implement a shared voice to guide everyone toward success by fostering a culture of collaboration, communication, and shared responsibility among all stakeholders. A shared voice, characterized by openness, inclusivity, and accountability, enables organizations to engage employees, customers, suppliers, and other partners in a collective effort to prioritize sustainability, align actions with values and goals, and drive positive change toward a more sustainable future.

A shared voice that values diverse perspectives, promotes transparency, and encourages dialogue can help organizations create a culture of mutual respect, trust, and empowerment where all stakeholders feel valued, heard, and invested in the organization's sustainability initiatives. This shared voice can help build consensus, foster collaboration, and drive collective action toward achieving sustainability goals and outcomes that benefit the organization, its stakeholders, and the broader community. A shared voice can provide a platform for sharing knowledge, best practices, and lessons learned, enabling individuals and groups to learn from each other, leverage their strengths, and overcome challenges together. By promoting open communication, active listening, and information-sharing, organizations can enhance their capacity for innovation, problem-solving, and continuous improvement in sustainability practices and performance. This collaborative approach can lead to greater resilience, agility, and adaptability in the face of external shocks, disruptions, or changes in the business environment.

In addition, a shared voice can enhance transparency, accountability, and trust within the organization by promoting a culture of integrity, honesty, and ethical conduct in all interactions and decisions. By encouraging open dialogue, constructive feedback, and collective decision-making, organizations can build trust, credibility, and engagement among their stakeholders, fostering a sense of ownership, loyalty, and commitment to the organization's sustainability goals and values. This shared commitment can help align individual actions with shared goals, values, and outcomes and drive positive change toward a more sustainable, responsible, and ethical organization. By implementing a shared voice to guide everyone toward success in achieving sustainability, organizations can overcome barriers, address challenges, and leverage opportunities to enhance their performance, reputation, and impact in the marketplace. A shared voice promotes a culture of collaboration, communication, and shared responsibility that empowers individuals and groups to work together toward common goals, values, and outcomes and fosters a sense of purpose, belonging, and pride in their contributions to sustainability and organizational success.

Failing to achieve sustainability within an organization can have far-reaching implications that impact its processes, performance, and long-term viability. By addressing the challenges and risks associated with sustainability failures and implementing a shared voice to guide everyone toward success, organizations can mitigate risks, enhance resilience, and drive positive change toward a more sustainable, responsible, and ethical future. A shared voice fosters a culture of collaboration, communication, and shared responsibility that empowers individuals and groups to work together toward achieving sustainability goals and outcomes that benefit the organization, its stakeholders, and the broader community. Achieving sustainability is paramount in organizational processes as it sets the foundation for long-term success, resilience, and adaptability in a rapidly evolving business landscape. Sustainability encompasses economic, environmental, and social considerations, striving to balance the needs of the present without compromising the ability of future generations to meet their own needs. When an organization fails to achieve sustainability, the repercussions can be severe, leading to operational inefficiencies, reputational damage, stakeholder distrust, and missed opportunities for growth and innovation.

One critical reason why organizational processes fail when sustainability is not achieved is the lack of alignment between business strategies and sustainability goals. Organizations that disregard sustainability considerations may experience resource depletion, environmental degradation, and increased operating costs, undermining their competitiveness and ability to respond to changing market dynamics. Without a robust sustainability strategy in place, businesses risk falling behind their more forward-thinking and sustainable competitors, limiting their potential for growth and long-term success. Another consequence of failing to achieve sustainability is the erosion of trust and credibility among stakeholders. In today's interconnected and socially conscious society, customers, investors, employees, and regulators expect organizations to demonstrate a commitment to sustainable practices, ethical conduct, and corporate responsibility. Failure to meet these expectations can lead to reputational harm, loss of stakeholder trust, and negative perceptions of the organization's values and integrity. This lack of trust can have far-reaching implications, affecting customer loyalty, employee engagement, and investor confidence, ultimately jeopardizing the organization's reputation and bottom line.

The absence of sustainability within organizational processes can result in inefficiencies, waste, and missed opportunities for innovation and growth. Sustainable practices such as resource conservation, waste reduction, and stakeholder engagement not only enhance operational efficiency and reduce costs but also drive innovation, differentiation, and competitive advantage in the market. Organizations that neglect sustainability risk being ill-prepared to adapt to changing consumer preferences, regulatory requirements, and market trends, putting themselves at a significant disadvantage in a rapidly changing business environment. To address these challenges and steer organizations toward sustainability success, a shared voice that promotes collaboration, communication, and collective responsibility is crucial. A shared voice fosters a culture of inclusivity, openness, and accountability, encouraging all stakeholders to actively engage in sustainability initiatives, align actions with values, and work toward common goals and outcomes. By fostering a culture of shared responsibility, organizations can leverage the collective wisdom, expertise, and insights of their stakeholders to drive meaningful change and achieve sustainable outcomes that benefit the organization and its broader ecosystem.

Fostering a culture of collaboration, communication, and shared responsibility among all stakeholders through a shared voice, organizations can harness the diverse perspectives, talents, and resources of their employees, customers, suppliers, and partners to address sustainability challenges, drive innovation, and create shared value for all stakeholders involved. A shared voice enables individuals to voice their opinions, concerns, and ideas, fostering a sense of ownership, empowerment, and accountability in driving sustainability initiatives and outcomes. This collective approach ensures that all stakeholders have a stake in the organization's sustainability efforts, feel valued and engaged in the process, and work collaboratively toward common goals and outcomes that benefit the organization and its broader community.

A shared voice can enhance transparency, integrity, and trust within the organization by promoting open communication, honest dialogue, and ethical conduct in all interactions and decisions. By fostering a culture of open communication, active listening, and information-sharing, organizations can build trust, credibility, and engagement among their stakeholders, creating a sense of unity, transparency, and shared purpose in achieving sustainability goals and outcomes. This shared commitment to sustainability fosters a culture of accountability, responsibility, and ethical behavior where all stakeholders feel valued, heard, and empowered to contribute to the organization's long-term success and sustainability.

Expansion of Responsibility of Reason beyond the Individual

The Responsibility of Reason within an organization must extend beyond individual employees or hierarchical levels to encompass a collective commitment to rational decision-making, ethical conduct, and shared goals and outcomes. While individual responsibility and reason are important in guiding personal actions and choices, it is imperative that organizations cultivate a culture of accountability, critical thinking, and collaborative problem-solving that transcends individual contributions and spans across teams, departments, and leadership levels. By expanding the Responsibility of Reason beyond one person or level, organizations can leverage diverse perspectives, expertise, and insights, foster a culture of transparency, integrity, and trust, and drive collective actions toward achieving common goals and organizational success.

Expanding the Responsibility of Reason beyond individual employees lies the importance of promoting a culture of shared values, ethical conduct, and critical thinking that guides decision-making, behaviors, and interactions at all levels of the organization. When reason is applied collectively, individuals are encouraged to seek out different viewpoints, challenge assumptions, and evaluate evidence objectively, leading to more informed, well-rounded decisions that consider the broader implications and consequences of their actions. By fostering a culture of responsibility and reason that extends beyond one person or level, organizations can ensure that ethical standards, logical reasoning, and shared values are upheld as core principles that guide organizational processes, strategies, and outcomes. Expanding the Responsibility of Reason beyond one level in the organization encourages leaders to model ethical behavior, integrity, and transparency in their decision-making processes, setting a clear example for others to follow. Leaders play a crucial role in shaping the organizational culture, values, and practices and are responsible for instilling a sense of accountability, critical thinking, and ethical conduct among their teams and peers. By demonstrating a commitment to reason and responsibility in their actions, decisions, and interactions, leaders can inspire trust, respect, and confidence among employees, fostering a culture of integrity, honesty, and ethical behavior that permeates throughout the organization.

Expanding the Responsibility of Reason enables organizations to build a culture of transparency, accountability, and trust where open communication, constructive feedback, and information-sharing are encouraged, and decision-making processes are informed by diverse perspectives and expertise. By promoting transparency and accountability across all levels of the organization, individuals are empowered to speak up, raise concerns, and offer input on critical issues, fostering a culture of openness, dialogue, and collaboration that values reason, integrity, and mutual respect. This collective approach to reason enables organizations to leverage the knowledge, insights, and expertise of their employees, customers, suppliers, and other stakeholders to drive innovation, enhance decision-making, and achieve shared goals and outcomes that benefit the organization and its broader ecosystem. Expanding the Responsibility of Reason helps build resilience, adaptability, and agility in response to external shocks, disruptions, or changes in the business environment. In a volatile and uncertain world, organizations must be able to anticipate, respond to, and capitalize on emerging trends, challenges, and opportunities by leveraging the collective intelligence, creativity, and problem-solving skills of their workforce. By fostering a culture of reason, curiosity, and continuous learning that transcends individual contributions and spans across teams and departments, organizations can enhance their capacity for innovation, agility, and adaptability, enabling them to thrive in a dynamic, competitive, and ever-evolving marketplace.

Expanding the Responsibility of Reason promotes a sense of shared ownership, accountability, and commitment to organizational goals, values, and outcomes. When reason is applied collectively, individuals are encouraged to align their actions, decisions, and behaviors with the organization's mission, vision, and values, fostering a sense of purpose, engagement, and pride in their contributions to the organization's success. By fostering a culture that values reason, integrity, and ethical conduct at all levels, organizations can create a sense of belonging, loyalty, and commitment among employees, customers, and other stakeholders, driving collective actions toward achieving common goals and outcomes that benefit the organization and its broader community.

Evolution and Fluidity of Responsibility of Reason

The Responsibility of Reason within an organization transcends individual actions and hierarchical levels to become a living and evolving entity that adapts to the dynamic and diverse organizational environment. To remain fluid and responsive in a diverse setting, the Responsibility of Reason must be ingrained in the organizational culture, values, and practices, guiding decision-making, behaviors, and interactions at all levels. By fostering a culture that values critical thinking, ethical conduct, and open communication, organizations can create an environment where reason becomes a dynamic and living entity that evolves in response to changing circumstances, challenges, and opportunities. The Responsibility of Reason becomes a living and evolving entity in a diverse organizational environment through the promotion of inclusive practices that value diverse perspectives, experiences, and insights. In a multicultural and globalized world, organizations are composed of individuals with different backgrounds, worldviews, and ways of thinking, requiring a nuanced approach to decision-making and problem-solving that considers a wide range of viewpoints. By embracing diversity and inclusivity, organizations can tap into the collective intelligence, creativity, and innovation of their workforce, fostering a culture of reason that values different perspectives, encourages dissenting opinions, and promotes dialogue and debate as a means to arrive at informed and well-rounded decisions.

The Responsibility of Reason can become a living and evolving entity by encouraging continuous learning, adaptability, and self-reflection among employees and leaders. In a rapidly changing business environment, organizations must be able to adapt to new challenges, technologies, and market trends by fostering a culture of curiosity, experimentation, and feedback that promotes ongoing growth and development. By encouraging individuals to question assumptions, challenge traditional norms, and seek out new insights and perspectives, organizations can create a culture of reason that values flexibility, innovation, and lifelong learning as essential components of success in a diverse and complex organizational environment. The Responsiblity of Reason will promote a culture of transparency, accountability, and ethical conduct that guides decision-making and actions in an open and honest manner. In an era of heightened scrutiny and accountability, organizations must uphold high standards of integrity, honesty, and ethical behavior in all interactions and decisions, fostering a culture of reason that values transparency, fairness, and trust, which is fundamental to organizational success. By promoting open communication, ethical conduct, and shared values, organizations can build a culture of reason that instills confidence, credibility, and respect among employees, customers, and other stakeholders, driving a sense of shared responsibility and accountability for upholding reason in all aspects of organizational life. Furthermore, the Responsibility of Reason can evolve into a dynamic and adaptable entity by fostering a culture of experimentation, innovation, and risk-taking that encourages individuals to explore new ideas, approaches, and solutions to complex challenges.

In a rapidly changing and competitive environment, organizations must be willing to take calculated risks, test assumptions, and pursue innovative strategies that drive growth and differentiation. By creating a culture that values creativity, flexibility, and resilience, organizations can foster a spirit of curiosity and exploration that fuels continuous improvement, adaptation, and innovation, allowing them to evolve in response to changing market dynamics, emerging trends, and disruptive technologies. By creating a participative and collaborative decision-making process, the organization can fully engage all stakeholders in shaping strategies, goals, and outcomes. In a diverse organizational environment, where individuals possess different interests, values, and priorities, it is crucial to involve employees, customers, suppliers, and other partners in the decision-making process to ensure that their perspectives, needs, and concerns are taken into account. By promoting a culture of inclusivity, collaboration, and shared ownership, organizations can empower individuals to contribute their unique insights, expertise, and knowledge to the decision-making process, fostering a sense of collective responsibility and commitment to achieving common goals and outcomes that reflect the diverse interests and values of all stakeholders involved.

Responsibility of reason can remain fluid and adaptable in a diverse organizational environment by encouraging a culture of constructive feedback, reflection, and continuous improvement that supports ongoing growth and development. By promoting a culture of open communication, active listening, and feedback, organizations can create an environment where individuals feel comfortable sharing their ideas, concerns, and perspectives and receive constructive input and support from their peers and leaders. By fostering a culture of reflection, self-awareness, and learning from past experiences, organizations can empower individuals to adapt, grow, and evolve in response to changing circumstances, challenges, and opportunities, allowing reason to develop and flourish in an environment that values critical thinking, self-awareness, and continuous improvement as essential components of individual and organizational success.

The Responsibility of Reason must have a solid foundation if it is to grow and develop value within an organization. This situation is very similar to a tree. For a tree to grow, its roots must be planted in rich soil. Water and the right conditions must exist for the tree to grow roots. Once the roots are grown, the tree will sprout up from the ground. As the tree grows, it will develop branches and leaves. Over time, the tree will become large and will provide shade, food, and resources to the natural environment around it. The tree was planted to give beauty and value to the current environment. Once the tree takes root, it will then be able to produce its own seeds to make more trees. As a result, the tree will be responsible for eventually planting a forest full of trees that give additional value to those in and around it.

The responsibility follows the same model as demonstrated in Figure 3. The foundation of responsibility for reason is education. Education is responsible for providing the ground or planting soil for the process to take place. The education theory, method, philosophy, and style used to support learning will determine how the seed is planted and in what direction it will grow. If there is a strong educational foundation, then the roots will take place. However, if there is little educational background, then the roots will not take place, causing the process to wither away and fail. Without a strong educational substructure, nothing can progress, and there will be no evidence of responsibility for reason.

When there is a solid educational philosophy, the "who, what, where, when, why," and "how" will expand and develop. These are critical components that stem from the seed of reason for responsibility. The "who" refers to the educator, leader, and follower who will use philosophy and knowledge. The "what" is the decision or action that will be conducted by the "who" in the organization. The "where" refers to the location where the knowledge will take place in the organizational hierarchy and its connection to the internal and external environments. The "when" is the time the knowledge or philosophy will be

FIGURE 3 Growth and development of responsibility of reason

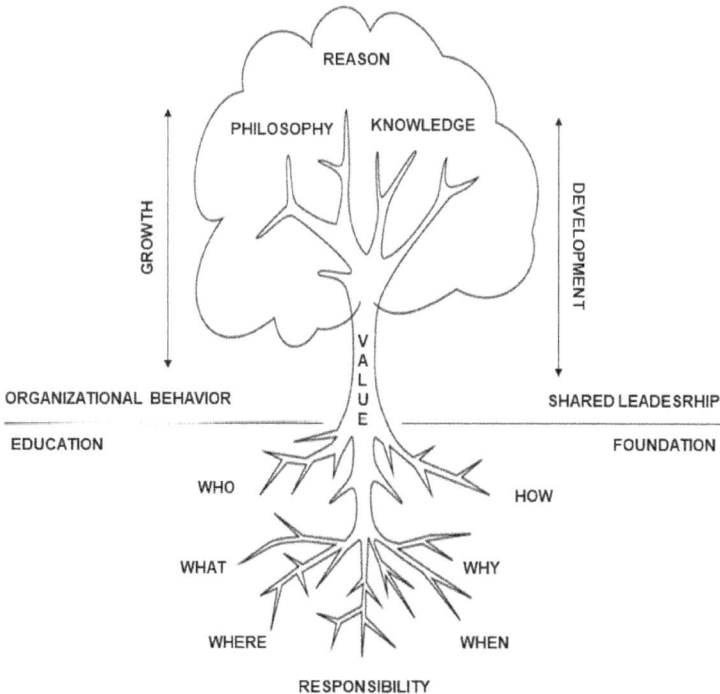

applied. This situation can be a one-time process or it can be recurring based on the need, situation, or event. The "why" is the reason for making the decision or taking the action to solve a current problem or achieve future success. Finally, the "how" is the plan or roadmap that will be used to pave the way to achieve both the individual and organizational objectives and goals.

Once the "who, what, where, when, why," and "how" have taken effect, then value will begin to grow in the organization. As value grows, it will begin to foster and develop organizational behavior and shared leadership within the company. Organizational behavior is based on how individuals interact to achieve positive performance driven by value. Based on the value, there will be different factors that will guide the behavior of both leaders and followers. Next, the value that is grown will also create shared leadership.

Shared leadership will take place when the leader or follower takes ownership of their decision-making process or actions on their own without being micromanaged or told to do something. When value becomes a part of shared leadership, there will be a shared purpose focused on the importance of a common goal, social support and interaction between members, effective communication within the company, and equal responsibility of everyone involved in the process. As a result, education will support the foundation that organizational behavior and shared leadership are based on. Value will be shared to unite the three elements of philosophy, knowledge, and reason in the Responsibility of Reason.

Simpleton Solution

The simple solution to the challenges of ethics and the Responsibility of Reason in an organization is for leaders and stakeholders to build a culture of collaboration, transparency, values, and shared beliefs. If the organization can create a unified culture where all members are focused on the success of each other and the success of the organization, then there is a great opportunity for success and growth. Regardless of the organization being in education or business, these principles of ethics and Responsibility of Reason become bedrocks of a well-developed and refined culture that will continue to grow and adapt. Organizations must have the flexibility of culture and structures that allow for change as circumstances change. As in education, businesses have a similar challenge of shifting expectations and regulations. If both types of organizations want to be successful, then the culture and systems that are being used must have the ability to change. Ethics and values are the processes organizations can use to help all stakeholders build understanding and acceptance of the goals and plans of the organization.

The Situation: The Secret Project

The school leadership teams were instructed to implement some school-wide changes. These changes would be mirrored in all the school buildings throughout the district. These changes were to address a growing concern about student attendance and student dropout rates. As school leaders began to meet to address these two issues, it became clear that there were going to be significant organizational challenges. School leaders were hesitant to openly share their current attendance concerns and the past strategies they used to address attendance. Additionally, they were reluctant to openly discuss action steps that could help to improve both student daily attendance as well as student dropouts. It could be heard within the groups of building leaders how they would never be honest in these meetings because they did not trust one of the district's senior leaders. They felt that this individual was vindictive and would target them because of their honesty. Also, this district leader did not meaningfully engage others in the decision-making process. He often wanted leaders to follow his specific instructions, regardless of whether these action steps worked well at the school or not. These meetings quickly degraded into reluctant participants who simply saw this as a waste of time.

The follow-up strategy from the school district was for this district leader to attend the building attendance and dropout team meetings. His participation was unwelcome and made school-level employees very uncomfortable. They felt as if they were being judged for the behaviors of students and families over which they had limited control or impact. The meetings he attended were guarded and unproductive, whereas the meetings he did not attend were far more productive and had a greater impact on changing student behaviors.

It also became abundantly clear that school leaders were not going to share with other school leaders what was being successful at their schools. This became the "secret project" among the district and school leaders. The lack of collaboration and communication created situations where schools either worked exponentially harder for success or did not meet with any success in changing student attendance behaviors. There were failures within the building within the school district that had to be addressed to improve attendance for an optimal learning environemnt.

Though this situation is an educational example of a failure of the system, the core struggles are like corporate and governmental organizations. The solutions and recommendations that could effect a positive change in the school district can be transferred to these organizations.

One of the most challenging aspects of leadership is to openly share that there is a problem or issue within the organization.

Figure 4 shows the iceberg effect of reason of responsibility. An iceberg is a solid piece of ice that broke off from a glacier and is floating alone in open water. Since icebergs are made up of frozen freshwater, they are less dense than the saltwater in the ocean. With ice being about 90 percent of the density of water, this leaves a 10 percent difference. As a result, much of an iceberg is found beneath the surface of the ocean, with only the top portion remaining above the waterline. Since most of the iceberg is hidden, it can make it hard to see without running into danger.

When describing the Responsibility of Reason, most of what makes it possible is the part that is not seen. Education, knowledge, and philosophy are established to add value and to achieve individual and organizational objectives and goals. Next, the responsibility of decisions and actions will be part of the organizational behavior that supports all levels within the hierarchy of the business. While you only see 10 percent of the iceberg or the reason, the responsibility is heavy below the baseline.

FIGURE 4 The iceberg effect of reason and responsibility.

Responsibility plays an important role in the support of reason. With responsibility, there is a duty or purpose. The duty or purpose then provides the individual or organization with accountability and the ability to take ownership and act independently without being sanctioned. Reason can only remain afloat when responsibility is dense and solid enough to support it. Responsibility is needed for reason to exist. However, responsibility without reason will not be able to remain afloat or be seen by the individual or organization. As a result, responsibility combined with reason will provide the correct buoyancy to exist in the organization, just like an iceberg floating in the ocean.

CHAPTER 4

LOOK OUT AHEAD IT'S THE CONSTANT AND EFFECTIVE COMMUNICATION PROCESS

The Situation: The Difference between What Is Said and What Is Meant

Tom and Pamela have been assigned to a new taskforce to implement a new production process for the company. Pam is a new employee and is eager and excited to show her value to the manager. However, Tom is less than thrilled. He has been with the company for many years and has seen many projects started but never finished. Tom and Pamela sit with the manager and listen as he goes over the directions. "You two will work together and complete this project." "Will you be here for guidance if we need it?" asks Pam.

Wait for it [...] thinks Tom to himself.

"About that," replies the manager. "I will be on vacation next week, but do not let that stop you from getting the work done. I believe that you two can handle it better than anyone else. Besides, you two are both here all week, while others in the office have other commitments with less time to dedicate to this project that I was tasked with completing."

Another day, another dollar covering for the manager who is never here, thought Tom.

"I know that I am leaving this project in good hands," said the manager. "Make sure to have everything completed by the time I return."

The manager then stood up. Tom could see him wearing flip-flops and watched as he flip-flopped out of his office, walked to the door, and then disappeared.

"I guess it's five o'clock somewhere," said Tom sarcastically.

Pamela did not share Tom's sentiment. "While it is five o'clock some-where," she said, "it is only 10 a.m. here. We have a lot of work to do. Let's hit the ground running."

"Whatever you say," said Tom.

Pamela and Tom both went back to their desks. Pamela dropped everything she was doing and focused on the project. She believed that the mission was the project given to her by the manager. Tom, on the other hand, completed all his assigned work for his position and said he would get to the project when he had time. All he kept thinking about was how, over the years, he had gone through the same scenario, seeing his work backed up to work on a special project that never amounted to anything. He had gotten "wise" to the situation and believed that Pamela was new and had not learned the ropes yet of how things really worked. The manager always left when he had his own work to do and passed it off to his staff as an important project. Tom knew that the real work never stopped and believed the mission and vision of the company was to do their daily tasks despite the projects that the manager had assigned before always going on vacation. When he finished his regular work, he started on the project to help Pamela.

The following Monday, Pamela and Tom arrived at work at eight o'clock on the dot and went right to work. About an hour and a half later, the manager casually walked in with his new suntan and still smelled of Coppertone. He sat down behind his desk and called for Pamela and Tom to come into his office. The manager sat there quietly for a moment. Tom noticed that the manager must have fallen asleep on the beach with his glasses on because there was a distinctive white outline where his glasses had rested on his face around his eyes. It was all Tom could do but laugh.

"It has come to my attention," said the manager, "that the project has been completed."

Pamela looked on happily since she had put a lot of pride and work into doing it, while Tom just sat there. "While the information is good, the company has decided to go in another direction."

Pamela sat there stunned. All her hopes and dreams of her hard work coming to fruition had just dried up and rotted away. She looked over at Tom, and he just shook his head. The look he gave said it all. He felt bad for her since it was her first time getting "burned" by the new manager.

The manager turned to Tom. "Tom," he said, "I am sure you understand and are good with this decision."

"You are the boss," he halfheartedly replied.

"Pamela," said the manager, "are you fine with this?"

"Oh yes," she replied, "I am FINE with this."

Arrrrr, she blows, thought Tom.

"That is great to hear," replied the manager.

"Do you have anything that you would like to say about this?"

"NOTHING at all," responded Pamela.

"That's great!" said the manager. "I knew you would see things this way. I will tell the board that they can go ahead and cancel this project idea."

"By all means," said Pamela, "GO AHEAD and do that!"

"By golly," said the manager, "I will do that right now!"

"WHATEVER," replied Pamela. "If you really think that is OK to do."

"I do," replied the manager. "I must say that I am really impressed with your attitude. You will keep us afloat. You will go far in this company."

"WHATEVER you say," replied Pamela. She then stood up and stormed back to her desk.

Now Arrrrr she goes, thought Tom. He just shook his head and wondered how the manager could be so clueless and lead his canoe into a giant ocean wave without a paddle of common sense [...].

The Impact of Communication on the Responsibility of Reason: RRRR She Blows to RRRRR She Goes

One of the most important components of Responsibility of Reason is communication. Communication is the process of sending and receiving information through messages using verbal and nonverbal methods. Next, communication is a dual channel that allows both parties to be the communicator and receiver of the message. For communication to occur, information must be sent and received in the form of a sign, opinion, or thought so a level of mutual understanding can be formed. As a result, communication attempts to give, receive, and share information and ideas through visual cues, writing, listening, reading, or speaking to one another.

Next, communication occurs between all horizontal and vertical levels within a corporation that includes the leaders, managers, and employees, to facilitate the inputs and outputs of the intent of the message. Within all aspects of education, management, and leadership, communication is the core of the organization. When serving in any role within an organization, effective communication is an essential job function to help bring synergy throughout the company and directly connect each group of stakeholders. It is the leader's responsibility to promote an open channel of communication and share thoughts, ideas, and information. Managers then take what is shared and put it into practice by working with employees to get their buy-in based on the knowledge that was shared.

Another important aspect of communication is to help improve the business flow and processes of the company. When looking at a universally designed system, all functions are connected to work together toward an end goal. First, education communicates what is learned and how it should be learned. This information is then incorporated by the leader in his or her vision and mission statement. Once the vision and mission statement has been developed, managers are then given the authority to create business practices and policies to communicate through thought and action how the details to success will be carried out. This situation links education, management, and leadership together through a shared process of inputs and outputs to enhance the coordination of a system's process based on communication as the core concept.

To be successful, each company must implement the communication process model. The beginning step is for the sender to initiate the communication process. The sender will initiate the creation and development of the idea. Once the sender starts this process, the information is then encoded into an actual message. Once the message has been transmitted, it is then received and decoded by the receiver. Based on what is transmitted and understood, the receiver sends feedback to the original sender. The sender will review the feedback to see if it aligns with what was intended to be communicated. If the feedback is supportive of the content, then the communication was successful. However, if the feedback expresses misunderstanding or confusion, then the communication channel was unsuccessful due to noise and other external factors. The goal of this structure is to create an environment of shared knowledge through the components of the communication process.

Within any framework of an organization, knowledge is the key to success. Gaining knowledge is a science and is based on gaining familiarity with an idea or subject through direct association or unique experiences. The more knowledge that is gained through shared communication and leadership, the more companies will experience an increase in workflow and productivity. One of the major ways communication has improved workflow and coordination within a systematic framework is through technology. Schools and companies now rely on communication technology to quickly disseminate information to their learners or employees.

Communication technology is a digital tool that is used to send and receive inputs and outputs through a shared channel of interaction. Types of communication technology include messaging systems such as email and voice messaging. Email is one of the most important business communication methods because it is efficient, effective, low-cost, and can be easily replicated. With the use of email, companies can easily transmit large quantities of data internally and externally to their stakeholders. While email is an effective method of providing a channel for fast communication, it can also create a high amount of noise for the receiver of the message within the organization. Most employees spend over two hours each workday sorting through spam, junk, or irrelevant email that detracts from the importance of other relevant work. Voice messaging is also helpful for companies since it can record verbal communications. Like email, voice messaging can also cause noise or static that can lead to distortion or confusion in the message.

When using communication technology, the main advantage is that it is more efficient. Second, it is a fast method of communication. Third, communication technology can be used to communicate and share information around the world using virtualization, making long-distance connections and faster decision-making possible. When used correctly, communication technology is an asset to any business. When it is not implemented properly, communication technology can create a barrier to communication. If the technology infrastructure fails, there is the potential that all communication will fail. Finally, communication technology can directly impact face-to-face interactions, leading to miscommunication and misinterpretation of information that leads to a decrease in shared knowledge and understanding within the company.

While most of this communication is verbal, businesses also rely on nonverbal methods to share information. With nonverbal communication, information is shared without using words. Instead, gestures, expressions, posture, and body language are used to encode or decode a message. The way a person reacts without words will provide visual cues to the sender or receiver based on how the person listens, looks, moves, or reacts to the message. One advantage of nonverbal communication is that it can strengthen the original message by strengthening the intent of the message through actions instead of only using words. Next, nonverbal communication can contradict a verbal message by showing the sender or receiver that the truth is not being spoken.

Another advantage of nonverbal communication is that it can be used as a substitute for verbal communication since facial expressions or gestures can be used to express detailed and graphic messages more effectively than words. Fourth, nonverbal communication is used to complement a verbal message to show additional support and approval. A firm handshake, a touch on the shoulder, or a salute can help reinforce the intent of a message from the sender to the receiver. Finally, nonverbal communication can accentuate the verbal message. Touching something or making a gesture like a fist can underscore or highlight the verbal message being made. When nonverbal communication is used to support verbal communication, the message is more likely to be encoded, decoded, and understood through the feedback loop than when one of these methods is used individually.

Once the method of communication is chosen, the direction of the flow of information must be determined. Downward communication is used by leaders to share information from the top-down instead of the bottom-up. The flow of information is used by leadership to disseminate the mission and vision throughout the business. When using this strategy, all decision-making is conducted at the top level and then is efficiently transmitted through the management chain down to the employees. When the information is received from the leader, employees are given specific tasks to complete based on the message that was received. While the tasks are delegated by the management team, they are ultimately completed by the employees at the direction or message from the leader.

The advantage of a downward communication model is that it links the processes together through the different levels by using messages and the sharing of knowledge and information. All information is transmitted using a high-to low-level strategy so that it reaches every worker, employee, and stakeholder. For downward communication to be effective, the leader must make sure that they are self-aware. Self-awareness enables the leader to know their strengths and weaknesses to help improve their ability to correspond and communicate with other individuals. Instead of only thinking about how they would perceive something, he or she would be more aware of what they are saying so it is more clearly understood by the intended recipient.

Next, downward communication relies on being able to write and speak effectively. What is spoken or written must be coherent and be able to be understood to guarantee knowledge between both parties. Downward communication initiated by the leader must be credible. The leaders of a company will need to be dependable and reliable. The words or gestures that are used will need to be carefully chosen to help enforce the true meaning of the message. All leaders will be required to be capable in their position and create and share effective messages that will be sent out throughout the entire business. Having reliable and valuable content contained within the message will be vital to the success of the message that will guide everyone toward the overall vision and mission to give Responsibility of Reason.

An effective channel should be used by leadership within an organization. A channel of communication is important to ensure that all information is spread to all stakeholders in the most effective and efficient way using technology, verbal, and nonverbal methods. With a downward communication method, the leaders will become the beginning of the channel, management the middle, and employees the end of the channel. This situation will provide a consistent approach for sharing the same information to various departments and people. As a result, communication becomes more streamlined and reliable when it comes from the top leadership team and travels throughout the organization.

Next, clarity is important to downward communication. Clarity is the ability of the leader to make their message simple and easy to understand. Since their information is coming from the top-down, the message will be delivered to multiple people and groups at the same time. If the message is not clear, there will be mass confusion and a general misunderstanding of the intended message. If clarity does not occur, then there will be a delay in the process, causing a lack of productivity and, in some cases, disengagement throughout the business. To support the clarity of the leader, effective listening is required. Effective listening is "active" listening, where the sender and receiver take the time to process what is being said and to understand the information that is being communicated. It is one thing for the message to be encoded and shared; it is another thing for the information to be decoded and heard.

If the message is successfully encoded and decoded, then feedback will result from the downward communication process. Since the information flowed down from the top, feedback will travel upward back to the leader through the employee and management team. Feedback will be received in the form of verbal acceptance, nonverbal cues of approval or disengagement, and through actions that support employee development and growth directly related to the flow of information. Based on the feedback received, leaders can better understand their workforce and become more aware of their thoughts, feelings, and needs. Using a strong downward communication model with upward feedback will help to connect people at each level within the corporate structure and bring everyone together to focus on the shared vision and mission of the business. As a result, empathy can be considered one of the most important components of a leader when implementing downward communication to help increase engagement and decrease employee dissatisfaction.

Not only does downward communication direct the flow of information, but it also works to connect all processes associated with communication. It is not just what someone says; it is also what they do. Effective communication will combine the "actions" with the "words" so there is symmetry in the business processes, goals, and objectives. Clear communication from leadership will guide each process so that all processes work together instead of competing with one another. Through this process, information is broadcast from the highest down to the lowest level of each process in the value chain of the business.

Before communication can begin, there are prerequisites for effective downward communication. First, "noise" or static should be eliminated. The elimination of noise or confusion will ensure that the message will be clear, concise, and accurate in its meaning. For leaders to get buy-in, the communication and message need to request support instead of being demanding. The ideas should be open to foster communication and community support. This strategy will make sure that people are not on the defensive and instead are open to new ideas and the change that is contained in the message. Finally, the leader will need to know their audience and use simple language so that the message will be easily understood by everyone.

Downward communication is used in education. It begins with the teacher giving information to students to help them learn. Once the information is learned, the learner then applies what they have learned to a process. This strategy is used by management to "manage" the process and to improve the information flow to the employees. Once the information is received by the employee, they will match the "words" with the "actions" so they can follow through on the leader's idea. When everyone is involved in this process, there is a Responsibility of Reason in education, management, leadership, and lifelong learning.

While downward communication is an effective method, it is not without problems. First, when communication comes from the top-down, information can be distorted. The leader might have good intentions, but the words used to communicate the information can be incorrect or misused. Next, since there is a huge amount of distance between the lower levels of the organization and the top hierarchy, this situation can lead to distortion and receiving slow feedback. Change will become a slow process due to the amount of time it takes to receive and process information from the message. There will also be problems with interpretation by people when understanding what is asked, especially when there is a "barrier" between them and the leader through the hierarchy of the organization. Due to this fact, morale can become low, creating disengagement in the workflow.

There are ways to improve downward communication. While communication will be coming from the top-down, information will still be received from the bottom-up through acceptance and feedback. To help improve the process, leaders need to remember to always ask encouraging questions and solicit feedback with any communication they send out. This approach will help get a "pulse" on the situation, to see where things are and what improvements can be made to enhance productivity and employee buy-in in the work environment. Next, the information received should be stored and easily accessible for recall so changes can be made while keeping an open line of communication at all levels of the organization. Third, the leader should always be informative and make sure that the message is clear so it can easily be encoded and decoded by the respondent. The final improvement in downward communication is to always be transparent and honest in what is being shared in your message. Honesty is the best policy in all aspects of business, but is extremely important in communication since it is required to build trust, acceptance, and sustainability within the company.

The second method of sharing information within an organization is upward communication. With upward communication, the flow of information is reversed. Communication travels from the bottom of the organization toward the top. The information does not come from the top-tier leaders but instead comes from the leadership of the employees. The employees initiate this form of communication for the managers and leaders to take notice and hear. The type of information that is usually involved in upward communication includes employee suggestions, ideas, and complaints.

Employees want to feel valued and know that their opinions are heard. When an employee feels valued, they become more invested and want to work hard to increase productivity and return on investment (ROI). Since employees are a company's most valuable asset, the leaders should listen to what they have to say so they can potentially benefit from their ideas that are shared through channels of communication. However, employees should also have a channel of communication to discuss and share their complaints. To be successful, leaders and managers should not dismiss the complaints that they receive. Instead, they should investigate the truth behind the complaints to see what, if any, changes are required to improve the working conditions or business processes. When a manager learns of a complaint from the bottom levels of the organizational hierarchy, they become aware that it is not just an employee problem but an organizational issue. To help improve the organization, the leaders should address all complaints and encourage employees to bring valid complaints to their attention so they can work on them together as a single entity.

Next, upward communication is a method that enables participatory interaction and involvement of employees with the leadership team of the business. Participatory interaction is a critical component of successful information exchange, so all individuals feel valued and an equal part of the team. Third, upward communication helps to create new policies used on the front line. Information received from frontline workers is important since they are the ones who do the work each day. Their input and feedback are critical to drafting new policies that should be adopted as part of the business process by upper management and leadership. Mutual trust is also developed through upward communication, as employees will see that they can bring issues or situations to managers and leadership without any negative repercussions or fear of voicing their opinions to make a positive change. Finally, feedback is gained through upward communication. Leaders and managers will gain feedback from employees that can be used to help improve the organizational structure and culture.

Examples of upward communication include a learner communicating with a teacher about their thoughts during the learning process. This feedback will help the teacher to know where the individual is within the learning process so he or she can adjust their learning with scaffolding and other educational teaching tools and techniques. Within a business, upward communication can be found in employee meetings. Employee meetings enable individuals to share thoughts and ideas to help benefit the company with fellow colleagues and management. The information collected by the manager is then shared with the leader or leadership team within the organization.

An open-door policy is also a form of upward communication. This policy is one where there is transparency in communication by allowing employees to come into the manager or leader's office at any time to voice concerns, share ideas, or give unsolicited feedback. This strategy is useful within a business since it creates a conducive and collaborative environment for open channels of communication. Next, employee letters are used as a written form of communication to share information, thoughts, or ideas that should be addressed. Email is the primary way for employees to provide written communication to their manager or leader within their organization. The advantage of employee letters or written communication is that it provides a documented record of the issue the manager or leader will address and can be used as part of the documentation for initiating change. Finally, upward communication focuses on social groups and participation within the company. Employees will get to join different groups and be able to make new connections with other employees, managers, and leaders within the company to build synergy and other direct connections.

When using upward communication, there are several methods that can be used to initiate the transmission of messages and information. First, managers and leaders can encourage employees to ask questions to gain valuable insight and feedback. Next, management and leaders can do management by walking around to observe employees in their natural work environment to get a realistic perspective of how things function and operate. Third, upward communication can be utilized in climate surveys. Climate surveys seek to determine individuals' thoughts about the culture, climate, and organizational behavior. The information gathered will be used to help gain employee support by including them as part of the process and culture through efforts of inclusion for equity and equality. Finally, upward communication can take advantage of 360-degree feedback. 360-degree feedback allows the leader and employee to give feedback to one another based on their perspectives. The evaluations are conducted and collected by all stakeholders to get a wide range of feedback to help create a realistic viewpoint of the situation of the entire business entity in its internal and external environments. As a result, participative management is being conducted to bring all parties together under a shared organizational culture.

The third communication method used in the Responsibility of Reason is through horizontal communication. Horizontal communication is information that is shared laterally or by people on the same level within the organization. This type of communication is helpful in departments of large organizations or small business environments. The idea behind horizontal communication is that everyone is in the same area at one time to share information and communicate openly with one another. As a result, horizontal communication is typically an informal method of sharing knowledge between individuals or groups of people within the same area.

The fourth communication method is diagonal communication. Diagonal communication is a method of sharing information that is a blend of horizontal and vertical communication. In this method of communication, managers and employees at all different levels within the organization can engage in open communication with people who are not in their direct chain of command. The idea behind diagonal communication is that it makes collaboration easier and brings different departments together under one umbrella. As a result, the different ranks and various departments will be able to coordinate with one another to develop a full picture of the organization and its internal and external environments.

While these forms of communication are formal, there are also informal channels of direct communication within an organization. First, there is the grapevine. The grapevine occurs when individuals gossip and share information about what they have heard from other sources or channels. The grapevine is based on perceptions and data that has not been verified. While the grapevine can be a good source of knowledge, it can be responsible for passing along bad or incorrect information. This situation means that if you hear something in the grapevine, it is important to verify the source and where the information came from before acting on what is said to be actual knowledge. Many times, information that is said is only rumors or information that does not directly support any form of real evidence and cannot be substantiated. As a result, the grapevine is a necessary part of any company but must be verified before the information becomes fact or part of the organizational behavior or culture.

Another way communication travels throughout an organization is by a communication network. There are five main types of communication network structures. The purpose of the communication network is to connect individuals who are the senders and receivers of information by creating the right channel to create and generate knowledge. The first type of communication network is the wheel network. The wheel network is used by teams, groups, departments, and organizations. With this structure, communication is centralized from the top and travels down through the organizational hierarchy until it reaches the managers, employees, and other stakeholders. One leader directs the communication flow to ensure fast and efficient communication throughout the organizational structure.

The second form of communication network is the chain network. The chain network was devised to help individuals within a business to communicate using a set sequence. While communication starts at the top from the leader, it then travels down through the hierarchy until it reaches each level within the business. This situation creates a chain that causes communication to pass through each "link" until it goes from the beginning to the end of the chain. The third type of communication network is the Y network. The Y network exists when two individuals directly report to a manager or leader. This situation creates a four-level hierarchy where the leader will speak to the manager, and then the manager in turn will speak to each of the individuals.

The fourth type of communication network is the circle network. The circle network is based on a three-level hierarchy where communication is shared between the leaders and employees. While this structure follows a sequence, there is also cross-communication or interaction at the necessary levels within the communication network. The final type of communication network is the star network. The star network revolves around a central hub or source of information. From the central hub, each employee or subordinate is directly linked, so information can be communicated to them. In this strategy, information is not hindered or blocked, and it enables a restriction-free environment for communication to exist. In most cases, technology is used to join users to the source of information to create a star network of communication.

While many forms of communication use direct verbal and nonverbal methods from a person, information can also be shared using technology. Email is one way to share massive amounts of information in a quick and reliable way using a computer and a program to track and record messages. While email is a necessary form of communication, many businesses or organizations can suffer from overuse by sending out unnecessary communications. This can delay responses to important messages, causing noise in the communication system. This situation can cause information overload for employees and become a disruptive part of the value chain.

Next, email can be viewed as being impersonal, causing a disconnect between the leader, manager, or employee when trying to communicate information and knowledge. Finally, email can lead to misunderstandings based on how the information is encoded or decoded. With email, there are no verbal or nonverbal cues to interpret. This situation causes the words, language, and tone of the email to be "blindly" interpreted by the decoder of the message. As a result, the same email can create a different message to each of its recipients, causing confusion, disruption, and potential disengagement between the individual and the organization. While email has become a critical component of any corporation, it should not be used to replace personal communication methods, especially when sharing important information.

Other forms of communication using technology include instant messaging, text messaging, social media networking, voicemail, blogs, videoconferencing, and digital presentations and training. Over the years, technology has advanced to provide several methods to transmit data and information. With the use of technology, the transmission of information has become faster and, in most cases, more reliable. However, companies must remember that technology is a tool to share information and should not be used as the only source of communication. Each of these electronic methods should always be followed up with in-person communication to avoid disengagement, misunderstandings, and potential conflicts that detract from the mission and vision of the organization.

There are barriers to communication that most businesses will face, including bias in the frame of reference when sending or receiving a message. Bias relates to the individual's personal preferences and can determine whether they support or reject an idea. The frame of reference is cognitive thinking, or how the person perceives the meaning of the message. When there is bias or an incorrect frame of reference, a barrier will be placed during the encoding and decoding of a message, creating a breakdown in the communication network. Next, filtering can cause a barrier to communication. Filtering occurs when there is distortion or something is not shared with another person to help manage their reactions. When this situation happens, the reaction that is received is not genuine since it has been engineered by one person to get a guided response from the second person. As a result, trust does not exist between the two individuals, and the actions can become counterproductive to the mission or vision based on incorrect data or opinions.

Another barrier to communication is the structure in which information is shared. If there is a high amount of bureaucracy within an organization, information can be transmitted slowly or become distorted as it passes through each level of the hierarchy. The rules, policies, and procedures can cause a delay in the true meaning of the information to be sent, ultimately leading to employee misunderstandings or being viewed as unnecessary by the individual. Since every individual operates and lives in the organization, it is important to share the right information correctly and equally with everyone so there is a high level of transparency to keep the employees connected with the managers and leaders to support the mission and vision of the business.

Information overload will also lead to a barrier to communication. With so many methods of receiving information, individuals can suffer from getting too much information at one time without having time to process what they have just received. This situation causes the individual to be focused in several different directions without being able to give any one topic the attention it deserves. When sending information, it is important to remember to send the message systematically so it can be digested, understood, and applied by the employee so they can put the idea into action in the workflow process. Next semantics can also lead to a barrier to communication. Semantics can develop with the words that are chosen in the message. While words can mean the same thing, the context they are used in can lead to a different interpretation of the information. This situation can lead to an unanticipated understanding of what was originally thought to have been communicated.

Another barrier to communication includes credibility. In email and other electronic forms of communication, there can be spam messages or viruses that cause miscommunication or misdirection from the actual communication that was intended by the leader to the employee. Individual perception is also a barrier to communication. Each person will interpret the message based on their own criteria and unique experiences and will filter the content of the message based on those beliefs. Differences in status or roles within the organization will create barriers to communication, since people may feel disengaged with those at other levels and do not believe that what they are saying directly impacts their position or job function.

A major barrier to communication is gender and the differences in how men and women use language or interpret information. Women and men both have different gender roles that can lead to stereotypes and personal differences when sending or receiving a message. While most of the time men will communicate a fact or an action, women will communicate to share their feelings and to create an opportunity to discuss a situation without providing a result or chosen action. To increase the barriers to communication, cultural differences can also create problems. Cultural barriers form when people from two different cultures try to communicate but have different perceptions, frames of reference, or internal understandings. As a result, cultural differences can impact cross-cultural communication through misunderstandings of language, politics, values, stereotypes, and conflicting moral values.

There are several methods that can be used to overcome barriers to communication. First, the sender of the information should make sure that it is the right time to transmit the message or share the data so it will be received clearly and accurately. Second, the language used in the message should be simple, clear, and related to the mission and vision of the business. Third, only communicate one idea at a time to maintain the clarity and focus of the message. Fourth, the sender and receiver of the message must respect each other equally so they will value the contents of the message, enabling the information to not get "lost in the sauce." Finally, the sender should always follow up with the receiver of the message to make sure that the information was understood and to provide additional support to the individual. This strategy will help to provide repetition and reinforcement of content and ideas, demonstrate empathy, and improve the general understanding within the company.

Overcoming barriers to communication will create a sustainable two-way communication channel, provide effective top-down and bottom-up feedback, and ensure efficient and effective communication throughout the organizational hierarchy. Next, active listening will become an integral part of overcoming barriers to communication. Active listening ensures that both parties are fully engaged in the communication process. While one person is speaking, the other individual is listening, processing, and understanding what is being communicated. When the first person, or the encoder, has finished speaking, then the second person, or decoder, will provide feedback. When the original decoder speaks, they become the encoder, while the original encoder becomes the new decoder. As the feedback is being given, the second party listens to what is being said to make sure that there is a clear line of communication and understanding.

Communication is one of the most, if not the most, important aspects of the Responsibility of Reason. When there is miscommunication, there is a breakdown from the top level to the bottom level of the organizational hierarchy. They say that someone is only as strong as their weakest link, and this is particularly true in the Responsibility of Reason. If communication fails, it will not be hard to get off course and become lost. However, if communication is strong, each person within the organization will be directly connected to one another through the communication channel, creating a positive and supportive environment of organizational culture and behavior. This situation will become clear with the following examples that explain the "'RRRR She Blows': The Impact of the Lack of Responsibility of Reason" and the "'RRRRRR She Goes: The Impact of the Use of Responsibility of Reason'" models.

When a business does not have an effective communication channel, it creates a sea of uncertainty. This sea of uncertainty causes people to become lost and washed along by the waves. Since people do not know what to expect due to a lack of clear or proper communication, there are rocky waters and large choppy waves that can cause the company to experience damage to its internal and external environments. The corporation should act as a large, sturdy ship to help all its employees weather the storm and achieve success. If the ship, or organization, is sound, then the journey will be smooth sailing. If the ship is unsound, then there is a greater chance for a shipwreck or failure within the business.

In this example, we see a person, or an individual traveling alone, trying to paddle safely in a canoe over a monstrous wave caused by the sea of uncertainty. Since there is no communication, the individual is unaware of the dangers they will face. Instead of avoiding the storm and setting a safer course, the individual must now try to paddle alone over a giant wave in a tiny canoe. While some smaller waves might be conquered, it will eventually become impossible for the individual to paddle over the giant wave and will soon be swallowed up. The canoe will break, and the individual will have to swim for their life before being destroyed by the giant wave caused by the sea of uncertainty.

What causes this sea of uncertainty? There are four main sources of problems that will develop from a lack of a strong communication channel within a business. First, a lack of communication will create resistance to change. Since the individual does not understand why they are doing something or the importance of what is being communicated, there will be an unwillingness to adopt new policies, procedures, or strategies. The main reason for the resistance to change is fear. While it may be fearful to adopt a new policy change, it can be more fearful to battle the harsh elements alone, like trying to sail a rickety canoe over a gigantic wave.

Next, there can be a restraint of vision due to a lack of communication. A restraint of vision occurs when the leader would like to decide but does not have all the information, facts, or employee support to make the new change a reality. While the company may need to adjust its strategy, it can become hampered by a lack of vision due to the overall support from internal and external factors that guide the mission of the leader. This situation causes the leader to reduce their vision based on being reactive to internal and external factors instead of being proactive and trying to get ahead of the upcoming storm of uncertainty due to a lack of communication.

Third, there is a reduction of mission with poor communication. When the leader is unable to get stakeholder support or buy-in, then the value chain of the organization will decrease, causing a lack of support for the mission of the company. This situation can cause the company to lose focus and get off course instead of following a well-designed path to success. Finally, a poor communication channel will impact the quality of purpose. The reinforcement of the quality of purpose can only be achieved when there is an efficient and effective communication channel. Without clear communication, individuals will become disconnected from the purpose of the company. This situation causes a decrease in quality and causes not only the individual but the company as well to be swallowed up by the sea of uncertainty. As a result, all that is left to say is "RRRR she blows!" as everything sinks down below, never to be seen or heard from again, as shown in Figure 5.

However, Figure 6 shows how a strong communication model can help to change the situation or status of an organization. This is done using the impact of the use of Responsibility of Reason with the "RRRRRR she goes!" model. When looking at this model, we can see that a strong communication channel will lead the sea of uncertainty to become the sea of tranquility. With the use of effective, clear, and relevant communication, there will be mutual understanding and trust that enable everyone to connect and work together toward a shared mission and vision. With this strategy, the sea of tranquility will help to support the six major functions of communication and improve the reason of responsibility by connecting education, management, and leadership skills.

First, information and knowledge are shared through a successful communication channel by releasing the knowledge to every individual. When information is shared, a shared knowledge base is developed within the company. This knowledge base becomes part of the organizational structure. With

FIGURE 5 The impact of "RRRR She Blows."

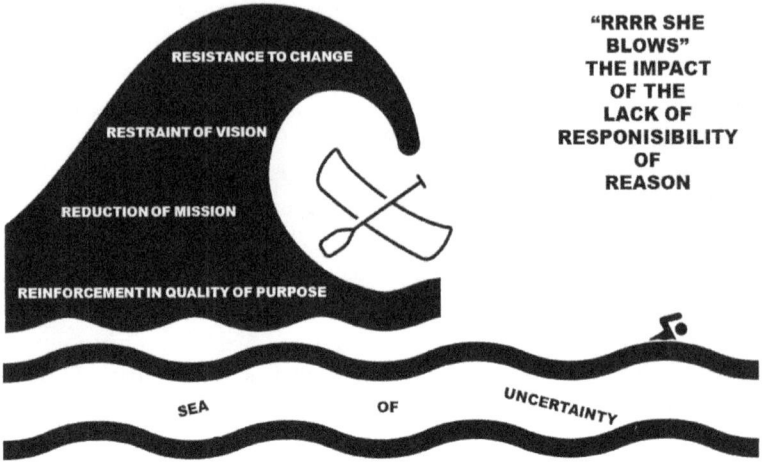

RESISTANCE TO CHANGE

RESTRAINT OF VISION

REDUCTION OF MISSION

REINFORCEMENT IN QUALITY OF PURPOSE

"RRRR SHE BLOWS" THE IMPACT OF THE LACK OF RESPONISIBILITY OF REASON

SEA   OF   UNCERTAINTY

FIGURE 6 The impact of "RRRRRR she goes."

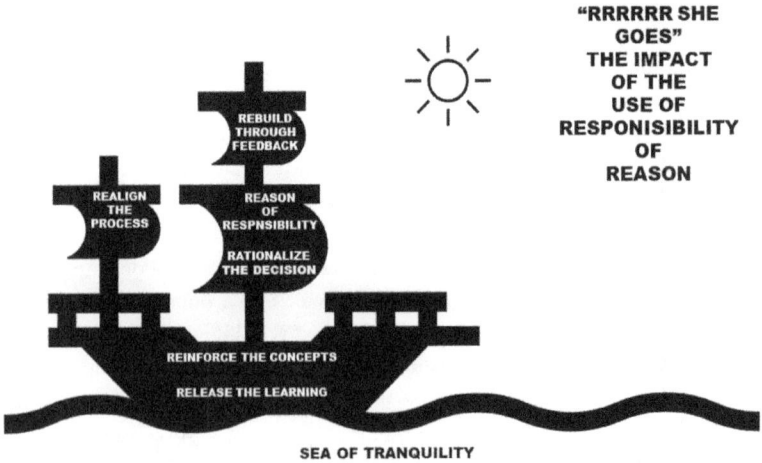

"RRRRRR SHE GOES" THE IMPACT OF THE USE OF RESPONISIBILITY OF REASON

REBUILD THROUGH FEEDBACK

REALIGN THE PROCESS

REASON OF RESPNSIBILITY

RATIONALIZE THE DECISION

REINFORCE THE CONCEPTS

RELEASE THE LEARNING

SEA OF TRANQUILITY

the knowledge released, everyone increases their responsibility, thus creating a tight ship. Next, a strong communication channel supports the reinforcement of concepts. Reinforcement of concepts is important since it provides additional support for the corporate mission and vision as determined by the leadership. When employees have increased knowledge, they are able to provide support based on their unique experiences and understanding.

The third function of a strong communication channel is to rationalize the decision-making process. When rationalizing a decision, the individual must have the information prior to taking action, so the process can be done with reason instead of by chance. Every action that is taken must be focused on the mission and vision if the company is to survive and avoid a sea of uncertainty. Only with clear communication and clarity can a ship sail on a sea of tranquility by rationalizing the decision. The fourth function is to realign the process. Realigning the process involves open communication between all levels within the organizational hierarchy. To realign the process, leaders, managers, and employees will need to work together and communicate so a 360-degree view of the organization can be understood to help strengthen its internal and external environments.

The fifth function of "RRRRRR she blows" is to rebuild through feedback. Companies can rebuild and become stronger by receiving feedback. Feedback comes not only from the top-down but also from the bottom-up. When feedback is received, the message that is sent will be guaranteed to be understood and to help bring everyone onto the same page to work together instead of separately in silos or competing departments. If there is no feedback, everyone in the organization will be left to their assumptions without any true facts of what is really happening or what is understood. This situation can cause uncertainty to take over and will lead to a non-Responsibility of Reason.

The final function of this model is the reason for responsibility. The Responsibility of Reason can only come when there is combined communication and feedback from the leaders, managers, and employees. Without knowledge or process, a valid reason cannot exist. The processes within a company must be aligned with the mission and vision of the leadership. Since an organization is made up of individuals, each person is required to take responsibility for their actions and make sure that everything they do supports the objectives and goals of the company. With the Responsibility of Reason, the organization will be able to institute SMART goals that enable specific, measurable, achievable, relevant, and time-bound targets. As a result, individuals work together to support the company in being SMART and to increase the goals of Responsibility of Reason. As a result, the company will experience smooth sailing on the sea of tranquility with its big, strong ship as it sails off into the sunset toward a brighter future with the leaders, managers, and employees all saying, "RRRRRR she goes!"

Simpleton Solution

Whether you are in education, management, or leadership, communication is an important process for sending and receiving information to help support the learning process. Communication can be conducted using verbal, nonverbal, or technological methods to share information. The main goal of communication is to increase knowledge. This situation supports a stronger Responsibility of Reason for both the individual and the organization. To ensure that there is effective and efficient communication, the right form of communication channel must be implemented to strengthen organizational behavior. If there is a failure to communicate, there will be a breakdown in the support of the mission and vision of the leadership. As in business, where cash is "king," communication is "king" in the Responsibility of Reason.

Here are the key takeaways from the chapter to remember:

- Communication is important from the top-down and bottom-up.
- Feedback is required to help strengthen the level of understanding and to create a process for support.
- The impact of the lack of Responsibility of Reason is based on the 4Rs of "RRRR She Blows!"
  - Resistance to change.
  - Restraint of vision.
  - Reduction of mission.
  - Reinforcement in quality of purpose.
- The impact of the use of Responsibility of Reason is based on the 6Rs of "RRRRRR She Goes!"
  - Releasing the learning.
  - Reinforce the concepts.
  - Rationalize the decision.
  - Realign the process.
  - Rebuild through feedback.
  - Reason of responsibility.

The main takeaway from this chapter is that communication is very important at all levels of an organizational hierarchy. While it is easy to say or send a message, the real struggle comes from ensuring that it is properly received and understood. Leaders cannot assume that what they said or what makes sense to them will be understood the same way by others. This situation causes leaders to make sure that all forms of communication are simple, clear, and aligned with the mission and vision of the business. When this strategy is used, the level of uncertainty is reduced, and organizations will increase their knowledge and improve their organizational culture. As a result, everyone in the hierarchy will be connected and become proactive instead of reactive to help improve sustainability in the future.

Figure 7 uses the example of pushing the buttons on a light switch. The two options are sanity and insanity. Sanity is when a person thinks and acts rationally in each situation based on a healthy state of mind. However, insanity is doing something when conventional logic tells us that something else will happen. When an individual constantly does the same unreasonable action repeatedly, expecting a logical result, this will result in insanity. To prevent insanity from developing, the individual or organization must push the sanity button.

For individuals and organizations, each decision or action requires the pushing of a button to guide the success or failure of the process. If a decision is made without knowledge, structure, or vision, then proceeding will create insanity in the organization since it will believe it can obtain high-level results with a low-level process. However, if the necessary amount of time has been put forward to understand the situation through knowledge, skills, abilities, and philosophy, then a sound decision will be made. The organization will be able to create policies and processes that support the shared vision of the leader.

As a result, this situation will prevent insane actions from occurring, which would cause a breakdown in the Responsibility of Reason in leadership,

FIGURE 7 The light switch effect of sanity vs. insanity.

management, and lifelong learning creation. Having a strong philosophy will lead to making logical decisions. Second, the leader will be able to establish a mission and vision for everyone to follow. Third, management will be able to act on that philosophy and create a sustainable process. Together, there will be a change from insanity to sanity by the flip of a switch. Now, let's remember to remain sane in an insane world by creating stability in organizational behavior and shared leadership using the voice and Responsibility of Reason.

CHAPTER 5

THE NEED FOR SPEED […] AND GREAT RESPONSIBILITY

The Situation: With Great Power There Is a Need for Great Responsibility

"With great power comes great responsibility" were the legendary words of wisdom that were first spoken by Uncle Ben before his tragic end. Ever since those (now) famous words were uttered to Peter, who was transforming himself into something new (a.k.a. Spider-Man), no one has been able to say it better. With this simple phrase, Ben Parker shared what it means to be leaders, to have power, and to promote an individual and collective Responsibility of Reason. With any form of power, there is a moral responsibility beyond the needs of oneself to serve the greater good. Having power should not be used only for personal gain. Instead, the position or responsibility of power is to have a strong commitment to others. This situation means that the more power or influence someone has, the greater amount of responsibility will exist. While it may be more fun to be the lone superhero and deal out our own justice with the phrase "I am Batman," the truth that lies under the mask is that we should all be like Spider-Man, and where we possess extraordinary abilities and take responsibility, make the world a safer place for everyone through leadership, management, and lifelong learning.

Let's take a closer look at the many important concepts found in the simple phrase "With great power comes great responsibility." First, we will look at accountability. Accountability occurs when someone has a great deal of power. While having power is necessary to make decisions for yourself, it is more important to be able to use that power to positively support those around you. As a result, anyone with power or in a position of power will need to be responsible for making ethical decisions for the common good.

Next, this statement incorporates the idea of power and trust. Trust is earned through proven responsibility. The more people act responsibly, the more they demonstrate the level at which they can be trusted. When there is trust, power will be sure to follow. People will be more inclined to listen to someone who is trustworthy than to someone who cannot be trusted. Finally, trust is directly linked to power and responsibility, enabling someone to influence others in a positive way. As a result, trust is established over time by demonstrating that you will do what you say and take responsibility for what you do.

The third aspect of this quote is respect. Respect is earned when someone acts ethically and responsibly beyond his or her own needs. Second, respect is used to influence others through authenticity. When someone is authentic, a positive relationship will develop between that person and the other group members. The more trust, authenticity, and integrity there are, the stronger the influence the person will have in the established relationship. Finally, respect is based on empathy and compassion. Empathy is understanding the other person's situation, and compassion is treating everyone equally and with respect for their unique characteristics and skills. As a result, the person's words will match their actions to show that they are authentic in both what they say and what they are willing to do to create a more positive environment.

The fourth component of this statement is sustainability. Sustainability is the ability to use power successfully over a long period of time. Power should be gained through positive interactions of supporting those in your environment. This situation will create a positive environment and a Responsibility of Reason. The results of the positive use of power will lead to long-term results and a positive culture. However, power can be used to coerce others into doing what you want. This situation occurs through coercion, manipulation, and unethical decision-making and behavior. When power is used incorrectly, actions will be short-lived. Negative consequences will also be implemented because of the incorrect use of power with a lack of responsibility.

The final aspect that pertains to the statement "with great power comes great responsibility" is leadership. Leadership is used by an individual to impact or guide a specific desired outcome. First, leadership skills can be inborn or can be developed and learned within a given situation or environment. This makes leadership a position of both formal and informal power. Next, leadership is demonstrated by any observable behavior or trait that is used to support positive results and decision-making processes. As a result, leaders who can demonstrate responsibility in their decisions and actions will be more likely to rally and motivate others. When this situation occurs, the leader will be able to enhance the amount of power and influence they have in the situation or environment.

As you can see, there is a great deal of Responsibility of Reason contained in the words of Uncle Ben. The main point of this quote is to demonstrate that each one of us can influence and change the environment around us with our actions. The actions can either be positive or negative. To have great power and responsibility, an individual will need to learn to establish and maintain trust. Next, great power will lead to great responsibility by demonstrating respect, empathy, and compassion toward others. Finally, great power combined with great responsibility will lead to a positive and sustainable culture and atmosphere. This situation will improve or enhance the power of both the leader and their followers, proving that "With great power comes great responsibility."

Now that we understand the importance of great power and the need for responsibility, let's discuss how this concept impacts an organization. Within an organization, power is distributed to various individuals, roles, and positions that include executive leadership, middle management, individual contributors, support staff, and stakeholders. The highest level of leadership is executive leadership. Executive leadership includes the chief executive officer (CEO), president, vice president, and other top-level positions. Executive leaders have the most power and influence over the organization. When it comes to decision-making authority, executive leaders are the ones who influence and determine the course of action that the company will take as it relates to vision, mission, values, and culture.

The next level of leadership is middle management. Middle management reports directly to the executive leadership team but supports both the upper and lower levels within the organizational hierarchy. Middle management positions include managers, department heads, team leaders, and project managers. Next, middle management positions have the authority and responsibility to make decisions that positively support their teams. Finally, middle managers can acquire and allocate resources to help ensure that the right priorities are achieved.

The third level of leadership in the organizational hierarchy is individual contributors. Individual contributors are the employees who do not occupy a management position within the hierarchy. These employees do not have the same high-level decision-making capabilities as the managers or executives. However, individual contributors still have power and influence based on their personal levels of knowledge, skills, abilities, and expertise. The skills of individual contributors can motivate and influence those within their organization through their reliability and Responsibility of Reason.

The fourth level is the support staff. The role of support staff is to assist other personnel in achieving organizational success. Positions that are included in the support staff include administrative and human resources. While these positions are not credited with directly influencing organizational decision-making, people within these roles do have the power to ensure that policies and processes are followed to support the work of other people. Human resources does not generate money for an organization, but it does provide the resources to influence a positive culture and improve employee retention.

The final level within an organizational hierarchy of power is the stake-holders. Stakeholders are not directly part of the organization. They are not employees who are hired by the company. Instead, stakeholders include share-holders, consumers, and community members who are directly impacted by the success of the organization. Stakeholders are unique in that they have the power and responsibility to influence the reputation or status of the company. With an improved reputation or standing in the environment, the organization will experience financial success, providing it with more power and greater influence over the community. With the increased amount of power, the various levels of power will be distributed to provide a greater amount of influence for both personal and shared success through the Responsibility of Reason in leadership, management, and lifelong learning.

Finally, it is important to remember that power is not just derived from the levels of organizational hierarchy. Instead, power comes from several other factors that include influence, expertise, the ability to acquire resources, and the capability of enacting and leading positive change. Within any organization, each person or component has some form or level of power. However, it is critical to understand the dynamic relationship between the different groups to help unite them and work together to achieve organizational success through power, shared leadership, and responsibility.

While power is divided among the various roles within an organization, responsibility is also dispersed among the various roles and people. The first group within an organization to bear responsibility is executive leadership. Executive leadership is responsible for setting the mission and vision of the company. Next, executive leadership determines the strategic strategy and direction for everyone to follow within the organization. Third, executive leadership ensures the financial safety and success of the company. As a result, executive leadership provides oversight of success by acting responsibly and establishing the reputation and culture of the business.

The second group that has responsibility within a company is middle management. Middle management is responsible for implementing and managing the policies and procedures that are established to assist in the vision and mission of the executive leadership. Next, middle management executes the business strategy required to be successful in the daily operations. This situation enables middle management to monitor and control essential resources. Third, middle management is responsible for overseeing the work of individual contributors or employees to ensure that everyone is being productive and working toward meeting the goals of the executive leadership.

The third responsible group is individual contributors. Individual contributors are workers or people who are not in management or executive positions. However, these individuals still have power and therefore have responsibilities as well. This group is responsible for completing assigned duties and tasks. Their main responsibility is to follow organizational policies and procedures. Next, individual contributors also meet the established expectations of performance standards based on a balanced scorecard. Finally, individual contributors work individually and together to achieve the shared mission and vision of the company.

The fourth group that has a level of responsibility is the support staff. The support staff are responsible for overseeing and facilitating the duty and work of other employees. Next, the support staff are responsible for ensuring that the organization is fully staffed and performing all the required functions for success. As a result, the support staff are found in all departments and levels within the organizational hierarchy. Finally, the support staff are responsible for addressing and solving employee issues and concerns so a positive organizational culture can exist within the company.

The final group that has responsibility within an organization is the stakeholders. Stakeholders are responsible for providing guidance to the company. One group of stakeholders are shareholders. Shareholders must vote on all major corporate decisions. The next group of stakeholders are customers. Customers are responsible for buying products and services. Customers are also responsible for providing valuable feedback to the company so it can adjust and better meet their needs. The final group of stakeholders is the community. The community has a responsibility to help keep the company ethical and accountable to all local, state, and federal laws and regulations.

While power is about having the authority or ability to direct or enforce a change, responsibility is about having accountability within each position in the organization. Each group or person within a company has both some form of power and responsibility built into their role or position. This situation makes it important for the leader and all followers within the organizational hierarchy to understand the dynamic relationship between the levels of operation. When the dynamic relationship is understood, then the organization can become more successful through the collaboration of power and responsibility.

With a strong responsibility of power, it becomes possible for an individual or leader to acquire the necessary resources to support the decision-making process. Having a good reason to gain resources to support the decision-making process is critical to the success of an organization. First, resources should be gained to increase efficiency. Efficiency relies on all resources that the company has access to. Types of organizational resources include human capital, financial, and material. In most situations, one or all of these resources will be limited, and there will be a competing need to claim them over someone else. When there is a positive reason to gain these resources, finances, human capital, and materials will be used more productively. This situation will eliminate organizational waste. As a result, the more effectively resources are used, the greater the level of efficiency.

Next, power and responsibility must be used to provide justification when requesting more resources. Justification is a well-defined reason that is used to explain why a certain resource is needed, why a decision was made, or why a specific action was taken. Next, it is important to have justification no matter which group you fall into within the organizational hierarchy, since decisions are either made or carried out. Justification will be needed by each group to explain their actions and thought processes to the board members, investors, stakeholders, and employees. As a result, justification is needed within each level of the organizational hierarchy and supports the position of power through responsibility.

Goal alignment is also needed to support the proper allocation of resources. When the decision to allocate resources aligns with the strategic goals, then goal alignment occurs. The better the reason provided by the leader or individual, the more critical it will be in ensuring that the resources used will be properly employed to support these goals. However, if resources are misused and are only used to support individual initiatives, then there will be a misalignment of goals with the mission and vision of the leader. To help ensure goal alignment, organizations must implement risk management. While each decision an organization makes contains a level of risk, having a good reason can reduce the negative impact of a decision by securing the necessary resources and remaining aligned with the overall goal or mission. As a result, organizations at all levels must work together to manage risk and reduce any potential threats by securing the necessary resources.

Finally, performance management requires having a clear goal or vision. Once the vision has been established, then all available resources should be allocated to support the shared vision. Performance management is used to help measure the use of resources and the level to which they impacted the overall performance of the decision-making process. Next, performance management provides a level of comparison between perceived and actual outcomes and performance levels. The expected outcome provides the reason and power for the decision-making process that can lead to the actual outcome. As a result, the ability to have a good reason to gain resources relies on accountability, transparency, and strategic alignment to the goals and decision-making process. Consequently, having a good reason combined with the power to gain resources will help to guarantee that each decision made will contribute to the success of the organization.

There are several advantages when individual and organizational power are combined. The first is collaboration. Collaboration will improve when each person takes responsibility for their own actions and decision-making processes. Through individual power, unique knowledge, skills, and abilities are used to help improve diversity and create a combined wealth of human capital resources. Each person within the organization is chosen for his or her knowledge and becomes an organizational resource. With the combined skills of everyone, they collectively represent the entire organization through collaboration. Finally, collaboration forms a synergy or bond between everyone within the company. This situation will lead to new and innovative decision-making processes and solutions.

The second advantage is empowerment. Empowerment develops through trust, power, and responsibility. When employees feel that they are recognized for their individual power, then he or she will be recognized by the organizational unit. This situation can lead to improved job satisfaction and employee performance. Next, productivity will increase for both the individual and the company. Third, motivation will improve for the individual since they are being recognized, which will lead to increased performance for the entire organization. As a result, empowerment enables employees to take the initiative and produce their best work for both themselves and the business.

Third, adaptability will be improved through individual and organizational power. Adaptability is the ability to make positive adjustments in a changing and dynamic environment. Individuals must take responsibility for their decisions and actions so organizations can take advantage and leverage both individual and organizational power to become more adaptable. When individuals and organizations become more adaptive, both parties will be able to effectively and efficiently direct positive change in the environment. To be adaptable, there must be a high level of diversity and inclusion. Diversity and inclusion allow the organization to recognize the power everyone possesses so they can harness it to support the shared vision and goal. When everyone is included, the organization will become diverse while allowing every individual to have a valued voice in the success of the business.

Finally, the advancement of leadership will begin to develop. When the organization recognizes individuals with knowledge, skills, abilities, and power, it will see their full potential and value. The organization will then begin to nurture and grow these individuals to be the next generation of potential leaders within their environment. Next, the organization will provide dedicated resources and support opportunities for the individual growth and development of each person to help them become individual and organizational leaders. As a result, individual and organizational power combine for many positive benefits to both the person and company, encouraging collaboration and mutual support to improve growth and development for everyone involved.

When individuals and the organizational units can work together, they will become more effective in achieving their desired results or goals. Next, the individuals and organization will work together to create a shared culture that enables the strengths of each person to be recognized within the organization. The more individual strengths that are identified, the greater the benefit there is for the organization. To effectively work together, there must be open communication to share information, ideas, and decision-making processes. Next, there must be mutual respect so that everyone is valued within the company. Third, there is a need for a shared vision so that all objectives and goals are aligned for a unified purpose, so that misalignment does not develop. This situation will create an environment for effective leadership that will balance the goals of the individuals with the needs of the organization. The power of the individuals will complement and support the power of the organization. As a result, both individuals and organization will use their power to propel one another to greater success.

Businesses that experience a higher level of accomplishment owe their success to their ability to empower their people within their hierarchy and organizational structure. The first method used to empower individuals is increased engagement of employees and departments. When employees are fully engaged and empowered, they are more likely to be committed to their jobs. Next, empowered individuals have a stronger sense of responsibility and ownership of their duties. This situation will cause empowered employees to become more productive and motivated to achieve both personal and organizational success.

Next, empowerment enables employees to become more innovative. When employees are trusted, they will use their knowledge, skills, and abilities to take more risks and chances in the workplace. This situation will help lead the person and the organization to take risks, and they can even come up with new innovations. Since they have become trusted and empowered, employees are not afraid to "think outside of the box" to develop and implement new ideas. Third, empowered employees are unafraid to challenge the current system or paradigm. These employees are willing to challenge the status quo to bring new and innovative ideas to the organization.

Third, there is improved decision-making within both individuals and the organization. When employees experience empowerment, they are closer to the decision-making process and more able to take part in day-to-day actions and activities. This situation will help the employees and the organization to become more informed about current business activities and functions. As a result, the entire organization will be more informed of the current situation, so more effective and efficient decisions and actions can be made to lead everyone to success in the future.

Fourth, empowered employees will lead to better and improved customer service. Better customer service will develop since employees are free to take new chances and go the extra mile. This situation will enable the employee to gain personal experience and meet all the actual and perceived needs of the customer. With each new success, the employee will continue to improve customer satisfaction. As customer satisfaction increases, so will the level of loyalty among all stakeholders. Fifth, personal growth will develop within empowered employees. Personal growth will lead to individual growth and the development of each employee. The more developed the employee becomes, the stronger and more diverse the organization becomes. Individual employees will gain both confidence and leadership skills that will be beneficial to their careers in the internal and external environments.

Last, empowered employees will be responsible for organizational agility. Organizational agility enables both the employee and the company to better adapt to changes within their environment. By being more empowered, the decision-making process can be performed faster than if employees were waiting to be told what to do. This situation will lead to quicker and more efficient actions. As a result, more actions and responsibilities can be handled at the same level instead of having a time delay by escalating them to a higher level for resolution. This situation makes it possible for management to focus on more advanced issues that can strengthen the objectives and goals of leadership due to individuals being empowered to handle more responsibility based on their knowledge, trust, dedication, and Responsibility of Reason.

Finally, employee empowerment will create an empowered organization. The success of empowerment is based on the amount of trust the organization places in each employee, followed by how responsible they have proven to be within a specific situation. Next, empowerment focuses on giving each employee the necessary tools, resources, and autonomy they will need to succeed. Not only does this situation benefit the individual but it also has a positive impact on the organization since upper management can handle more complex situations and issues that can arise in the internal and external environments.

When looking at individual and organizational power, there are also different forms of power. The first form of power is legitimate power. Legitimate power is associated with a formal position within a company or hierarchical structure. With legitimate power, the role and its responsibilities define the amount and type of power the position will hold. For the individual within that position, they are given a certain amount of scope and authority to make decisions. Next, legitimate power enables an individual to delegate and assign tasks to others within the organization. Third, legitimate power is used to drive change within the scope of responsibility of the specific position within the business.

While legitimate power will benefit the individual through their assigned role, it will also improve the organization. Legitimate power is used within organizations to establish a clear hierarchy. Having an established hierarchy is important for making clear decisions and taking the necessary or appropriate actions in a specific situation. Next, legitimate power will enable the organization to streamline its business processes to become more effective and efficient in its operations. Third, legitimate power will improve coordination and collaboration between all individuals and departments within the organizational hierarchy, creating a more cohesive unit. Finally, legitimate power will seek to enhance the efficiency of business operations by having clear-cut roles, duties, and skills associated with each position, so work is not duplicated and creates a critical path to success within a learning organization.

The second form of power is influential power. Influential power is the power that derives from the personal attributes of an individual. These unique attributes include charisma, expertise, and relationships. Charisma is the attractiveness, charm, or ability to influence another individual. Expertise is the knowledge and skill of a person within a certain area or field. Relationships are important and define how the individual can bridge the gap between the "in" group and the "out" group to form a special relationship focused on shared goals and outcomes. As a result, influential power is the ability to finesse a situation toward a chosen outcome or desired result. Once the result has been achieved, the individual will change their focus to a new goal, or a new leader with the necessary influence will emerge to help achieve the new objective.

For the individual, each person can meet, engage, or inspire others using their unique abilities and defining characteristics. Regardless of their formal position, a person can possess influential power to be instrumental in the success of the outcome. This situation will cause a person to gain respect, trust, and responsibility not based on their formal position but instead on their character traits. For the organization, influential power will help to foster and increase leadership within the hierarchy of the company. Next, influential power will encourage innovation by motivating its employees. Finally, influential power will support an organization by creating and strengthening teams through mutual support, respect, responsibility, and collaboration.

The main goal of legitimate power is to ensure order and efficiency. While legitimate power is necessary to have formalization within the organization, influential power is used by leaders at all levels of the organization to encourage innovation. Next, influential power is a critical component of leadership since it helps to strengthen the team environment. This situation will create unity among all individuals within the company. Finally, influential power is necessary for team cohesion and collaboration. As a result, it is important to have a balance of legitimate and influential power for both the individual and organization to be successful in their future endeavors. The combination of individual and organizational power will create a supportive internal and external environment to foster sustainable leadership, management, and life-long learning within the supported structure.

Responsibility plays a critical part in both influential and legitimate power. The first area we see this happening in is ethical conduct. Ethical conduct is how individuals and organizations use their values and moral compass to operate fairly and with honesty, integrity, and a good faith effort. When power is combined with ethics, it can have a positive impact by aligning everyone around a shared value or goal. This situation is more likely to produce ethical decision-making for both the individual and the organization. However, if power is misused, unethical conduct will lead to poor decision-making and actions that do not support the shared mission or vision of the organization. When responsibility is used in ethical conduct, it will ensure that the use of legitimate and influential power will produce a positive benefit for both the individual and the organization.

Next, responsibility will lead to an increased level of trust and respect. Trust develops when one has the confidence or belief that they will make the right decision or action based on reliability, honesty, and integrity for the greater good. Respect is the appreciation or recognition that someone earns based on their worth, value, and dignity through the support of mutual understanding and a history of their beliefs. The responsible use of power will work to build the relationship of trust and respect among individuals, team members, and leaders within the organization. Finally, the responsibility of power will be shown through each action taken since the decision-making process includes the respect and value of the entire group's contributions instead of being based on the needs of the individual.

Third, accountability will benefit from the responsibility of power. Accountability is focused on the willingness and obligation of an individual or organization to accept responsibility for both their decisions and actions. When a decision is made or an action is taken, the respective party will be held liable or responsible for the who, what, where, when, why, and how of their choice. The decision or action of the party will have results that either support or detract from their decisions. People or positions of power are placed in roles whose decisions and actions will have significant impacts on everyone involved. Responsibility will ensure that accountability is included within all decisions that are carried out and that the consequences of the choices that are made are fully understood.

Fourth, sustainability relies heavily on the need for responsibility of power. Sustainability is the ability to maintain or support a process or system over a long period of time. Each organization faces the use of limited resources. To prevent the depletion of resources, decisions and actions need to be made to support the long-term mission and vision of the leader instead of only supporting short-term personal objectives and goals. With the responsible use of power, everyone, whether a manager or department, can contribute and support the positive organizational culture. Next, sustainability will ensure ethical behavior, inclusion and collaboration, and fairness in decision-making and actions. To achieve long-term success, everyone must use their legitimate and influential power to make choices that will support long-term goals instead of self-serving short-term objectives.

Fifth, the responsibility of power will effectively promote improved leadership. Leadership involves guiding a person or group of people toward a common goal or specific outcome. For effective leadership to occur, it requires responsibility in the use of legitimate and influential power. Leaders who use both types of power responsibly will become more effective and efficient in their decision-making and actions. With each positive decision or action, the leader will encourage and empower individuals to become more motivated and to collaborate with one another to achieve a higher level of success. This situation will increase both morale and productivity. With responsible power and leadership, the leader can guide, inspire, direct, and enable positive changes within the environment.

Responsibility and power must work together to support a shared vision. However, responsibility and power serve as two different sides of the same coin. While power is the ability to have authority, responsibility serves as its counterweight. Power can lead to long-term decisions and actions. However, the job of a leader is not just about making decisions. Instead, it is about making the right decisions that inspire and motivate others based on their best interests and the needs of the organization. As a result, it is important to properly align responsibility and power so that the influence of legitimate and influential power can be used properly within the internal and external environments of the learning organization.

It is not necessarily about what "I" can do, but rather what "We" can do together to support one another for future growth and development. Finally, it is necessary to distinguish legitimate power from influential power to align each decision and action that will lead to the empowerment of individuals. When power is properly aligned, individuals will be motivated to collaborate with one another to form a solid "in" group that will lead to a positive organizational culture. Through the alignment of legitimate and influential power, critical components of success within the organization will be established. These critical components include the balance of power, empowerment, positive culture, leadership development, and organizational success.

The balance of power is based on both types of power. First, legitimate power is derived from the position of an individual provided by the organization through a position title or job description. However, influential power is obtained from an individual's personal attributes and characteristics. To be successful, there needs to be an equal balance of power that is used by each person. When there is too much reliance on legitimate power, the position can be used to make decisions or actions that are not necessarily in the best interest of everyone involved. This situation causes a high level of bureaucracy in the organizational hierarchy. As a result, autocratic leadership begins to take shape, causing people to abuse their power based on their title or position for personal gain instead of making decisions that support the common good.

However, the overuse of influential power can also cause problems within the organization. Too much reliance on influential power can lead to a high degree of ambiguity in decision-making because others were "influenced" by the leader or person to make a decision that does not necessarily reflect the vision of the leadership. This situation can cause problems with guiding their chosen "in" group members and allowing them to develop autonomy. Instead, too much influential leadership can cause disengagement and higher turnover rates due to a lack of shared interest or employee support. As a result, it becomes important to always maintain a balance of power and to know the appropriate time to implement legitimate or influential power.

Next, empowerment can only develop with the alignment of both legitimate and influential power. Empowerment is the decision or action to allow someone else to do something under their own right or power. With empowerment, a person is trusted to make reliable decisions to perform a duty or task. Next, empowerment enables a person to become a stronger resource through improved confidence and motivation. When individuals within an organization understand that power is not just associated with a position, they will see that it is instead associated with the knowledge, skills, and abilities of the right person or leader within the given situation. This situation enables everyone to understand and know that they can contribute to the organizational goals in a meaningful and worthwhile way. As a result, empowerment created with the balance of influential and legitimate power will lead to positive outcomes for both the person and the organization.

Third, the alignment of legitimate and influential power will lead to the creation and development of a positive organizational culture. A positive and influential organizational culture must include shared beliefs, values, norms, assumptions, and symbols that shape the psychological and social environment of the people within the company. Next, organizational culture should provide identity and define the sense of a shared character among all its members to eliminate the divide between the "out" group and the "in" group. The main aspects of organizational culture include the historical rituals and symbols of its founders as a collective experience, the social construction that has been created and preserved by its members, being deeply engrained in principles and values for long-term sustainability, having cultural assumptions that are unforgettable to build a sense of community and purpose, and having behavioral patterns that are used to shape how people act and perform together. When an organizational culture has an alignment of the different types of power, it is more likely to be collaborative, inclusive, and innovative. Finally, a positive organizational culture based on the balance of power will respect both the hierarchy of each position or person while also appreciating and valuing the influence and skills of everyone. As a result, the balance of power will create an organizational culture that promotes and fosters a positive work environment.

Fourth, organizational success is dependent on the alignment of both legitimate and influential power. In general, organizational success is the company's ability to achieve its objectives and goals to fulfill the vision of its leader. Successful organizational change includes the ability to adapt to changes in the internal and external environments. Next, organizational success is focused on goal attainment that is established by the stakeholders. Third, organizational success achieves strategic fulfillment. Strategic fulfillment is achieved when the strategic plan has been completed and new and unexpected opportunities have been developed to respond, adapt, and align with the new diverse environment, creating a learning organization.

In the end, the alignment of legitimate and influential power is necessary for organizations to experience success. With the balance of power, both legitimate and influential, the individual and organization will work to facilitate effective decision-making among everyone that is streamlined with the mission and vision. Next, the balance of power will promote employee engagement, which will lead to increased motivation, satisfaction, and production. Finally, the balance of power will be used to drive innovation. Innovation can be fostered by encouraging a culture of curiosity and experimentation among employees and departments, providing new resources for learning, training, and development, creating a matrix of cross-functional collaboration, creating a platform for idea generation and implementation, having leaders and managers support and champion change by leading by example, developing a flexible work environment and layout to promote "out of the box" thinking, embracing failure and learning from mistakes, allocating time to creative thinking and business practices, and focusing on entrepreneurship where employees serve as internal entrepreneurs within the company to grow and test their new ideas to support external outputs.

Using both legitimate and influential power to foster organizational success is a dynamic, not static, process. It must be used as a continual and ongoing process that requires the commitment and dedication of leadership, management, and individuals who are lifelong learners so all stakeholders remain willing and able to adapt to the changing circumstances in the internal and external environments. As a result, it is essential to distinguish and align both influential and legitimate power to properly leverage and control the wide variety of resources available to the organization. This will cause a change from the focus of what "I" can do to what "we" can do. This situation will create a learning and educational environment that supports a collaboration

of both personal and professional knowledge and growth. The proper alignment of legitimate and influential power will create an environment where
each individual feels empowered and valued. As a result, individuals will gain
the power to make decisions and act, be given responsibility for the success of
their outcomes, and will collaborate to create a positive culture that is sustainable within the organization.

The goal is to change from "Got [...] nothing" to "Got something!" In
most organizations, employees feel isolated or bottled up. Their responses and
feedback go unheard, like being trapped inside a milk bottle. They can see
what is going on but are unable to interact. This causes a lack of empowerment,
disengagement, and a lack of organizational learning. What should occur is for
everyone to be in the same environment. Following with the example of the
milk bottle, everyone should be poured out and placed into a large milk jug.
The concept of that large milk jug is that everyone is in it together. As a collective unit, they fill the milk jug with their unique attributes. Next, the individuals will adopt a shared culture through direct and collaborative experiences.
Third, everyone will benefit at all levels from improved design, support, and
implementation practices that support the education, management, and leadership goals of the organization.

Figure 8 uses the simple example of a milk bottle. Back in the day, homes
did not have refrigerators. Milk had to be delivered daily to homes by the milkman. The milkman was the homeowner's direct link to fresh milk that would
not spoil before they could drink it. Next, the milkman used glass bottles since
it made it easy to make deliveries. Finally, glass bottles were used to help the
dairy farmers know and track how much milk their customers had drunk and
were paying for. As a result, the glass bottle served several purposes like leadership, management, and lifelong learning.

The responsibility is a lot like the milk bottle. The "milk bottle" of reason
can help to keep ideas fresh and unspoiled. Next, this idea can help decisions
and ideas to be delivered in a safe and sturdy way. Third, the "milk bottle"
of reason will track how much the followers are using and embracing the
organizational culture and shared leadership through their common voice. As
a result, the "milk bottle of reason" can provide many benefits. If not allowed
to breathe, the "milk" or ideas inside the milk bottle will spoil inside the glass,
causing disengagement and employees to become spoiled before they have a
chance to show their potential.

However, if the milk bottle is always empty, then employees will become
stuck without anything to drink. Ideas will dry up or spoil before they become
implemented. Second, if the milk bottle remains empty, the employees will lose

FIGURE 8 Got [...] nothing!: no WEEDU.

focus, direction, and voice. This situation will cause the employees to be stuck behind glass walls. Inside these walls, they can see the organization's goals, but they become distorted from behind the glass. The question becomes what "we do" inside the glass. The "we" can be an individual or group operating separately from the organization, causing a breakdown in success. A common goal or shared vision of leadership is crucial. As a result, there is no WEEDU in the Responsibility of Reason.

Figure 9 demonstrates what happens when the milk bottle is full and provides the essential minerals and nutrients to its employees. By using the acronym WEEDU, we can see how the organization "Got [...] Something!" instead of "Got [...] Nothing!" helping them stand out from the many failing companies in the fields of education, management, and leadership. This situation will cause a change from "we do" inside the milk bottle to "WEEDU" that will be poured out to help everyone in the organization grow healthy and strong through support and acknowledgment of value and voice.

First, there must be a win-win relationship. When individuals or organizations use philosophy and education, ownership of the process will be created. Through the ownership of the process, a sustainable individual or group process can be implemented around the mission or vision of the leader. Second, the milk bottle will be filled with an early adoption of process and culture. An early adoption of process and culture will help to create stability and sustainability within the shared environment. Next, early adoption will create a system for both individuals and the organization to follow that is focused on an established philosophy and shared vision.

Third, it is important to effectively create supply and demand of Responsibility of Reason. Supply is the amount of Responsibility of Reason that is available from the leader. Next, demand is the amount of responsibility that the followers or employees are willing to want or accept. When there is a high supply and demand, there will be a strong Responsibility of Reason that is shared by the leader and followers. Fourth, the individual and organization will directly experience success when goals are aligned to the outcomes from education that is directly linked to leadership. When there is a direct experience of success when goals are aligned to the outcomes, the individual will become more central to the shared vision and goals. This situation will enable the individual to embrace education and learning, to become a more integral component of the sustainable process, and to be in the "in-group" of the leader-member exchange in the pursuit of a common goal.

FIGURE 9 Got [...] something! WEEDU.

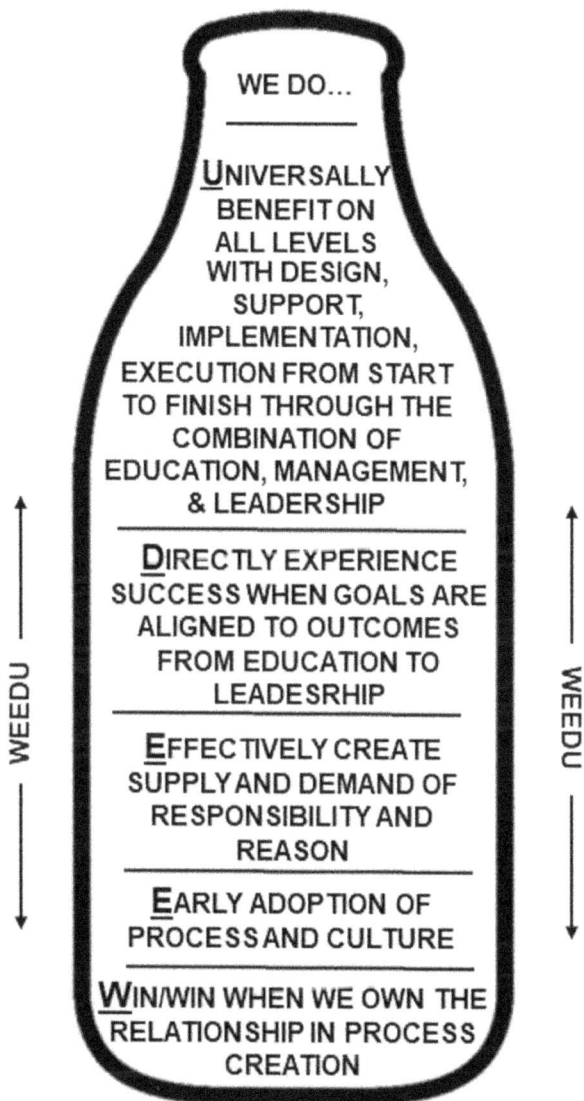

WE DO...

UNIVERSALLY
BENEFIT ON
ALL LEVELS
WITH DESIGN,
SUPPORT,
IMPLEMENTATION,
EXECUTION FROM START
TO FINISH THROUGH THE
COMBINATION OF
EDUCATION, MANAGEMENT,
& LEADERSHIP

DIRECTLY EXPERIENCE
SUCCESS WHEN GOALS ARE
ALIGNED TO OUTCOMES
FROM EDUCATION TO
LEADESRHIP

EFFECTIVELY CREATE
SUPPLY AND DEMAND OF
RESPONSIBILITY AND
REASON

EARLY ADOPTION OF
PROCESS AND CULTURE

WIN/WIN WHEN WE OWN THE
RELATIONSHIP IN PROCESS
CREATION

WEEDU   WEEDU

Finally, there is a universal benefit on all levels with design, support, and implementation. This process relies on execution from start to finish through a combination of and respect for education, management, and leadership. Education is directly linked to establishing the philosophy and knowledge required to make a reasonable decision or to act. Next, education will guide the management process by helping the individual to plan, organize, and direct activities for the individual and the company. Human capital and material resources are required to obtain short-term objectives and long-term goals. Finally, management will create leadership as the final part of the organizational process to change what the individual or "we" does and instead focus on "WEEDU," or what we, as educators and lifelong learners, share together as a group.

Always remember that WEEDU is:

- **W**in-win when we own the relationship in process creation.
- **E**arly adoption of process and culture.
- **E**ffectively create supply and demand of responsibility and reason.
- **D**irectly experience success when goals are aligned to outcomes from education to leadership;
- **U**niversally benefit on all levels with design, support, implementation, and execution from start to finish through a combination of education, management, and leadership.

Simpleton Solution

No matter what business or organization you work for, it is important to recognize that having power also requires having responsibility. With the responsibility of power, it is important that it is broken down into several components:

- Accountability to make decisions and take action that impacts everyone positively.
- Trust is based on the responsibility to demonstrate trustworthiness and create followers.
- Respect from others that is translated into influence.
- Sustainability for long-term goals through ethical means.
- Leadership to empower others and to motivate others to become inspired.

The responsibility of power is spread across various roles within the organization that include:

- Executive leadership that includes the CEO, president, and other top executives who are responsible for using their power to establish a mission and vision.
- Middle Management that includes department heads, team leaders, and project managers, and the authority and resources that are allocated to each area.
- Individual contributors who do not hold a management position but whose power and responsibility come from their knowledge and expertise in their job.
- Support staff who directly provide support and service to others through facilitation.
- Stakeholders who influence the organization's reputation and financial success.

Having responsibility and power will be used to improve:

- Efficiency in the use of resources.
- Justification for why a decision or action is made.
- Goal alignment to unite everyone toward achieving the strategic goals and vision.
- Risk management to manage threats when making a decision or using valuable resources.
- Performance management to measure the performance of each individual and the organization so that true outcomes correspond with expected outcomes.

When individual power is combined with organizational power, the benefits will include:

- Collaboration with individuals, managers, and leaders toward a shared goal.
- Empowerment to increase responsibility, satisfaction, and innovation.
- Adaptability to overcome unpredictable or new changes in the environment.

- Diversity and Inclusion to value the voice and diversity of each skilled individual.
- Leadership development to promote opportunities for new leaders to emerge.

Empowerment of people will improve the organizational structure by:

- Increasing engagement by fostering ownership and responsibility of tasks to increase productivity.
- Innovation to enable individuals to challenge the status quo and create new ideas and solutions.
- Organizational ability to adapt quickly to changes in the internal and external environments.

There are different types of power that include legitimate and influential power, which must be combined and balanced:

- Legitimate power is given to a position of autocratic authority.
- Influential power is derived from personal attributes such as charisma, expertise, and relationships.
- The balance of legitimate and influential power will create a positive mix of authority and influence.
- Empowerment will develop to lead people to contribute toto meaningful outcomes regardless of their position in the organization.
- Positive culture can improve inclusivity, collaboration, and innovation to foster a positive culture and environment
- Leadership development to identify and nurture future leaders.
- Organizational success will be achieved through the facilitation of effective decision-making, employee engagement, and driving innovation to increase growth and performance outcomes.

Always remember that WEEDU is:

- **W**in-win when we own the relationship in process creation.
- **E**arly adoption of process and culture.
- **E**ffectively create supply and demand of responsibility and reason.

- **D**irectly experience success when goals are aligned to outcomes from education to leadership.
- **U**niversally benefit on all levels with design, support, implementation, and execution from start to finish through a combination of education, management, and leadership.

CHAPTER 6

THE GAP IN THE PROCESS: BLAME VERSUS RESPONSIBILITY

Organizational behavior and leadership: the importance of voice and shared leadership cannot be understated. These concepts have been proven to enhance employee engagement, promote creativity and innovation, and increase overall organizational effectiveness. However, there exists a significant gap in the process when these principles are implemented without accompanying responsibility. Voice refers to the extent to which individuals feel comfortable expressing their opinions, ideas, and concerns within an organization. It is closely tied to employee empowerment and engagement, as individuals who feel that their voices are heard and valued are more likely to be motivated and committed to their work. Shared leadership, on the other hand, involves the distribution of leadership responsibilities and decision-making among team members rather than being concentrated solely at the top of the organizational hierarchy. This approach has been shown to enhance team performance, promote collaboration, and drive innovation.

When voice and shared leadership are implemented effectively, organizations can achieve significant benefits. Employees are more likely to feel connected to their work and their colleagues, leading to increased job satisfaction and retention. Teams can tap into the diverse perspectives and skill sets of their members, resulting in more creative solutions to complex problems. Organizations are better equipped to adapt to a rapidly changing environment, as decision-making is distributed among those who are closest to the front lines of operations. However, a gap in the process arises when organizations prioritize voice and shared leadership without also emphasizing responsibility. Individuals are given the freedom to express their opinions and take on leadership roles, but they are not held accountable for their actions or decisions. This can lead to a lack of alignment between individual contributions and organizational goals, as well as a sense of chaos and confusion within the organization.

The gap in process creates the potential for conflict and power struggles within the organization. When individuals are given the freedom to express their opinions and take on leadership roles without being held accountable for their actions, it can create an environment in which competing agendas and egos clash. This can lead to a breakdown in communication, decreased trust among team members, and ultimately, a decline in team performance. When individuals are not held accountable for their decisions and behaviors, there is little incentive for them to act in the best interests of the organization. This can lead to a lack of commitment, motivation, and engagement among employees, as well as a sense of unfairness and inequity within the organization. To address this gap in the process, organizations must prioritize both voice and shared leadership alongside responsibility. This involves creating a culture that values open communication, collaboration, and accountability. Leaders must set clear expectations for individual and team performance, provide opportunities for feedback and reflection, and hold individuals accountable for their actions and decisions.

By establishing mechanisms for feedback and continuous improvement, organizations can implement regular performance reviews, peer evaluations, and feedback processes to assess individual and team contributions, identify areas for improvement, and hold individuals accountable for their actions. This can help to create a culture of transparency, trust, and recognition within the organization, as well as provide a platform for individuals to learn from their mistakes and grow as leaders. By promoting a culture of shared responsibility and collective ownership, organizations can encourage teams to collaborate on decision-making, problem-solving, and goal setting rather than relying solely on individual leaders to drive outcomes. This can help to distribute leadership responsibilities more evenly among team members, foster a sense of community and belonging, and ensure that everyone is invested in the success of the organization.

Organizations can provide training and development opportunities for employees to enhance their leadership skills, improve their communication abilities, and build their emotional intelligence. By investing in the growth and development of their employees, organizations can empower individuals to take on leadership roles, voice their opinions, and contribute meaningfully to the organization. This can help to create a more inclusive, diverse, and dynamic workforce, as well as build a pipeline of future leaders who are equipped to navigate the complexities of the modern business landscape.

Miscommunications when There Is No Responsibility of Reason

In the realm of organizational behavior and leadership, the absence of responsibility can lead to a range of issues and miscommunications that can hinder the effectiveness and efficiency of a team or organization. When individuals are not held accountable for their actions or decisions, it creates a vacuum of leadership and accountability that can result in confusion, conflict, and ultimately, a breakdown in trust and collaboration within the organization.

When there is no responsibility, there is a lack of clarity and direction within the organization. Without individuals being held accountable for their actions, decisions, and performance, it can be difficult to determine who is responsible for specific tasks, projects, or outcomes. This can lead to a lack of ownership and commitment among team members, as well as a sense of disorganization and chaos within the organization. Miscommunications also often occur when there is no responsibility in place. Without clear lines of accountability, it can be challenging for team members to effectively communicate with one another, share information, and coordinate their efforts. This can result in misunderstandings, conflicts, and missed deadlines, as individuals may not be aware of their roles and responsibilities within the team or organization.

The absence of responsibility can create a sense of unfairness and inequity among team members. When individuals are not held accountable for their actions, it can foster a culture of favoritism, nepotism, and injustice within the organization. This can lead to resentment, animosity, and a lack of trust among team members, as well as undermine the overall morale and motivation of the team or organization. When there is no responsibility, there is a lack of transparency and accountability. Without individuals being held responsible for their decisions and behaviors, it can be challenging to track and monitor the performance and progress of team members. This can hinder the ability of leaders to identify areas for improvement, provide feedback and coaching, and ultimately drive the success and growth of the organization. The absence of responsibility can lead to a culture of blame and finger-pointing within the organization. When individuals are not held accountable for their actions, it can create a culture in which everyone is quick to assign blame to others for mistakes, failures, and shortcomings. This can erode trust, collaboration, and teamwork within the organization, as well as create a toxic and negative work environment that stifles creativity and innovation.

To address these issues and miscommunications that arise when there is no responsibility, organizations must prioritize accountability, transparency, and clear communication. Leaders must set clear expectations for individual and team performance, hold individuals accountable for their actions and decisions, and provide regular feedback and support to help team members succeed. By establishing mechanisms for tracking and monitoring performance, providing opportunities for open and honest communication, and fostering a culture of accountability and ownership, organizations can address the root causes of miscommunications and conflicts that arise when there is no responsibility in place. By implementing performance management systems that track and monitor individual and team performance, and by setting clear goals, objectives, and key performance indicators for team members, leaders can provide a roadmap for success and hold individuals accountable for their contributions to the team or organization. Regular performance reviews, feedback sessions, and coaching opportunities can help to identify areas for improvement, celebrate successes, and provide support and guidance to team members as needed. Promoting a culture of open and honest communication within the organization. Leaders must create opportunities for team members to voice their opinions, share their ideas, and provide feedback on their experiences within the organization. By fostering a culture of transparency, trust, and respect, organizations can create a safe and inclusive environment where team members feel comfortable expressing their thoughts and concerns.

Organizations can promote a culture of accountability and ownership by encouraging team members to take responsibility for their actions and decisions. Leaders must lead by example and demonstrate a commitment to holding themselves accountable for their behavior and performance. By establishing a culture of accountability from the top-down, organizations can create a sense of fairness, trust, and integrity among team members, as well as foster a shared sense of purpose and vision. The absence of responsibility can lead to a range of issues within an organization, including a lack of clarity and direction, miscommunications, a sense of unfairness and inequity, a lack of transparency, and a culture of blame and finger-pointing. To address these challenges, organizations must prioritize accountability, transparency, and clear communication within their teams. By establishing mechanisms for tracking and monitoring performance, promoting open and honest communication, and fostering a culture of accountability and ownership, organizations can mitigate the negative impacts of the absence of responsibility and create an environment where individuals are empowered to take ownership of their actions and decisions.

Self-serving versus Shared Responsibility and Commitment

Organizational behavior and leadership can address the conflict between self-serving behavior versus shared responsibility and commitment. These types of behaviors can play a critical role in determining the success and effectiveness of a team or organization. Self-serving behaviors focus on individual interests, goals, and actions, while shared responsibility and commitment emphasize collective goals, collaboration, and accountability. Understanding the differences between these two approaches is essential for promoting a healthy and productive work environment. Self-serving behaviors are characterized by a focus on individual success and advancement, often at the expense of others or the team. Individuals who exhibit self-serving behaviors may prioritize their own needs, desires, and goals over those of their colleagues or the organization. This can lead to competition, conflicts of interest, and a lack of cooperation within the team or organization. Shared responsibility and commitment involve a collective focus on achieving common goals, supporting one another, and holding each other accountable for individual and team performance. Individuals who demonstrate shared responsibility and commitment are willing to collaborate, communicate openly, and work toward the greater good of the team or organization. This approach fosters a sense of trust, collaboration, and mutual respect among team members.

A key difference between self-serving and shared responsibility and commitment is the impact on team dynamics and performance. Self-serving behaviors can create a sense of competition and mistrust within the team, as individuals may be more concerned with advancing their own interests rather than working together toward shared goals. This can lead to conflicts, power struggles, and a lack of cohesion within the team, ultimately hindering the team's ability to achieve its objectives. In contrast, shared responsibility and commitment promote a culture of collaboration, trust, and mutual support within the team. Individuals who demonstrate shared responsibility are willing to share the workload, support their colleagues, and hold themselves and others accountable for their actions and decisions. This approach fosters a sense of unity, teamwork, and commitment to achieving collective goals, ultimately leading to improved team performance and outcomes.

An important distinction between self-serving and shared responsibility and commitment is the impact on organizational culture and employee engagement. Self-serving behaviors can create a toxic work environment characterized by competition, distrust, and a lack of cooperation among team members.

This can lead to low morale, high turnover rates, and decreased employee satisfaction and engagement. Shared responsibility and commitment promote a positive organizational culture characterized by collaboration, open communication, and a shared sense of purpose and belonging. Individuals who feel a sense of shared responsibility are more likely to be engaged, motivated, and committed to their work, as they see themselves as part of a larger team working toward common goals. This can lead to higher levels of employee satisfaction, retention, and productivity, as well as a stronger sense of camaraderie and unity within the organization.

The distinction between self-serving and shared responsibility and commitment can also impact decision-making processes within the organization. Self-serving behaviors may result in individuals making decisions that are solely in their own self-interest without considering the broader implications for the team or organization. This can lead to shortsighted decisions, conflicts of interest, and a lack of alignment with organizational goals. In contrast, shared responsibility and commitment promote a collaborative approach to decision-making, where individuals consider the perspectives and needs of others before making choices that impact the team or organization. This can lead to more informed, inclusive, and strategic decision-making processes, as well as a greater sense of ownership and accountability among team members for the outcomes of those decisions.

To promote a culture of shared responsibility and commitment within the organization, leaders must lead by example and demonstrate a commitment to fostering a collaborative and inclusive work environment. Leaders can set clear expectations for individual and team performance, provide opportunities for open communication and feedback, and encourage team members to support one another and work toward common goals. Leaders can also establish mechanisms for recognizing and rewarding shared responsibility and commitment, such as team-based incentives, recognition programs, and opportunities for professional development and growth. By highlighting and celebrating instances of teamwork, collaboration, and accountability, leaders can reinforce the importance of shared responsibility and commitment within the organization. Leaders can promote a culture of shared responsibility and commitment by providing training and development opportunities for team members to enhance their collaboration skills, communication abilities, and emotional intelligence. By investing in the growth and development of their employees, leaders can empower individuals to take on leadership roles, support their colleagues, and contribute to the success of the team or organization.

The Blame Game: Why It Is Important to Work Together

The blame game is a common phenomenon that can have detrimental effects on team dynamics and organizational performance. The blame game refers to a situation in which individuals within a team or organization engage in a pattern of assigning blame to others for mistakes, failures, or shortcomings rather than taking responsibility for their own actions and decisions. This behavior can create a toxic work environment characterized by mistrust, defensiveness, and a lack of collaboration, ultimately hindering the team's ability to work effectively toward its goals. One of the key reasons why it is important to work together and avoid the blame game within a team or organization is to promote a culture of accountability and responsibility. When individuals engage in the blame game, they are essentially avoiding taking ownership of their actions and deflecting responsibility onto others. This can create a culture of finger-pointing, deflection, and conflict within the team, as individuals may become defensive, resentful, and unwilling to collaborate with their colleagues.

When individuals work together and hold themselves and others accountable for their actions and decisions, it fosters a culture of trust, transparency, and collaboration within the team or organization. By taking ownership of their mistakes and failures, individuals demonstrate integrity, humility, and a commitment to learning and growth. This can create a positive work environment in which team members feel supported, valued, and empowered to work together toward common goals. Working together also promotes a sense of shared responsibility and commitment among team members. When individuals collaborate and support one another, they are more likely to feel a sense of unity, camaraderie, and mutual respect within the team. This can lead to higher levels of teamwork, communication, and collaboration, as individuals are more willing to share ideas, provide support, and work toward common objectives without fear of being blamed or criticized. When individuals collaborate and share ideas, perspectives, and expertise, they can tap into the diverse skills and experiences of the team to find innovative and effective solutions to complex challenges. This can result in higher levels of creativity, productivity, and performance, as well as a greater sense of accomplishment and satisfaction among team members. Working together can enhance overall team effectiveness and performance. When individuals collaborate and support one another, they can leverage the strengths and talents of each team member to achieve common goals and objectives. This can lead to improved communication, coordination, and alignment within the team, as well as facilitate a greater sense of cohesion and synergy among team members. By working together toward a shared vision and purpose, teams are better equipped to overcome obstacles, adapt to change, and achieve success in a dynamic and competitive business environment. When individuals feel supported, valued, and respected within the team, they are more likely to be motivated, committed, and invested in their work. This can lead to higher levels of job satisfaction, retention, and loyalty among employees, as well as a sense of pride and fulfillment in being part of a collaborative and high-performing team.

Miscommunication: How to Improve Each Person's Accountability for the Process

Miscommunication can occur in various forms within a team or organization, leading to confusion, conflict, and inefficiency. It is crucial for individuals to take accountability for their role in the communication process and strive to improve communication methods to ensure clarity, collaboration, and understanding among team members. One form of miscommunication is poor listening skills. When individuals fail to listen actively and attentively to others, messages may be misunderstood or misinterpreted. To address this issue, individuals must take accountability for their listening skills by practicing empathy, maintaining eye contact, and providing feedback to demonstrate understanding. By actively listening to others, individuals can enhance communication effectiveness and avoid misunderstandings. Miscommunication in the process of messaging can create a lack of clarity. Messages that are vague, ambiguous, or lacking detail can lead to confusion and misinterpretation. To improve communication clarity, individuals must take accountability for their message delivery by articulating their thoughts clearly, providing context, and confirming through feedback. By ensuring that messages are expressed clearly and concisely, individuals can enhance communication effectiveness and reduce the risk of miscommunication.

Nonverbal communication can also contribute to miscommunication. Body language, tone of voice, and facial expressions play a significant role in conveying messages, and misalignment between verbal and nonverbal cues can lead to mixed signals and confusion. Individuals must take accountability for their nonverbal communication by being aware of their body language, maintaining a positive tone, and aligning their verbal and nonverbal cues to convey a consistent message. By paying attention to nonverbal cues, individuals can enhance communication effectiveness and foster understanding among team members. Assumptions can lead to misunderstandings and errors in communication, as individuals may misinterpret information or make inaccurate assumptions about others' intentions. To address this issue, individuals must take accountability for seeking clarification by asking questions, paraphrasing, and confirming understanding. By clarifying information and avoiding assumptions, individuals can improve communication accuracy and avoid misunderstandings.

Emotional barriers can also hinder effective communication. Emotions such as anger, frustration, or anxiety can impact communication dynamics and lead to defensive responses or conflict. Individuals must take accountability for managing their emotions by practicing active listening, using empathy, and maintaining a positive attitude during interactions. By controlling emotional responses and fostering a supportive communication environment, individuals can enhance communication effectiveness and build stronger relationships with team members. Cultural differences and language barriers can also contribute to miscommunication. Diverse teams may face challenges in understanding cultural norms, language differences, and communication styles, leading to misunderstandings and conflicts. Individuals must take accountability for bridging cultural and language gaps by promoting inclusion, cultural sensitivity, and language proficiency within the team. By fostering a culture of respect and inclusivity, individuals can enhance cross-cultural communication, build trust among team members, and leverage diversity as a strength in achieving common goals.

To improve communication methods and address miscommunication, individuals must also take accountability for proactively seeking feedback and iterating on their communication approach. By soliciting input from team members, reflecting on past communication challenges, and adapting their communication style based on feedback, individuals can continuously improve their communication effectiveness and refine their interpersonal skills. By demonstrating a willingness to learn and grow in their communication abilities, individuals can foster a culture of continuous improvement and collaboration within the team. Stakeholders must take accountability for building trust and rapport with team members to promote open and honest communication. Trust is a foundational element of effective communication, as it creates a sense of psychological safety and mutual respect among team members. By demonstrating integrity, reliability, and transparency in their interactions, individuals can establish trust within the team and create a supportive communication environment where ideas can be freely shared, feedback can be constructively given and received, and conflicts can be resolved collaboratively. Stakeholders must take accountability for promoting a shared understanding of goals, objectives, and expectations within the team. Clear alignment of common objectives is essential for effective communication, as it ensures that team members are working toward a common purpose and are aware of each other's roles and responsibilities. By fostering a shared vision and sense of purpose, individuals can enhance communication clarity, coordination, and collaboration, leading to improved team performance and outcomes.

Self-serving Goals Replaced with Team Goals

In organizational behavior and leadership, the shift from self-serving goals to team commitment, shared goals, and common objectives is crucial for fostering a culture of collaboration, productivity, and success within a team or organization. When individuals prioritize self-serving goals over collective interests, it can lead to conflicts, competition, and a lack of cohesion within the team. By aligning individual efforts with team commitments, goals, and objectives, organizations can drive improved performance, creativity, and synergy among team members. This shift can be achieved through the Responsibility of Reason, where individuals take ownership of their actions, decisions, and behaviors in service of the greater good of the team. Self-serving goals are centered around individual interests, achievements, and aspirations, often at the expense of team collaboration and success. When individuals focus solely on advancing their own agendas and desires, it can create silos, distrust, and a lack of unity within the team. This can lead to conflicts over resources, recognition, and credit for accomplishments, hindering the team's ability to work together toward common objectives and achieve shared goals.

Team commitment involves a dedication to working collaboratively toward shared goals and objectives, putting the team's success above individual accomplishments. When team members align their efforts and energies toward common goals, it fosters a sense of unity, cooperation, and mutual support within the team. This can lead to increased motivation, engagement, and accountability among team members, as well as improved communication, coordination, and performance toward achieving collective success. Achieving a shift from self-serving goals to team commitment, shared goals, and common objectives requires individuals to embrace the Responsibility of Reason. This entails taking ownership of one's actions, decisions, and behaviors and considering the impact of these choices on the team. By exercising reason and sound judgment in their actions, individuals can contribute to the greater good of the team, foster trust and collaboration, and drive progress toward achieving shared goals and objectives.

Responsibility of Reason also involves aligning individual values, motivations, and behaviors with the team's mission, vision, and objectives. By recognizing the interconnectedness of individual actions and team outcomes, individuals can make decisions that prioritize the team's success over personal gain or recognition. This shift in mindset from self-interest to collective interest can help to build a culture of accountability, transparency, and collaboration within the team, fostering a sense of shared purpose and commitment toward achieving common goals. The Responsibility of Reason requires individuals to exercise critical thinking and problem-solving skills in their decision-making process. This involves evaluating the potential impact of one's actions on the team, considering alternative perspectives, and making choices that are in the best interest of the collective rather than solely focusing on individual benefits. By engaging in reasoned decision-making, individuals can contribute to a culture of teamwork, communication, and collaboration that drives organizational success and achievement of shared goals. Taking responsibility for reason involves actively listening to others, seeking feedback, and demonstrating empathy and understanding toward team members. By fostering open communication, trust, and respect within the team, individuals can create a supportive environment where ideas can be shared, conflicts can be resolved constructively, and collaboration can thrive. This can lead to improved performance, creativity, and innovation within the team, as well as a greater sense of ownership and commitment to achieving common objectives. The Responsibility of Reason calls for individuals to set aside personal biases, prejudices, and egos in service of the team's success. By approaching interactions and decision-making with integrity, humility, and a focus on the greater good, individuals can overcome obstacles, bridge differences, and build strong relationships with team members. This can help to build a cohesive, high-performing team that is aligned toward a common vision and committed to achieving shared goals and objectives.

Developing a checklist of questions can help ensure that decisions are not only ethical but also promote unity and shared leadership and management within an organization. By encouraging individuals at all levels to take ownership of their actions and align them with the common good, organizations can foster a culture of accountability, collaboration, and success. The following checklist of questions can be used to guide decision-making processes and actions that prioritize the collective good over self-serving interests:

1. Have I considered the impact of this decision on all stakeholders, including employees, customers, suppliers, and the community?
2. Is this decision aligned with the organization's values, mission, and long-term goals?
3. Have I consulted with relevant team members, leaders, and stakeholders to gather diverse perspectives and insights?
4. How does this decision contribute to promoting unity, collaboration, and shared leadership within the organization?
5. Am I transparent and open in my communication about the rationale behind this decision and its potential implications?
6. Have I considered any potential conflicts of interest or biases that may influence this decision?
7. Does this decision prioritize the common good and benefit of the organization rather than individual gain or recognition?
8. How will this decision impact the overall morale, engagement, and motivation of team members and stakeholders?
9. Have I considered any ethical considerations, principles, or guidelines that apply to this decision?
10. How does this decision promote a culture of accountability, responsibility, and shared ownership of actions at all levels of the organization?
11. What steps can be taken to involve and empower team members in the implementation and execution of this decision?
12. Are there mechanisms in place to monitor and evaluate the outcomes and impact of this decision on the organization and its stakeholders?
13. How can this decision contribute to building trust, respect, and collaboration among team members and leaders?
14. Have I considered the long-term implications and sustainability of this decision for the organization and its stakeholders?
15. What opportunities exist to involve team members in the decision-making process and encourage their input, feedback, and participation?

By using this checklist of questions, individuals at all levels of the organization can assess their decisions and actions to ensure that they are ethical, promote unity, shared leadership and management, and uphold the common good of the organization. Encouraging a culture of accountability, collaboration, and shared ownership within the organization can lead to improved decision-making processes, enhanced teamwork, and ultimately, organizational success and achievement of shared goals and objectives.

Shift from Blaming Others to Working Together

A culture of blame can be detrimental to teamwork, trust, and overall performance. When individuals resort to blaming others for mistakes or failures, it creates a toxic work environment characterized by defensiveness, mistrust, and a lack of collaboration. To shift from blaming others to working together and sharing responsibility for solutions, organizations must promote a culture of accountability, open communication, and collective problem-solving. This transformation can be achieved through a deliberate and strategic approach that emphasizes cooperation, empathy, and a shared commitment to achieving common goals. It is essential to address the root causes of the blame culture within the organization. Leadership plays a crucial role in setting the tone and expectations for behavior within the organization. Leaders must model accountability, transparency, and a willingness to take ownership of their actions and decisions. By leading by example, leaders can inspire others to follow suit and prioritize working together toward solutions rather than assigning blame.

Communication is key to changing the blame culture within an organization. Open and transparent communication channels should be established to encourage dialogue, feedback, and the sharing of ideas among team members. By fostering an environment where individuals feel heard, valued, and respected, organizations can create a culture of trust and collaboration that mitigates the need for blame and fosters a sense of shared responsibility for finding solutions. Empathy and understanding are essential components of shifting from blame to collaboration within an organization. Individuals must learn to see things from others' perspectives, acknowledge the challenges they face, and work together to find common ground and solutions. By practicing empathy and actively listening to others' concerns, organizations can cultivate a culture of mutual respect and empathy, where team members support one another and work together toward shared goals. Shared responsibility for finding solutions is another crucial aspect of changing the blame culture within an organization. Rather than assigning blame for mistakes or failures, individuals should focus on identifying root causes, analyzing the situation, and collaboratively developing solutions that address the underlying issues. By working together toward solutions, organizations can foster a sense of collective ownership and accountability that motivates team members to take proactive steps toward achieving positive outcomes.

Leadership development and training can also play a significant role in shifting from blame to collaboration within an organization. Leaders should be equipped with the skills, knowledge, and tools to effectively manage conflicts, facilitate dialogue, and promote a culture of open communication and teamwork. By empowering leaders to foster a collaborative and accountable culture, organizations can create a supportive environment where team members feel empowered to take ownership of their actions and work together toward solutions.

Recognizing and celebrating successes are also important factors in changing the culture within an organization. By acknowledging and rewarding collaborative efforts, problem-solving skills, and shared responsibility for solutions, organizations can reinforce the desired behaviors and values that promote teamwork and accountability. Celebrating small wins, milestones, and achievements can help build momentum and motivate team members to continue working together toward common goals.

Training and development programs focused on communication, conflict resolution, and teamwork can also be instrumental in changing the blame culture within an organization. By providing team members with the necessary skills and tools to navigate difficult situations, communicate effectively, and collaborate with others, organizations can empower individuals to work together toward solutions rather than resorting to blame. These programs can help build a common language, understanding, and approach to problem-solving that emphasizes collective responsibility and shared commitment to achieving positive outcomes.

Incorporating feedback mechanisms into the organization's processes and practices can also support the shift toward a culture of collaboration and shared responsibility for solutions. By soliciting input, ideas, and feedback from team members, leaders, and stakeholders, organizations can create a culture of continuous improvement, learning, and growth. Feedback loops can help identify areas for improvement, address concerns, and foster a sense of inclusivity and empowerment among team members.

Establishing clear roles, responsibilities, and expectations can clarify expectations and promote accountability within the organization. By defining individual and team goals, outlining key responsibilities, and setting performance metrics, organizations can create a structure that encourages individuals to take ownership of their actions and contribute to collective solutions. Clear communication of roles and responsibilities can help prevent misunderstandings, conflicts, and the need for assigning blame, as individuals are aware of their obligations and contributions to the team.

Creating a culture of trust and psychological safety is essential for fostering collaboration and shared responsibility within an organization. Team members should feel comfortable speaking up, sharing ideas, and challenging the status quo without fear of reprisal or judgment. Building trust through transparent communication, mutual respect, and a commitment to openness and integrity can create a safe space where individuals feel empowered to take risks, experiment, and work together toward solutions.

Ultimately, changing the culture of blame within an organization requires a concerted effort from leaders, team members, and stakeholders at all levels. By focusing on promoting accountability, open communication, empathy, shared responsibility for solutions, recognition of successes, leadership development, training, feedback mechanisms, clear roles and responsibilities, and a culture of trust and psychological safety, organizations can create an environment that values collaboration, teamwork, and shared ownership of actions. By working together toward a common goal of fostering collaboration and embracing a culture of accountability, organizations can overcome the pitfalls of blame and empower individuals to work together toward shared success. This transformation requires a commitment from all individuals within the organization to prioritize the common good, foster trust, and actively engage in problem-solving and decision-making processes that promote unity and shared responsibility. By taking deliberate steps to address the root causes of the blame culture, communicate openly and empathetically, foster a sense of collective ownership for solutions, provide leadership development and training, recognize successes, incorporate feedback mechanisms, clarify roles and responsibilities, and build a culture of trust and psychological safety, organizations can create an environment where individuals feel empowered to take ownership of their actions, collaborate effectively, and drive positive outcomes. Through a collective effort to shift from blame to collaboration and shared responsibility, organizations can create a culture of teamwork, trust, and mutual support that fuels success and achievement of common goals and objectives.

Simpleton Solution

In Figure 10, we can see how education and organizational behavior are directly related to WEEDU. An hourglass is the best example to give when discussing the flow between knowledge, the Responsibility of Reason, the leader and manager, and the worker as it relates to individual and external value. An hourglass is a device that measures the passage of time from one area to another. Inside the hourglass, sand is passed down through a narrow funnel into the bottom container. As the sand falls, it passes from the top until the bottom section of the hourglass is full. As a result, once all the sand has passed, the time is up, and the task should be completed.

When we look at the top-down perspective of the Responsibility of Reason, we begin with organizational behavior. Organizational behavior encompasses all the components of WEEDU. These components include achieving a win-win when we own the relationship in process creation, the early adoption of process and culture, effectively creating supply and demand for responsibility and reason, directly experiencing success when goals are aligned with outcomes from education to leadership, and universally benefiting on all levels through the design, support, implementation, and execution from start to finish via a combination of education, management, and leadership. The knowledge gained and created through WEEDU should then be used to create a Responsibility of Reason. Most organizations are lacking this step, causing knowledge or philosophy to be directly passed on to the leader and manager without validity or reliability.

From the leader and manager, the organizational behavior is then passed on to the worker through policies and procedures to help them complete objectives and goals. Without a Responsibility of Reason, the leader and manager will be unable to provide support to the worker to create individual or external value. However, if there is Responsibility of Reason, the knowledge and philosophy will create internal and external value that will be embraced by the

FIGURE 10 The Multidirectional Perspective of The Responsibility of Reason.

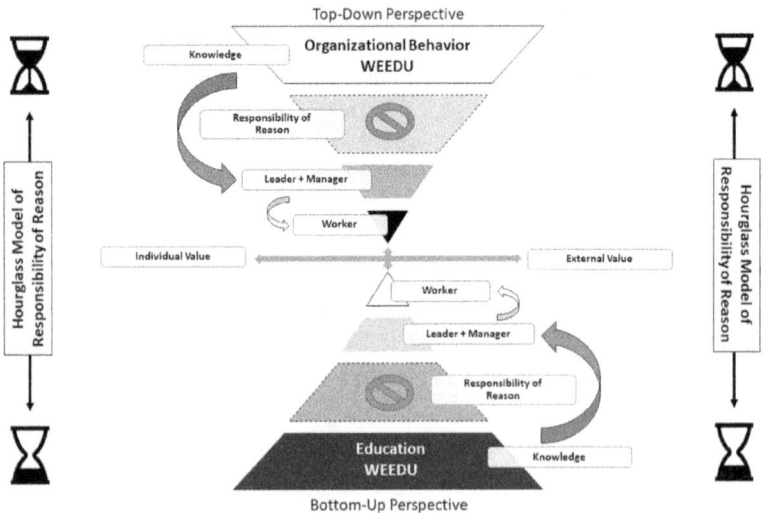

leader and manager, and then passed down to the worker, who will then use it to create additional value for the organization through the bottom-up perspective of Responsibility of Reason.

First, the bottom-up perspective will use education to create WEEDU. The WEEDU will be originally passed down from the top-down but then will be modified with added value and perspective by more intelligent workers to strengthen WEEDU from the bottom-up. Next, the knowledge and education from the workers will flow to the next phase, which is the Responsibility of Reason. During this phase, what is learned is then used to create a logical reason for making responsible decisions and actions. However, if there is no Responsibility of Reason, then the knowledge of the workers will not be implemented in the decision-making process. Therefore, it is important to have Responsibility of Reason.

Once there is Responsibility of Reason, knowledge can have value to be passed on to the leader and manager. This situation will enable the leader and manager to practice servant leadership and become the workers so they can implement what was shared by the employees to build a better value chain and sustainable process within the internal and external environments. Finally, the hourglass model demonstrates how organizational knowledge flows down to education through the hierarchy until it influences education and WEEDU. In turn, WEEDU and education will then flow and pass through the organizational hierarchy to organizational behavior. As a result, there should be a constant flow of Responsibility of Reason to enhance and improve organizational behavior and WEEDU for the individual and organization.

CHAPTER 7

THE BIG IMPACT OF RESPONSIBILITY OF REASON IN THE SMALL BUSINESS MARKET

The Situation: It's Story Time Everyone

You have just returned from a well-deserved weeklong vacation. Since your return to the grind this morning, you have been working your tail off to get caught back up. With all the emails and voicemails to return, you feel you are surrounded by an endless barrage of complaints and questions that should have been handled by your manager while you were gone. Instead, each message you listen to repeats the same message. "I spoke to your manager, and he said you would handle my problem first thing when you returned. Here is what I need […]."

You have a strong work ethic and believe that every customer is important, especially in a small business where it can be difficult to maintain loyal customers. You do your best to answer every question, but you look at the clock and see time ticking away from you. You turn and see your manager in his glass-walled office. He looks hard at work, but you catch a reflection of his computer screen from the picture frame hanging behind his desk. You see that he is, in fact, busy playing solitaire. To make matters worse, you see him cheating at the game and then being proud of himself for winning as if he were an underdog winning a major fight.

With the day halfway done, your stomach starts to growl from your hard work. "It's time for lunch," you say to yourself. "I should be able to get to the rest of these emails and voicemails after lunch." You go to lunch and enjoy a nice ham and cheese sandwich while you sit outside on the park bench. As you eat the last bite, and with your belly full, you feel confident that you can complete the daunting task ahead of you. "Time to get back to work," you say as you stand up and head back inside to the office.

When you get back inside, you see your manager, still on cloud nine from his victory in solitaire, come out of the office. "Everyone," says the manager, "important meeting in my office in five minutes. Get comfortable. It could take a while. We have a lot of ground to cover."

Everyone, along with you, looks at each other and makes eye contact, not sure of what to expect. "Do you know what this meeting is about?" asks Gertrude.

"I have no idea," replied Tom, "but it sounds important."

You know that you have a mountain of work to do, but if a manager calls a meeting, you believe that it must be to give essential information to the entire staff. "I will have to rearrange my schedule," you say. "This sounds serious."

You grab your notepad and a cup of coffee and head into the conference room. All the other employees follow you in and take a seat around the table. The last one to enter is the manager. He quietly walks around and sits in the chair at the head of the table. "It has come to my attention," says the manager as he clicks open his briefcase, "that there is a new book that I wanted to share with you."

As a wannabe manager one day, you are interested in any book that gives insight on how to improve business production, customer service, and increase revenue. *This should be* good, you think to yourself. *I wonder if it's a new book by one of the greatest like Jim Collins, Ken Blanchard, or Spencer Johnson.*

Eagerly waiting to hear what knowledge lies in this secret new book that generated an immediate need for a meeting with such great importance that it would disrupt the entire rest of the day, you see the manager pick up the book. The manager holds it up to the right of his head and uses his left hand to point to the words on the title. "It's story time," he says. "Let's read *Everyone Poops.*"

The manager proceeds to have story time and reads through the entire book to his team of employees. If that was not enough, he expounds on the brilliance of each drawing in the picture book. This goes on for two hours, and your cup of coffee has gone cold. When the manager finishes the last page, he closes the pages of the book and places it back in his briefcase, securing it safely inside.

The manager sits in silence and looks at his staff. Then, after a long moment, he gets up, walks out of the room, and goes back into his office, presumably to play another round of solitaire. You and your coworkers are left sitting there wondering what just happened.

Dazed and confused, you try to think about what the point was of what you just heard, but all you can do is sit in silence and think about all the customers you did not get back in touch with who needed your help. "What was the point of the meeting?" asked Jerry.

"I think it was to tell us that sometimes life can be messy," replied Gertrude.

"I think his point of reading that book is to teach us the basics in life," said Suzie.

"I think you have it all wrong," said Tom. "I believe he was saying that even though we are all different, we still have basic things in common to build a stronger foundation. What do you think, Fergil?"

You sit there in disbelief from all the nonsense that has transpired throughout the day, keeping you from getting real work done. You are hoping for some moment of clarity that will save the day. *Come on, Fergil, bring it home. Make some sense out of today that makes all this worth it. You got this!*

"It's all so simple," replies Fergil. "Everyone poops."

All you can do is shake your head in disbelief at the events of the day. "Yep," is all you can muster. "I think you nailed it […]"

The Big Impact of Small Business and the Critical Need for Responsibility of Reason

Figure 11 demonstrates the potential issues individuals and organizations face. When there is no responsibility or reason, it is easy to become overwhelmed and overcome by the situations and problems in both the internal and external environments. When weeds grow, they entangle with the good roots until they become choked and strangled. Eventually, the weeds will overtake the good plants, causing them to wilt and suffocate. As a result, the weeds will flourish, while the good plants will quickly wither away and die.

Many different issues serve as issues in the internal and external environments of an organization. The first issue is not having a common core goal. A common core is important, so there is a center and locus of control to help guide everyone within the company. Next, poor communication can be an issue since it causes misunderstandings or disagreements in the workplace. As a result, ineffective or miscommunication will create a breakdown of support and understanding between workers, managers, and leader. The third issue, or weed, is a lack of organization. When there is a lack of organization, there is no control or sustainable process. With no maintenance, the weeds will continue to grow, causing a breakdown and discontent in the workplace.

The fourth weed is no guidance. This issue is a result of poor leadership. If the leader does not have Responsibility of Reason in their vision, then there

FIGURE 11 Getting lost in the weeds.

will not be a common objective or goal to work toward. The fifth weed that can unwantedly grow is no voice. When an employee or follower does not have the ability to speak or be heard, he or she will feel disconnected and become disengaged from the vision of the leader. The sixth issue is no consistency. Having no consistency will create turbulence and chaos in the organization that will result in misdirection and competition for shared resources, which will negatively impact the business.

The seventh weed is not having a culture within the organization. A lack of culture will cause the individuals to not be conducive to success. Next, ineffective culture will cause employees to only focus on short-term issues and not long to remain in the organization for the long term. The eighth weed is a lack of follow-through. No follow-through will cause employees or followers to not make any progress in their personal or professional goals. This situation will cause employees to lose faith, trust, and hope in believing that positive change is possible.

Ninth, there is no mission or vision. A mission is the core beliefs and values of organizations that are uniquely specific to their business. The vision communicates the long-term goals of the business. Next, the vision statement provides a "roadmap" to help align the philosophy, management, and leadership within the company. Next, when there is a "me" instead of "we" attitude, then people will work for themselves and not for the business. As a result, this will cause many individual goals to be pursued instead of a shared or common goal. The major weed that organizations face is the lack of reason and a lack of responsibility. When there is no reason or responsibility, there is no basis of cause for a given action. As a result, there will be a lack of sustainability throughout the hierarchy of the business. In organizations, it is important to have a strong focus on the mission and vision of the leader. Management and the followers will need to have guidance from the leader, so they do not get lost in the weeds. While weeds can impact a large corporation, they will have more of a stronghold and cause a negative environment in small businesses.

The business world is no longer dominated by large corporations and organizations. Instead, the focus has changed to smaller companies that provide the same goods and services. Small businesses have become the backbone of the economy in the United States. With over 33 million small businesses in existence in the private sector, they have been responsible for creating jobs and new opportunities. This situation has created a critical need to give small businesses the necessary Responsibility of Reason. However, while there are successful small businesses, over 65 percent fail within the first 10 years of operation, and only 25 percent of new businesses survive to reach fifteen years.

The reason so many small businesses struggle is changing dynamics in the economy, a lack of shared leadership, no shared voice, and low Responsibility of Reason. Barriers to market entry for small businesses involve capital expenditure requirements, the competitive advantage of executive firms, the local and global business environments, and the educational background of the owners. Once small businesses have been established and officially entered the competitive market, there are several additional factors that have historically increased the risk to their survival that include active restructuring reforms, a division of operating cash flow by current short- and long-term liabilities, cash flow requirements, and owner's equity.

While a 65 percent failure rate seems high, it has improved in the past few years. This situation provides evidence that small businesses are taking greater Responsibility of Reason in their decision-making, making them a stronger competitive force in the global market. Next, small businesses are more effectively using the theoretical foundation that includes the 5Ps strategic direction and management model. Research has been done in Management and Leadership Skills That Affect Small Business Survival: A Resource Guide for Small Businesses Everywhere to show that effective management and leadership were essential for small business success; however, research terms have only defined these in general terms.

One of the major themes discussed was that there was a lack of focus and vision. This situation caused management to lack the ability to carry out a mission that was based on a responsible vision that would negatively impacted the small business's success rate. A manager's lack of focus would result in the inability to complete daily tasks and duties. Next, managers without a focus from a lack of understanding of leadership would instead cause managers to hyperfocus on individual tasks instead of seeing the big picture. This excessive focus on their daily tasks would derail small businesses' growth potential through failure to attend to future possibilities for the business. Third, managers who failed to provide sufficient focus for their small business team undesirably impacted the forecasted success of the small business by allowing employees to invest energies into non-industrious behaviors that did not support a vision through shared leadership.

The book suggests that leaders who promoted and influenced a shared vision for the business were able to foster team processes that moved the small business toward shared goals. Leaders who use the strategy of setting clear goals for their staff will be more successful through shared voice and leadership. For small businesses that survived beyond the ten-year benchmark, the leaders improved organizational behavior more successfully through transparency and sharing the challenges and obstacles with employees, in addition to the business's goals. When there is a shared vision, there is a universal focus that will lead employees to think critically about what created the problem and how to overcome the situation through the Responsibility of Reason.

The second major theme is communication, or the lack thereof, within small business operations and organizational behavior. With a lack of communication, small business management faced the problem of having no direction, which led to an unsuccessful and unsustainable business plan. Since communication began at the top, insufficient communication skills were associated with poor interpersonal skills in managers and leaders. Next, it was strongly suggested that lack of communication might result in managers endorsing business decisions that did not blend with the leader's vision, which negatively influenced the success of the small business. As a result, interpersonal skills play an important role in developing sustainable organizational behavior and culture that promote the success of small businesses everywhere. Small businesses operate in both internal and external environments. While it is important to have strong communication skills internally, the small business must also develop effective and efficient communication skills and interpersonal relationships with external customers to maintain long-term, mutually beneficial partnerships to provide and sell products and services.

With a lack of understanding and poor communication channels, small businesses suffered as a result of leaders' inability to understand the responsibilities, roles, and relationships with each individual team member. Leaders and managers who did not understand their roles were viewed as either absent or weak leaders by the employees. The lack of comprehension of the roles and responsibilities of employees was a potential issue in the leadership of small businesses. Leaders and managers who did not understand their employees' daily tasks and responsibilities lacked a definitive understanding of how the business functions on a day-to-day basis and failed to have Responsibility of Reason in their decision-making process or when performing action steps.

Another significant theme that developed from *Management and Leadership Skills that Affected Small Businesses Survival* was the lack of employee support. A lack of employee support will negatively impact the ability of a small business to survive beyond the 10-year benchmark. The leader's failure to provide support to employees will cause problems for the manager and for the small business. To be successful, managers and leaders need to exhibit understanding and support for employees for them to be successful in their specific roles. This situation will lead employees to become more productive when they are fulfilled and happy in their jobs. As a result, manager support becomes critical in promoting a positive experience for every employee for individual and company success. When there is support from management, there will be increased productivity from employees that contributes to higher return on investment (ROI) and profits. The more engaged the manager or leader is with their employees, the more likely there is a reduction in employee turnover, leading to a greater chance of success for the small business.

Within small businesses, communication issues lead to a leadership challenge that increases the level of unnecessary risk for small businesses. Communication problems between leaders, managers, and employees result in issues that cause employee uncertainty and misunderstandings about the expectations of the leader. Leaders who have inadequate contact with employees damage the team environment by promoting an "us versus them" atmosphere. As a result, it is important for the success of small businesses to have clear communication and social skills that can address the needs of the diverse workforce to increase productivity while reducing the level of risk within the small business. When there is a lack of focus, leaders are unable to create objectivity in a situation that negatively impacts success.

A major theme that was discovered is the lack of company focus within small businesses. A lack of company focus characterized a management problem that negatively impacted the success of small businesses. Managers and leaders who were only focused on their own success caused damage to the small business by promoting their own self-interests and neglecting the shared needs of the company. Managers and leaders who did not have company focus failed to develop successful human resources (HR) methods. Managers and leaders are required to maintain high employee performance standards to uphold the success of small businesses, and this means hiring effective employees and training or dismissing ineffective employees. Instead, managers who are company-focused will have to implement decisions that benefit the entire company, even if the decisions that must be made might be unpopular with their employees. As a result, the leader's failure to focus on the needs of the business endangered the long-term success of small businesses. Performance feedback for employees was a key management function that enhanced the success of small businesses everywhere.

What causes small businesses to be different from large corporations is the potential lack of resources to support each necessary business function. Since there is typically a lack of capital and they are family operated, small businesses do not have a HR department. This situation causes the managers to serve as the HR liaison or department, creating additional responsibilities that take away from ensuring the success of daily operations. The need for small business leaders to handle each job function of HR alone creates management problems that influence the negative impact on the success of small businesses. Financial challenges and a lack of capital causes major problems for most small businesses. Inventory problems, insufficient cash flow, non-liquidity, and lack of financing cause small businesses to focus only on short-term needs instead of long-term goals, increasing the failure rate of most small businesses. Since financing is an issue, the small business was limited to undesirable locations that impacted their success and ability to retain employees and customers.

There is a need for equal parts of leadership and management within small businesses to create Responsibility of Reason. Both management and leadership are relied upon to promote the success of small businesses. Small business own-ers are more likely to be successful if they themselves had performed in both management and leadership roles to understand the required duties. Both management and leadership are necessary for the success of small businesses, but different groups might fulfill these functions. Management and leadership skills are important and underline the symbiotic relationship between manage-ment and leadership roles. Leaders are responsible for inspiring individuals and teams, while managers are responsible for enforcing rules, regulations, and policies. Communication skills in leaders and managers are essential for the long-term success of small businesses everywhere. Leaders and managers need to maintain open and clear communication channels to remain aware of each other's perspectives in the diverse economic environment. Leaders and managers need to sustain open communication with employees to create a strong and reliable team approach. When there is a strong team, everyone will work toward the shared goals and vision of the small business.

Shared knowledge, leadership, and vision are decisive management and leadership skills that lead to the success of a small business. Leaders and man-agers must develop and maintain a cooperative attitude among all employees of the small business. Next, leaders and managers must foster a cooperative cul-ture by supporting employees to develop based upon their shared experience, making them a part of a shared voice leading to Responsibility of Reason. It is important for leaders and managers to share knowledge and information with one another. The sharing of knowledge will support a unified strategic plan for the small business.

When sharing leadership throughout the company, the leaders will be able to promote success for the small business through gained experience and unique learning experiences. Small business leaders are more important com-pared to managers because their role requires a specialized, rare, and unique skill set to operate in an unfamiliar environment and to compete against larger competitors. Success in the leadership of small businesses hinges upon recogni-tion of the meaning of "success" for the small business based on the mission and vision of the manager or leader. Leaders must first establish and define "success" for their company and then create objectives and goals that will move the small business in the chosen direction.

The results helped to identify management and leadership skills that con-tributed to the success and failure of small businesses. This information was used to help small business owners develop a winning strategy that combines the roles of management and leadership. Management and Leadership Skills That Affect Small Business Survival studied and provided new perspectives and experiences of current and former small business owners regarding the leadership and management skills that affected their survival rates. With the help of the resources found in this book, small businesses have increased their survival rate by making smarter choices, implementing shared leadership, and developing a Responsibility of Reason for all future decisions and actions.

For small businesses to survive, leaders must not be afraid to work with managers and employees to create organizational reframing. Within any business, there will be a political frame or environment. Every organization is going to encounter politics for people or resources of some kind. Politics within a business can either be viewed as being positive or negative since it's up to the leader to make the necessary decisions to determine how to allocate limited resources to support their mission and vision. Next, leaders and managers rely on politics to constructively gain power to channel their business in a positive direction. This means that every action or decision that is made within an organization is, in some form, based on politics. However, politics should be used constructively to make the best decisions for the company, relying on Responsibility of Reason. Constructive politics must always be considered since it can change the course of action that the small business will choose to implement and follow in the dynamic environment.

The political frame views organizations as a living political arena that contains a complex web of different individual and group interests. This situation is based on five political assumptions. First, those organizations are coalitions of diverse individuals and groups with competing interests. Second, there are enduring differences among the individuals and groups due to beliefs, values, interests, and their perception of the situation. Third, those organizations will experience limited resources. Fourth, that there is a conflict in the way that the limited resources are used within the organization and that this causes an underground power struggle. Any final decisions or goals are only achieved after bargaining, negotiating, and jockeying for a position among the other competing stakeholders.

It is critical for managers to understand this concept, so they can become a better politician as a leader on behalf of their team within their specific organizational arena. Managers must understand what type of politics the organization will encounter to make the best argument to secure the funding and resources required to ensure sustainability. This situation will enable the manager to become a constructive politician and make the organization more effective. Good political managers can then set the organization's agenda, map the political terrain, create a network of support, and negotiate with both allies and adversaries through the political frame. Small businesses are arenas for both internal and external politics, and managers need to learn how to work within these environments. In working in a political arena, the management of an organization can help determine who the major players are and what interests will then be pursued. When a manager acts as an agent, they use their organization as a tool to support their team and the goals of the company.

In today's diverse business world, small businesses find themselves in a battle over gathering and controlling information. While most large corporations have used human resources to support their needs, small businesses have only begun to implement these resources. Companies must use HR to transform themselves to improve their ability to develop intangible assets and remain sustainable for the future. An organization's ability to use its intangible assets is becoming more crucial than its ability to control its physical assets for small businesses. Due to this trend, small businesses are relying on the use of the balanced scorecard. The balanced scorecard allows small businesses to monitor and track their financial results while examining the progress in creating the resources they would need for future growth. Today, some businesses have been able to find additional value in the balanced scorecard approach. This situation has helped to create a stronger new strategic management system that small businesses can use to improve their sustainability. The traditional management system of the past meant that small businesses relied only on financial data, which showed little correlation to the achievement of long-term strategic objectives of the organization.

The balanced scorecard uses a combination of four perspectives that help small businesses connect long-term objectives with their short-term actions. The four integrated perspectives are financial, customer, internal business process, and learning and growth. The first process in helping companies achieve full integration is translating the vision. This process helps managers to form a unified understanding of the organization's strategy and vision. The better managers can understand the company as a single entity, the more likely they are to make decisions that will match the organization's overall mission and objectives. The second process is communicating and linking information to an objective or goal. This process helps managers to effectively communicate their strategy throughout the entire organization and to directly link it to both individual and departmental goals. This strategy will help organizational leaders to understand and manage each department while bringing them together as a whole unit. As a result, each employee in the company will understand the purpose of everyone's position to help the organization become more tightly aligned.

Business planning allows companies to integrate their business and financial plans into their mission and vision. This process helps businesses to achieve their long-term results by relying on accurate data that is based on the integrated factors of the entire organization. The fourth process for businesses is feedback and learning. Feedback and learning help to give companies the ability to experience strategic learning to grow and remain sustainable with a focus on shared goals and leadership. In business, there are two types of learning. The first type is single-loop learning, which means that the object of the organization remains constant throughout the entire process. The second type of learning is double-loop learning, which allows companies to constantly look at new threats and opportunities. As a result, organizations can better understand the cause-and-effect relationship of the events to create relationships and to improve the Responsibility of Reason.

By using this method, it has been proven that traditional budgeting is inefficient and is fast becoming obsolete. Next, traditional budgeting lacks the ability to motivate the right behaviors to help an organization become more strategically focused throughout its various layers. Traditional budgeting creates a lack of congruence with the organization's strategic plan. Instead, budgeting must become integrated as part of the strategic practice, combining the different business functions under one united goal of the leader to achieve success. As a result, small businesses have been able to experience a dynamic and forward-looking approach to business planning. Implementing a strategy-focused business plan that also combines budgeting will help to advance the organization instead of hindering its strategic plan.

With the combination of planning and budgeting into one process, business planning becomes reliable and consistent throughout the entire company. The strategy-focused business plan helps objectives and targets become the common goals of the organization. A strategy-focused business plan will allow organizations to have a continuously aligned reporting process. A continuous measurement process will help organizations to develop a clear understanding of their business strategy so they can make more efficient and effective decisions. This strategy will also allow organizations to adjust their priorities depending on the conditions of the market and economy. Incorporating a strategy-focused business plan will enable organizations to experience increased strategic results by creating an aligned and fully integrated planning process.

The strategy-focused business plan has four main principles. The first principle is to align the strategic and operational planning with budgeting. Aligning strategic planning with budgeting will help to optimize the organization's strategic execution of its goals. Having a strong alignment will help the organization to better align its objectives and targets as a whole entity. The second principle is to adapt quickly to change through continuous planning and forecasting. Continuous planning and forecasting will help organizations to have up-to-date information and to develop rolling forecasts to predict future conditions. This process will allow organizations to have a constant strategic and performance management plan.

The third principle is to assign and reallocate resources vigorously through management. Management will need to be involved in establishing the priorities of the organization so it can determine how to best utilize the company's resources on an ongoing basis. The fourth principle is to reduce the detail and effort in the planning process. Reducing the detail and effort will help organizations to achieve increased planning results by using the right information and analytical tools that support the strategic business plan of the organization.

Implementing the strategy-focused business plan relates to both Michael Porter's and the balanced scorecard approach to business. Before organizations can implement a strategy-focused business plan, they will need to understand their markets. Once the markets have been determined, organizations will need to look at their internal and external environments to determine what their strengths, weaknesses, opportunities, and threats are. After a SWOT analysis has been created, organizations will be able to develop a fully integrated business strategy that will allow them to become more efficient in their company's operations. Combining planning and budgeting will help organizations to fully understand its entire operation. This strategy will help to provide useful data that will help to ensure the success of the organization's strategic goals and future success.

Due to different ideologies, religions, and mistrust among cultures, the world has become more fragmented than at any time in the past. World War II was the last major turning point that has caused the world to become more segregated. Despite the world's differences and political agendas, organizations and their business operations continue to expand all over the world. Since organizations operate globally, managers and executives will have to figure out ways to run their businesses effectively and efficiently in a diverse global environment. Small businesses will need to create the proper management structure to support this process to equally balance between the local, regional, and global demands that are forced on companies that choose to operate globally. In the world of transnational organizations, there is no such thing as a "universal" global manager. However, there are three groups of specialists that can help to create a strong global management team.

The first group of specialists is the business managers. Business managers have three main responsibilities: to act as a strategist, architect, and coordinator. As strategists, business managers help to plan the direction of their operations. Next, they help to create a strong structure for the organization to operate. Finally, business managers help to coordinate the entire business process. The second group of specialists is the country managers. The three main challenges that they face are to act as a sensor, builder, and contributor. First, country managers must be able to sift through all the information to determine what the best course of action for the business will be. Next, they will have to work as builders to set up the partnerships that will be required for the organization to compete. Finally, country managers will need to become contributors and to help build strategic leverage so the company can successfully operate and achieve its goals.

The third group of specialists is the functional managers. The role of the functional managers is to act as scanners, cross-pollinators, and champions. As a scanner, it is their job to gain knowledge and become specialized in business operations. Cross-pollinators help to spread the information to create stronger ways of using business channels in the global markets to help solidify business. Finally, functional managers act as champions by successfully overcoming any weaknesses and threats to the organization. At the corporate level, there are top executives who manage the complex interactions between these three groups of specialists. The top executives can then identify and develop the individual into the talented professional that is needed to become a successful global manager.

The structure of small business organizations allows them to integrate assets, resources, and people into their products or services around the world by developing partnerships and becoming transnational competitors. Business managers, country managers, and functional managers can form one balanced unit that works efficiently together. This structure allows transnational companies to become efficient on a global scale, to have national flexibility and responsiveness, and to have a multi-market capacity to leverage their learning on a global scale. To be successful, transnational organizations rely on understanding their competitive advantage and their business environment. They also rely on the balanced scorecard to help stay focused on their organizational goals. As a result, small business managers can lead their organizations into global markets and become successful transnational competitors in the global market to become more sustainable in the current environment.

Small businesses must be aware of their core competencies and how they use their resources to rethink how they operate. Before the 1990s, organizations used to focus on their portfolio of businesses instead of focusing on their portfolio of competencies. In the 1990s, the top executives of corporations were judged by their ability to identify and produce the core competencies of their company. In the 2000s, small businesses developed and outnumbered corporations. Once the core competencies have been identified, the top executives must exploit their unique competencies to help the small business experience future growth. Companies and upper management will need to rethink and better understand the concept of the small business itself to create a new path that leads to success.

Upper management has the important task of creating an organization that invents products or services that have a wide range of functionality. Management must develop products that customers will need but have yet to be created. Focusing on the company's core competencies will give upper management a better opportunity to create highly functional and needed products for consumers. Core competencies allow upper management to improve their communication, which allows the corporation to become a stronger competitor. Core competencies develop through collective learning throughout the small business. A small business' management team can more efficiently coordinate its diverse production skills with the use of new technological processes. The core competencies of small businesses have three main characteristics. The first characteristic is that a core competency provides access to a wide range of market segments. This allows the small business to increase its target market and increase its profits. Second, a core competency must make an important contribution to the value of the product or service purchased by the customer. The more value a small business can put into a product, the more a customer will come to depend on that product. This will help small businesses ensure future sales and create a strong bond between the customer and the business. Third, a core competency needs to be hard for other companies to imitate. The harder it is to imitate a core competency, the more of a competitive advantage the small business will have in the global environment.

It is important for small businesses to understand and restructure themselves around their core competencies to survive. Since core competencies play an important part in a company's survival, upper management needs to spend a significant amount of time understanding their competencies so they can better lead the business. Once the core competencies of a business are understood, management can then create a tightly aligned organizational structure focused on these competencies. Upper management will then become more strategically aligned and centered on the entire company that is focused on achieving their desired results. As a result, the small business will increase the learning within the corporation for the development of new core competencies. Understanding a small business's core competencies also relates to Porter's definition of strategy. The Porter strategy is the organization's ability to create unique and valuable positions. To accomplish this task, companies need to know what their strengths and weaknesses are when competing against other firms. Knowing the strengths and weaknesses of the business is extremely important for top management when making strategic decisions. Centering the business on a few key core competencies will give management a tighter direction on exactly what to manage. This situation will help the entire organization create products or services that are all centered on its strengths and opportunities while avoiding its weaknesses and potential threats. Small businesses that understand their core competencies will be able to create unique and valued positions in the marketplace and will remain strong competitors in the market segment.

One of the key aspects of small business survival is the way in which the HR function must become strategically integrated with the company that it supports. One of the ways this can be achieved is by having an HR leader who has a "seat at the table" when organizational decisions are made. In most cases, the owner of the small business serves as the leader, manager, and head of HR. As the HR leader of the small business, there are five actions that can be taken to ensure that the HR function is or will become strategically integrated into the organization. For HR to have a "seat at the table" when organizational decisions are made, HR will need to act on integrating HR policies with line managers by creating an HR scorecard. HR will also need to improve the metrics, staffing, evaluating employee performance, and employee rewards and compensation. Each of these five actions will work together to help the employees and the organization become part of an "upward spiral."

The first action that would ensure the HR function is becoming strategically integrated would be to fully align HR with the line managers of the organization. HR would be able to create an HR scorecard with the line managers to help create a better, more compliant organization. With the changing business needs of the organization, it becomes important for the line managers and HR to have a liaison or to create cross-functional teams to meet these new demands. This new integrated structure would replace the traditional structure of employees being disconnected from HR. With HR and the line managers working more closely together, there will be a better opportunity to help create new policies and procedures that are more closely related to the organization's goals. These new policies and procedures will help the employees to better adapt to their working environment and to form a more cohesive bond with their colleagues to help create a more aligned organization.

HR would also become more integrated with the line managers by working with them to build an agenda to reduce risk and increase sustainability. This agenda would need to accomplish four sequential tasks to create a meaningful integrated HR strategy. First, HR would have to work with the top managers to become a part of the organization's philosophies and themes. The human resources of an organization become the main priority of the line managers when they know what the leader of the business values most. This situation would seek to define the role of each employee and to help relate each employee to the overall vision and goal.

HR would use the agenda to work with the line managers to create compliant business-unit people plans. This strategy would help each business unit to create its own plan. With the help of HR and the line managers, the business-unit people plan will be structured around the strategic and operating plans of the whole organization. This will help to improve the strategic alignment of the small business to its goals. The third part of the agenda would be for HR to work with the line managers to establish organizational HR priorities. This would help to integrate all the HR practices that are needed across the various business units. Integrating all the business units with HR, the leader, and the manager will allow the small business to move forward in its business endeavors instead of merely trying to maintain its current existence.

With the integration between HR and the line managers, new positions and layers in the company will be created. This will create new core competencies that are important to the small business. These unique core competencies will determine which direction the company will choose to follow based on the vision of the leadership. Once the direction is determined, HR will then be able to take other actions that will allow them to remain fully integrated with the line managers within the organization.

Once the agenda for the organization has been determined, the partnership between HR and the line managers will need to work on promoting the integration process. The second action that should be looked at is the metrics that will be used within the organization. HR and the line managers will have a good opportunity to make some changes in the use of the organization's metrics to ensure a better fit with the goals of the leader and manager. Metrics are important for an organization to use. They play an important part in the organization's HR scorecard. The HR scorecard relies on metrics to help link the line managers and their subordinates to the business strategy so better decisions and actions can be implemented.

As the HR leader of the small business, it is the leader's job to make sure that the organization stays on track with its goals. The only way to accomplish this is by using the proper metrics. Most organizations use metrics that are easy to measure but do not provide useful feedback to the company. Line managers look for things that can measure their profits and productivity. In the past, small businesses forgot to measure the human element of what was happening. By integrating HR through shared leadership, new metrics can then be used to better measure everything that is vital to the organization's mission. HR will need to work with the line managers to agree on the new, improved metrics for the organization. The first metric they will need to look at is the people. HR will want to make sure that the line managers have the most productive people. They will need to develop a metric to determine who their hardest workers are. They will also have to determine if the line managers have the proper number of staff to run the small business operation. Some divisions may find that they are overstaffed or inadequately staffed. Creating a metric to measure this will help to realign the organization so that it can become more productive and strategically integrated.

Another metric that HR can use to work with small business managers is to look at the customer satisfaction rate of their product or service. A division may be efficient at producing a product, but if a customer is not happy, then the organization loses its value. Being the fastest producer of a product is not always enough. The employee and customer need to be considered in an organization's metric system. The most important metric that HR will need to work with the line managers on is determining if the employees really do make a difference for the company. They need to look at the "critical success factor" of each employee and see how much of what they do contributes to the organization. Everyone from the owner, leader, manager, to HR should be concerned with this metric. It is important for HR to meet with leadership so they can create metrics that will help to achieve the goals of the organization. The small business managers can then use these metrics to help run their divisions more efficiently, which will add value to the organization.

The third action that can be taken to ensure that HR will be strategically integrated into the small business is to use HR to assess the company's staffing needs. The ability to attract and retain good employees is important to the small business. In many situations, a company just fills positions with whoever is available to satisfy the vacancies. No thought is given to the needs of the person or to the company. There is no consideration given to what the job demands and the effects the job will have on the employee after a period. HR will be able to help small business managers with the process of putting the right person in the position. Next, HR will be able to make this decision by working with small business managers to understand the different personalities of their workers and to better understand what motivates them. Every employee is different, and they each have different needs. It is important for HR and the small business managers to take action to make sure that these needs are recognized.

Within a small business, employees are your most important resource. Each employee will have a hierarchy of needs. These needs revolve around physiological, safety, love and belongingness, esteem, and self-actualization. No matter what sector the business operates in, every employee has these basic needs. Everyone needs food and water to live. Working for an organization and earning money allows this need to be met. Employees want to feel safe, and knowing that they are in a stable position within the company will help them to fulfill this need. People need to feel loved and that they belong. When an organization is out of alignment, this need is not met. When HR and the small business manager work together, they can become more aligned and make the employees feel that they are truly a part of the organization. Employees also want to feel good about what they are doing.

It is important for HR to ensure that small business managers recognize their subordinates when they do something good. Finally, employees have needs of self-actualization. This is where HR wants to support each of their employees based on their unqiue needs and wants. When an employee can experience self-actualization, then they have achieved the rest of their needs. This allows the employees to further develop who they are within the organization. When the needs of the employee are met, then small business management and HR will do their job, which will allow HR to have continuous, ongoing actions within the organization.

Within organizations, an employee receives an appraisal of their performance once a year. The evaluation needs to be a two-way street for open communication between the employee and the small business manager. This appraisal is based on metrics that the organization can measure. These measures are usually based around efficiency and profits. These measures fail to analyze the human element of the job, and they are a poor indicator of how the employee is doing. HR will need to take a more active role in working with the leaders and managers to come up with an improved performance evaluation for the small business. This new performance management system will be used to get a better idea of how the employees and the organization are doing. HR will need to move the organization away from traditional employee evaluation systems to a performance management system that will focus on employee development and on organizational improvement.

Another major function of HR in small business management is to properly define the purpose of an employee's job, job duties, and responsibilities. HR will need to define the performance goals that will have measurable outcomes. Third, the priority of each job will need to be evaluated with its primary goal. Next, the performance standards for the main components of the job will need to be defined. Finally, HR will have to provide relevant feedback to employees, small business managers, and leaders. One way to accomplish this is for HR to institute 360-degree evaluations. 360-degree evaluations allow the employee to be evaluated by their line manager and for the line manager to receive feedback from the employee. This concept is important for HR to implement and act on because it allows both sides to share their views of what is happening. The 360-degree evaluation helps to provide HR with firm feedback on the entire situation. HR can then use this data to make sure that the organization is using the right metrics in the evaluations. HR can also see if both the line manager and the employee share the same opinions. If they do, then the division is in proper alignment. If they are different, then HR knows that corrections need to be made.

The HR leader will want to act on making sure that the rewards are attracting and retaining employees. Rewards are very important to employees. They help an employee to feel valued. The rewards that an organization offers to its employees will determine to what extent an employee will perform and what their retention rate will be. There are essentially three types of rewards. These rewards are money, personal, and award programs. Organizations should remember that monetary rewards are not always used as the prime motivator for all people. Money is used to keep employees satisfied with what they are doing. Money does not give the job any more value, but it does provide some level of compensation for the work that is being done. Money allows the individual to satisfy their basic needs to live. As a result, money is a hygiene factor and not necessarily a motivating factor to have a sustained increase in performance and value.

Personal rewards are more meaningful to the employee. Each employee is different, and organizations need to remember that when they are thinking about rewards. What one person values, another may not care about. HR needs to work with the organization to become more integrated so they can create personal rewards that do not alienate any of its employees. When an employee does something good for the organization, HR needs to make sure that the line managers are praising the employee. It is not the amount of recognition that is given but the quality that matters the most to the employee. When an employee sees that the organization is genuine in its appreciation, then the employee feels personally rewarded.

As the HR leader of a small business, it is important to see that HR integrates these five actions within the organization. Creating an HR scorecard to integrate with the small business managers, developing applicable metrics, properly staffing the organization, giving employee evaluations, and creating rewards and compensation are all important HR functions that an organization can benefit from. All these actions are closely related and help to add value to an organization. Each of these actions builds on the others and is crucial to each other's successes. By having integrated policies with line managers, HR will be able to get everyone in the organization more aligned with the mission and goals. By making the small business managers more aware of the need for HR, they will be able to better communicate the information to their employees. This will allow the employees to have easier access to the company's policies and procedures. HR will also help the organization to benefit from new and improved metrics. With HR working with the leader and small business managers, they will be able to create useful metrics that measure both productivity and the human element. This will help the organization to become more aware of what is going on. This will also help the organization to have a competitive advantage in their human capital, as well as in their productivity and efficiencies.

Staffing will also be used to increase the value of the organization. Since HR will be more aligned with the organization, they will be able to better understand the staffing needs. This will help the organization to put the right person in each job at the right time. This situation will also help the organization to look at its structure and to make the necessary changes if a department, division, or job function is over or understaffed. Employee evaluations will also add value to the organization. Both the employee and the organization will better understand what is expected from the 360-degree performance evaluation. This will help to provide continuous positive feedback so the organization can continue to grow. Finally, HR will be able to improve the organization's employee reward system. As a result, HR will be able to create rewards that are more integrated with the organization and the employee. This will help to increase employee morale and promote employee development, which will lead to long-term loyalty to the small business, increasing the chance for sustainability and success.

All these functions and actions that HR oversees are used to create value for the organization. HR realizes that people are what make an organization. Organizations need to remember this value when dealing with their employees. Each employee contributes to the organization, and they need to be considered in every decision. When HR is aligned and strategically integrated with the organization, more can be accomplished, and it is easier to achieve these goals. HR uses the human element as a competitive advantage for the organization, which helps the organization to grow. The more integrated HR is with the organization, the more successful it will be. HR is an important part of any small business and should always be strategically aligned with the organization so it can help to ensure its success in the future.

Another successful HR tool that has improved small business success is the use of performance appraisal. Even though many small businesses consist of family members, they must be evaluated as employees to determine the strengths, weaknesses, opportunities, and threats each person is responsible for within the company. The performance appraisal, and its process, is a fundamental leadership responsibility. The performance appraisal can be a source of stress and tension, as well as a time for celebration. Performance appraisals are a vehicle to validate and refine organizational actions. They are also used to provide feedback to employees with an eye on improving future performance. In my leadership situation, there are five actions that can be taken to make the performance appraisal process more effective. These actions will help to reduce the likelihood of a surprise at performance appraisal time, and they are all centered on result-oriented measures for the organization. The five actions are to create an appropriate evaluation based on relevant metrics, conduct peer reviews, employee self-reviews, upward assessments, and 360-degree reviews. These actions will help the small business manager and the employee to establish a clear channel of communication about what the evaluation is really for and how it will be used to help benefit the organization.

The first action that can make the performance appraisal system less stressful is to create a relevant performance review based on metrics. The metrics that will be used in the performance appraisal will need to relate to both the manager and the employee. In traditional appraisal systems, the manager uses an evaluation form that focuses on the employee's job from a certain perspective. Most of the time, the metrics used to evaluate an employee are based on productivity and dollar amounts. The metrics fail to evaluate an employee's human element and any other contributions they have made to the organization. Not everything that the employee does or is responsible for is measured in the performance appraisal. This situation can cause an employee to not receive a favorable ranking based on these metrics. This causes the employee to feel stressed, devalued, and apprehensive when it is time to receive their performance appraisal.

The metrics that are used in performance appraisals also have a hard time clarifying what qualifies as a "good" performance rating. Since appraisals can be very subjective, they can be viewed in many ways depending on the manager who is giving the appraisal. This also causes the employee to feel stressed when receiving this appraisal. Performance reviews are usually done once a year, so if that review is bad, it will set the tone for the employees' morale for the following year. This will cause a "negative" or "downward" spiral. When the employee is tense about the performance appraisal, they will not be able to gain a mutual understanding of what needs to be done. The employee will become defensive, which means there is no clear communication with the small business manager, causing disengagement and low morale within the company.

Using metrics that contain a mix of efficiency and the human element helps the manager to give a fair rating to each employee. On some performance appraisals, the manager is forced to rate the employee on a scale. The manager will then have to choose a specific, predefined rating for the employee that may not accurately represent their true value, worth, or performance. HR will need to work with the small business managers of the organization to create a well-balanced performance appraisal system that uses useful criteria for both the employee and the organization. This strategy will help to relieve the tension the employee feels during their evaluation, and it will also help to provide clear, constructive communication between the organization and the employee.

Second, when peer reviews are used, the employee can experience a better workplace, and they will not become frustrated with their level of performance. Peer reviews also help to benefit the organization by creating a bond between employees and allowing them to engage with one another to better understand their purpose and job function. When the employee can see benefits and be less tense or stressed, they are able to work harder to provide a higher level of performance. This also helps to eliminate the employees' tension because it helps them to focus on their job instead of spending too much of their time worrying about the company's politics. Next, peer reviews are also good because they are not used to set pay, give promotions, or administer disciplinary actions. This helps the employee engage in their job without having to worry about doing something wrong. The employee can have a more positive attitude in their job, which will ultimately lead to higher performance when it is time for them to receive their next performance appraisal to see if there has been positive progress during the year that will help to benefit the small business. The third action that the leaders in an organization can implement into their performance appraisal system is self-reviews. Self-reviews are a good idea because they are based on what the employee is most familiar with in their work. Employees have the most involvement in the jobs that are performed, and they are a good judge of what each job encompasses. With self-reviews, employees can rate themselves on a rating scale number using different criteria. This can be done with a standard survey form that also suggests areas for improvement. Self-reviews help the employee to clarify their own goals and to expose any areas of weakness. This helps the employee to focus on the positive experiences in their job and gives them a chance to improve on the areas of their job that are not being performed correctly.

Self-reviews are helpful to the performance appraisal system. Self-reviews leave the manager out of the process, and they help to boost the employee's understanding of what needs to be done at their own level. They allow the employee to become their own manager of their performance and support both the shared leadership and value of voice of the company. The employee can counsel themselves instead of feeling judged. This helps to give the employees more dignity and respect, and it also enhances their appreciation for what their manager is trying to accomplish, creating a positive culture and organizational behavior. Finally, self-reviews allow the employee to discuss how he or she is doing with the manager and to provide input into their performance evaluation.

The fourth action that can be taken is to incorporate upward assessments into the performance appraisal system. Upward assessments are used in many small businesses and large corporations. Next, upward assessments can result in significant improvements within the organization. Upward assessments help small business managers to realize that what they say does not always match what they do. Managers can understand the employee's frustration during an evaluation when the employees are trying to follow what the managers say but do something that is different. The upward assessments help to keep the managers' actions and words consistent, so they can be more easily understood by the employees. This also helps the managers to work on their credibility with the employees so that everyone's performance improves and creates an "upward" spiral that leads to improved success and performance.

The process of upward assessment is what is important to the performance appraisal system. It allows both the employee and the manager to open a clear line of communication. This strategy helps them both to "open up" and discuss what is going on in a non-threatening way. Upward assessments are usually done by a third-party consultant who helps to provide constructive feedback. This brings the employee and the manager onto the same playing field so they can work on the task together. This helps the manager to check their progress so they can provide better support for their employees and become a better leader. When the individual can become a better manager, they will work on becoming a better leader to provide improved results. The employees will appreciate the upward assessment because it shows them that even managers must go through the same process. This situation helps to create unity within the organization to work harder and improve the overall level of performance.

The fifth action that can be taken in a leadership role to improve the performance evaluation process is to have 360-degree reviews. 360-degree feedback is the most comprehensive and costly type of appraisal to facilitate. However, it is also the most necessary when doing an employee performance evaluation. It focuses on getting feedback from everyone in the division or organization. The 360-degree review gives people the opportunity to see how they are viewed by others, identify their strengths and weaknesses, and improve communication among other people within the company. The 360-degree review helps to bring out every aspect of an employee to support strengths and improve weaknesses.

Each of these five actions is important when improving the employee performance process. The traditional way that companies are accustomed to using is not beneficial to the employee. The employee is forced to be ranked or put into categories that are not a fair representation of their performance. By changing the traditional format to a new format, the employee will not be as tense or negative about getting evaluated and will be more open to listening to the results that come from the appraisal process. Relevant metrics, peer reviews, self-reviews, upward assessments, and 360-degree reviews are all needed in creating a productive performance appraisal process. Metrics are important in defining the necessary criteria for the evaluation. The metrics need to include characteristics from an efficiency standpoint and from a human element standpoint to get an accurate evaluation.

The small business can also incorporate peer reviews into its culture. This will enable the employees to have more constructive relationships with their group. Peer reviews will help to provide a more positive work environment for the employees and it will reduce the amount of stress felt by the employees at work. Self-reviews will help to ease the tension of the appraisal process because they allow employees to monitor themselves. This situation helps to improve employee confidence because they can focus on what they are doing right and they are also able to make corrections to what is going wrong before being formally evaluated. Upward assessments are necessary because they show employees that their manager must go through a similar evaluation process. This helps the manager to grow into a better leader and it also forms a more cohesive bond between the manager and employees. Finally, 360-degree reviews are the most important. The 360-degree review allows everyone to be part of the performance appraisal process. Everyone gets to have input in the decision-making process.

The primary goal that HR will need to accomplish within a small business is to make the performance appraisal process less stressful and tense is provide the employee with continuous feedback. Honest feedback from the employee's manager or peers will help to increase communication. Communicating the necessary feedback will allow improvements to be made. Next, feedback can be given formally or informally to the employee. The feedback needs to be given, and received, throughout the year. These different types of review systems help the organization communicate with the employees. This situation makes the performance appraisal process a two-way street to improve shared leadership, create a collective voice, and create a Responsibility of Reason. As a result, peer reviews help the small business manager and the employee to set realistic measures.

Small businesses want their employees to have a positive work environment. Good organizations know that a positive work environment will increase an employee's contributions to the organization. Great organizations build on identified strengths and use them to create new opportunities. This situation will cause the employee to become more relaxed and not worry about receiving performance appraisals. If the organization uses the right metrics and incorporates these informal review processes, the employee will know exactly how they are doing. The employee will also know what is expected of them. This will help the employee and the organization to work together and promote an "upward spiral" for both parties. In the past, small businesses have lived in the "here and now." However, to be sustainable, they must also plan and forecast for the future. While the future is unknown, small companies constantly make assessments and decisions based on their perceptions of the future. As an HR leader in a small business, it is important to understand the impacts of what the organization does. The processes that the organization uses today will determine its outcome in the future. There are certain things that should be monitored to understand their future impact on the organization and the HR function. The HR leader needs to be informed of all the current developments within the organization. Since the HR manager is often the leader and/

or manager, this strategy will help HR to help predict the right course of action for the organization.

The first thing that needs to be accomplished is to monitor the staffing within the small business. It is important to monitor staffing since recruitment decisions are central to effectively managing, and restructuring, organizations. As an HR leader, it would be my responsibility to work with the leader and small business managers to make sure that each division is operating efficiently. Efficiency can be slowed down by having too many or not enough people working in a department. The right mix will need to be determined within the small business. Next, staffing is important since it looks at the types of employees the organization needs in each position. An organization may have the right number of employees, but the current employees may not be best suited for the position. HR and the rest of the organization will want to make sure that they staff the positions with the most dedicated employees, placing them in positions where they can individually grow and for the small business to increase its productivity.

Organizations will become more diverse in the future. Companies will need to make sure that the rewards they offer to their employees are relevant. The HR leader will need to work with the leader and small business managers to determine the appropriate salaries for their employees. With organizations competing in a more global environment, employees will always be asked to do more than what was originally expected. The employees' salaries will need to be adjusted to meet the new requirements of their jobs. HR will need to work with the managers to design new job descriptions so that the pay scale can be determined for each level of job. Next, organizations will need to monitor the external environment to see what the competitors' standards are. Once these standards are determined, the organization can then set benchmarks for the employees' jobs to provide the appropriate level of compensation.

These rewards will need to be monitored to make sure that they are aligned with the organization. The organization could offer small gifts of appreciation to employees that would also symbolize their loyalty to the company. This will help make the employees feel like they are a part of the organization's behavior and culture. This will also help to promote long-term loyalty with the employees to the small business. Finally, the HR leader will want to make sure that the employees' compensation is in line with the organization. The HR leader will need to monitor pay options such as merit pay, lump-sum bonuses, incentives, commissions, stock options, gains sharing, profit sharing, and seniority-based pay, which are benefits that all small businesses can benefit from since there is little room for upward mobility given the flat organizational structure.

The HR leader will need to remember that there is no correct answer to an employee's pay scale, so this will need to be carefully assessed and adjusted to meet the needs of the current and future workforce.

Organizations are growing and changing every day. HR will need to work with the leader to determine what the core competencies of the organization are going to be responsible for. HR will then need to align itself with those core competencies. When the core competencies are determined, HR will then need to decide what functions it will outsource. Outsourcing will cause the organization to restructure. The organization will then become dependent on another company to perform some of its administrative functions. HR will then act as the liaison between the two companies to ensure that things are running smoothly. Outsourcing will help HR to focus on more important strategic decisions that are more aligned with the organization's goals. The HR leader will need to closely monitor the risk that is associated with outsourcing the functions of the organization. HR will also need to monitor the efficiency of the outsourcing decision. If it is not helping the organization, then outsourcing is not the right decision to make. Third, the strategic capabilities will need to be assessed. Outsourcing should create additional value for the organization and allow it to become more aligned in its daily operations. Finally, the HR leader will need to monitor the flexibility of the organization's ability to outsource. If a company wants to try a new function and is unsure of its success, then it might want to outsource this activity. If the organization is truly committed to the project that will help give them a competitive advantage, then they would want to keep that project internal so the information does not leak out, causing a decrease.

HR will need to monitor integration throughout the small business. Integration is extremely important to the organization. Organizations constantly change the way they do things to compete in today's environment. As the leader of HR, it is their job to make sure that everyone has a "seat at the table" when the decisions for the future are being made to create an inclusive organizational culture, share voice, and Responsibility of Reason. The leader of HR will need to have a close relationship with the leaders in keeping HR aligned with the small business. Finally, HR will need to play an important role in working with the small business managers to help them better understand the human element of their staff.

The HR leader will have to monitor the changes from the role of just implementing guidelines, procedures, and business plans to a more integrated role. Human resources will now have a more integral role in the organization's planning and strategic goals. Human resources' new role in the organization's line integration is important when dealing with company growth and when facing global competition. Organizations have learned that it is their people that help to give them a competitive advantage and that their people need to be properly taken care of. If this situation does not happen, then the employees can go to work somewhere else, causing a new external threat to the organization.

HR managers will have to examine the use of technology. Technology can play an important role in an organization. It can help an organization save money on operational costs, and it can also help to better align the company around its goals for the small business. The HR leader will need to monitor the best ways to take advantage of new technologies. The first way that HR can take advantage of technology is to use the Internet. HR could use the Internet to post the necessary information that would be relevant to the organization's employees. Within a small business, it is important to get the right information out there for potential employees since there is a wide range of competition. Next, HR will need to work with the leadership and small business managers to create a website with all the HR forms, benefit information, policy changes, and procedures that the employees would need to become aware of. While this may sound commonplace, there are still several small businesses out there that do not use these features and suffer from their own lack of knowledge.

The HR leader would use technology to work with upper management to ensure that the organization remained in compliance with the rules and regulations of the government. The HR leader needs to invest in the Employment Law Information Network and the HRN Management group to use a wide range of human resources Management Compliance software for today's organizations. The software packages that the HR leader would use to monitor the organization's compliance are Performance Pro, Employment Law Guide, Surveys Online, HR Suite, Employment Law Self Audit, and Job Descriptions+. Each of these human resources software packages is a practical and efficient HR solution that is time-tested, subject-rich, and on the cutting edge of technology. Today, these software packages are created to help simplify and better improve how their organizations manage the human resources department so that they remain in regulatory compliance. Finally, each one of these software packages is essential to maintaining a proper human resources department, and they are something that every HR leader of any small business should consider a necessary investment.

The HR leader would also work with the leaders and management of the small business to create new work schedules. Today, most organizations have made it possible for their employees to telecommute to work. This could be done at a low cost for the organization to improve its bottom line and at the same time provide a huge benefit for the employees. This situation means that the employee can work virtually from home without having to physically come to work. HR can use this technology as a good incentive for employees. The same amount of work will be required of them, but it is up to the employee to plan out their day. The employee will not feel the tension of a manager watching over them. They will be allowed to work in their own environment and at their own speed. HR realizes that the employee will recognize this as an added benefit of working for the company because telecommuting will also allow them to spend more time with their family. This will help to provide long-term loyalty and appreciation from the employee, which will improve the overall performance of the organization.

As an HR leader, it is important to closely examine these factors if they ever plan to grapple with the "real world." Each of these factors helps to contribute to the future of HR within the organization and has a future impact on where the company will go and what the company will achieve. The HR leader will have to focus on defining the necessary staffing needs of the organization. It is important for HR to monitor the attraction rate of new employees, along with the retention rate of employees in each job. This will help bring each division of the organization into tighter alignment. Next, HR will ensure that the staff is properly rewarded for their work. The HR leader will need to track how successful the rewards are in improving employee performance. The rewards will need to be monitored to make sure that they properly motivate employees to improve their performance. HR will need to keep the employees of the small business content so they will not lose them to a competitor.

If they choose to, HR and the line managers will need to work closely with each other and establish a liaison with the outsourcing firm. The HR leader will need to ensure that value is being added to the firm. Once a function is outsourced, HR will need to measure the improvement of the organization's core competencies and effectiveness. This will help to promote stability and greater integration within the organization. Fourth, HR will need to be closely integrated with the line managers. HR will want to make sure that they have regularly scheduled meetings with them so they can share the necessary information. HR will want to work closely with the line managers to help keep them in compliance and to avoid any regulatory issues. For the organization to succeed, HR and the line managers will have to become a cohesive unit.

The HR leader can monitor the use of technology to see if it helps to keep the organization more compliant, if it is adding to their employee retention rate, and if it is helping to improve the organization's core competencies. If the HR manager can successfully use technology, then they will be able to give the organization additional value and to also improve its bottom line. By improving an organization's bottom line and adding value, they will be able to have a competitive advantage over other firms. This will help the organization grow and be an industry leader in the future economy. The HR leader needs to "have a seat" at the table so they can help guide the organization in the right direction. If the HR leader does their job, the organization will become more strategically aligned and will operate in a more efficient manner.

In today's diverse environment, employees have different needs. They are motivated by varying levels of internal and external rewards. It becomes important for small businesses to understand these motivations and devise effective reward systems. Organizational leaders need to ensure that the reward system is aligned with the organizational goals. The reward systems will also need to enhance the organization's chances for successful change. No reward system is perfect. Some adaptations will need to be made to achieve the goal of having successful change. If no adaptations are made, then employees will not be focused on changing the organization. There are four items that can be recommended to help an organization improve its reward system to promote successful change. The four items are: what's in it for me (WIIFM); align the reward system to the mission and goals of the organization; promote the development of new paradigms; and incorporate terminal values in the reward system.

The phrase "what's in it for me" is important for organizational leaders to consider when improving the reward system of an organization. The most valuable resource for any organization is its people. The employees are responsible for helping the organization to flourish toward its long-term goals. Organizations accomplish their goals by "people protecting" methods. Employees respect and work hard to help the organization achieve its goals, and the organization needs to respect its employees. This will help the employees see that the organization does want to properly reward them for their hard efforts. However, not every employee has the same views on relevant rewards.

Organizational leaders need to take the time to get the right people in the right place so they can help guide the organization in the correct direction. This will help the organization succeed and keep the reward system meaningful to each employee. Each employee will be working toward the goals of the organization. He or she will be properly compensated using a properly aligned reward system. Managers and employees will be able to understand "what's in it for me" and will experience meaningful rewards. Employees will be able to feel good about what they have accomplished, and the organization will continue to flourish.

The reward system needs to be aligned with the mission and goals of the organization. An organization's reward system is a representation of its values. These values are what guide the organization throughout its business. It is important for employees to understand these values. An important job of organizational leaders is to make sure that employees are being rewarded for following the goals of the organization. Leaders in the organization need to do this by setting a good example for the employees to follow. If an organization has the right people on the bus and in the right seats, it makes it easy for the organization to succeed.

Small businesses that have survived beyond the 10-year benchmark did so by creating new paradigms and innovative ideas. The reward system that an organization uses helps to ensure the chance for successful change. Organizational leaders want to make sure that the reward system promotes innovative ideas. When employees are rewarded, they will see a direct benefit in becoming more dedicated to the organization. Organizations and people tend to live in paradigms, a structured model based on a set of assumptions, concepts, or values of the organization. Paradigms help establish the boundaries of organizations and provide a framework for their employees. By nature, organizations follow paradigms because they make reality easier to understand. However, paradigms cause organizations to pass on new innovative ideas. Employees use the organization's old paradigms as a form of stability, so they will not have to change. Organizational leaders need to find a way to incorporate creating new paradigms into the reward system. The world is constantly changing, and new products and processes will need to be developed. Organizational leaders want to encourage their employees to create these new ideas. Employees are an organization's most valuable resource, and the employees should be viewed as innovative change agents.

For employees to come up with new innovative ideas, the organization needs to create a reward structure to help the employees think "outside of the box." New and innovative thinking will help organizations establish a new paradigm. This will cause a new paradigm to take effect. The organization will then be following the "going back to zero" rule. This means that organizations will constantly be changing their products and processes. Employees will continuously be asked to help come up with new innovative ideas that will benefit the organization. The reward structure that is established will promote innovative thinking and help the organization deal with change successfully. Directly linking employees to the reward system will bring them into alignment with the organization, creating an "upward spiral."

The reward system should incorporate terminal values within the small business. Terminal values are a fundamental part of what makes up the organization and are the moral backbone of the company. Organizational leaders need to incorporate terminal values into the reward system to help make it more beneficial to the employees. The reward system is the organization's way of thanking its employees for doing a good job. An organization wants to make sure that it is rewarding the right types of behavioral actions. Terminal values help to build trust between the employee and organization. Rewarding terminal values helps ensure that employees are following the organization's values and mission.

Terminal values are needed in the reward system because they help provide structure for the organization. These values are what the organization is about. When an employee reviews the reward system, he or she should be able to know what the organization expects. The reward system will then function as a moral compass for the employee. The employee will know that by doing the right thing, he or she will be properly compensated. If the terminal values are not followed, then the employee is out of alignment with the organization. This situation will result in the organization being unable to undergo any type of positive change. It is also important to integrate terminal values into the reward system to involve each employee. Employees all have a sense of morals and values. By placing values into the reward system, the organization makes the employee an integral part of the process. This situation allows the employees to share common ground and to better relate to one another. Terminal values help to form unity within the organization. Organizational leaders need to take advantage of terminal values to help the organization grow and to provide successful changes in the future.

These four items are an important part of an organization's reward system. The employees and organization need to know that the reward system lets them know "what's in it for me (WIIFM)," needs to be aligned with the mission and goals, needs to encourage new paradigms, and needs to address the organization's terminal values. Each of these items is needed to help keep the employees aligned with the organization. Organizational leaders need to know how to manage the reward system to better guide their employees. The reward system is the organization's way of thanking its employees for being loyal and doing a good job and is a fair representation of what small businesses believe. When employees know "what's in it for me," then they will be more willing to make themselves a part of the change. The employees will be able to see how they will be affected and what needs to be done. Aligning the reward system with the organization's mission and goals is also important.

This question helps small businesses think about the importance of the reward system. Organizational leaders need to use reward systems to encourage their employees to work harder. The reward system helps ensure a tight alignment within the organization and is a vital part of helping employees adapt to the changes that need to be made. Organizational leaders need to make sure that the reward system is relevant to the employees' needs, and it can help an organization and its employees better adapt to change. The reward system will also ensure that the change is effective, so the organization can experience success in the future. Another method used to help small businesses improve their level of sustainability is for the leaders, managers, and employees to look at the metrics that are used within their company.

The balanced HR scorecard is important to consider when analyzing metrics within an organization. Human Resources should play an important role in the organization when aligning employees with the organization. Human Resources set the rules and regulations for the employees to follow. It is the small business manager's job to ensure that their employees are aware of the policies and procedures. Organizational leaders need to make sure that the organization's message is made available to every employee. They need to make sure that the line managers are acting as the human resources liaison to the employees. Organizational leaders need to make sure that the HR department is in constant communication with the line managers. Constant communication between the two departments will help to improve the employees' knowledge of what is expected of them.

Human resources work with the organizational leaders to determine what metrics are relevant and which ones are outdated or irrelevant. Organizational leaders need to ensure that HR and the line managers are not just looking at the short-term financial results. Most managers get caught up in trying to manipulate the numbers instead of looking at the company's long-term goals. This situation can cause organizations to lose focus on what they are trying to accomplish. Organizational leaders need to prevent this from happening with the use of a balanced HR scorecard. A balanced HR scorecard will help organizations have a balanced metric system. A balanced metric system will help organizational leaders accurately gauge employee performance. The HR scorecard will look at all different types of metrics and will also focus on the company's financials. It will look at the organization to see if it is making money for the year and will help them determine where it should concentrate its efforts. More importantly, the only short-term financial metric it will use is whether the organization can make payroll on Friday. The rest of the balanced scorecard looks at indirect employee roles and contributions.

The balanced HR scorecard will look at factors such as employee morale and the retention rate. One sign of a good organization is if its employees are happy. The higher the retention rate, the happier employees are. Organizations will also want to look at factors such as employee productivity and empowerment. Organizational leaders need to be aware of each employee's contributions. Not all employee contributions can be measured accurately against short-term financial metrics. Instead, leaders need to look at the indirect contributions of employees to the organization's goals. Employees are the most important resource to an organization, and all their contributions need to be properly measured to ensure successful change.

Part of an organizational leader's job is to keep the organization properly aligned. Organizational alignment is crucial in accomplishing the mission and helping the organization achieve a successful change. Employees and line managers are responsible for performing daily jobs in the organization. They have direct and firsthand experience with how the entire process works. Organizational leaders need to listen to the employees so improvements can be implemented. How the employees view the daily job process and responsibilities is an extremely reliable metric. As a result, employees can offer a new perspective on the issue that might help the organization become tighter aligned. Organizational leaders will be able to determine what metrics are relevant to the employees' jobs based on the evaluations.

The metrics of an organization's performance appraisal need to be directly related to the reward system. Aligning the performance appraisal to the reward system helps the organizational leaders determine the company's success. Performance appraisals are used to provide the employee with feedback on how well he or she has performed over the year. Unfortunately, most of the time, performance appraisals are either done in a negative way or are not given at all. Performance appraisals become a process that both the employee and manager do not appreciate. Instead of bringing the employee and manager into closer alignment, the performance appraisal can cause a split between the two sides. Organizational leaders need to find a way to tie performance appraisals to the reward system. This alignment helps bring the employees into closer communication with the rest of the organization.

Linking the performance appraisals to the reward system will also help the small business to determine if it is rewarding the right types of behavior. Organizational leaders want to make sure that the reward system is focused on the organization's goals. Organizational leaders do not want to use metrics or a reward system that promotes the wrong type of behavior. A properly structured reward system that is tied to the performance appraisal is a good metric for organizational leaders. Organizational leaders can use performance appraisals to improve their company's metrics to ensure successful changes in the future. The ability of an organization to make transitions and change is an important metric for organizational leaders. In today's economy, businesses will constantly undergo changes. How the organizations deal with change is important to their survival.

Organizational leaders want to be able to measure the ability to undergo change so they can ensure effective company change. Managers will want to incorporate a metric that measures the S-Curve. The S-Curve is how long it takes employees to complete the change process. Organizational leaders will want to study the amount of time it takes for employees to accept change. The amount of time that it takes employees to accept change will help determine the organization's capabilities. Organizational leaders need to make sure that the employees maintain a positive view of change. This situation will ensure effective changes in the future. Small business leaders will need to have the ability to change part of the organization's culture. Once it is a part of the culture, leaders and managers can then incorporate the ability to change into the reward system. Rewards can then be given based on employees' performance appraisals. Organizational leaders can better ensure organizational success when they know that employees are more open to change. Transition and the ability to change are important metrics for organizational leaders to use. The organization's ability to change is very important when making leadership decisions. Organizational leaders need to be able to know what the company's ability is to make successful and effective changes. If a successful change fails to occur, the organization and its employees will become misaligned.

The balanced HR scorecard, 360-degree evaluations, performance appraisals, and the ability to change are very important to an organization's metric system. Measuring metrics is an important job for organizational leaders, as they help measure how well the organization is doing. Metrics are used to determine the future success and effectiveness of the organization. Finally, metrics help to ensure that the organization's activities are measured appropriately. Organizational leaders must rely on metrics to help enhance the organization's chances for successful change.

Organizational leaders will need to make sure that the company is using a balanced HR scorecard. A balanced HR scorecard will help to ensure that the metrics that will be used are diverse and will not just focus on short-term financial goals. The balanced HR scorecard will look at all the employees' contributions to the organization. The HR scorecard will help to create a more accurate representation of every employee. Next, organizational leaders can use 360-degree evaluations to help improve the metrics used in the organization. 360-degree evaluations help bring employees and management together. Both sides can come together to offer their perspectives on the situation. This perspective is very important for future change in the organization. Organizational leaders need to be able to measure the relationship between the performance appraisal and reward system. This relationship will help the organization see how effective its reward system is for the employees. If there is a tight alignment, then the reward system will be an effective measure to guide change. Organizational leaders will need to be able to measure the employees' ability to transition positively through change. Change is a major process in any organization. Leaders will need to measure how long it will take the organization to get through the S-Curve, so they can determine how effective the organization will be in the future. Each of these four items will help improve the organization's metric system and ensure effective change.

Organizational leaders need to use the right metrics to help determine each employee's contribution to the company. The metrics an organizational leader chooses to use are very important. Employees help keep the organization tightly aligned and let both the manager and the employee know what is expected. Metrics are an important part of helping employees relate to the organization. Organizational leaders need to make sure that the metric system is relevant to the employees. Relevant metrics are necessary for organizational leaders to ensure successful change for the company in the future. Small businesses must address the issue of market targeting and strategic positioning. This is important to remember when looking at high-performance marketing. First, organizations must identify a targeting strategy. This strategy needs to consist of identifying and analyzing the segments in a product market, deciding which segment(s) to target, and designing and implementing a positioning strategy for each target. High-performance marketing plays an important role in this situation. Strategic marketing helps determine what market segment an organization is going to target. The target segment can either be micro-segmented or macro-segmented. Once the target market has been selected, the organization must determine how it will best use high-performance marketing to confront the targeting factors. For an organization to effectively use high-performance marketing, it will need to use marketing to determine the stage of maturity of the market, the diversity in its preferences, the industry structure, all the capabilities and resources, and the prospects of competitive advantage.

Organizations can use high-performance marketing to address all these issues. Before an organization enters a market, it will want to make sure that it can compete in this market. The organization should look at all these factors.

The organization also needs to make sure that it has the right customer relationship management system in place to better meet the customers' needs. Organizations will want to make sure that they are using their marketing department to meet customers' needs instead of trying to control them. This will help the organization to become more customer-centric. This will help small business marketing to break out of its "do" instead of "lead role" that has prevented marketing from becoming a change agent for the organization. Next, small businesses will need to determine their marketing strategy. An organization can have a product strategy that focuses just on its merchandise. There is a value-chain strategy that allows an organization to focus on its relationship with retailers and consumers. A pricing strategy allows companies to compete based on the price of a product. Promotion strategies are used to help companies to create a unique way to sell their products. Through these strategies, an organization hopes to gain a competitive advantage over its competition.

High-performance marketing is important in determining the effectiveness of the organization's position. High-performance marketing creates a way that combines all the resources in the organization into creating a bond with the consumer. This helps the organization to become more profitable by becoming customer-centric. It also helps the organization to become investment-oriented by making more thought-out business decisions. High-performance marketing also helps to involve the entire organization, which promotes systems thinking. This will prevent the organization from becoming too incrementally focused on the market segment. Finally, high-performance marketing is a combination of using each marketing strategy to create a systematic strategy that guides the entire organization. High-performance marketing can help to combine each strategy to better meet the customers' needs. This situation will cause the small business to no longer experience a gap between the market segment and the company's products or services.

High-performance marketing helps organizations face these complexities and to create systematic strategies to address these issues. First, high-performance marketing helps organizations to better allocate their resources. This helps to ensure that better investments are being made, which allows for an increase in the organization's financial standing. Next, high-performance marketing helps the organization to work as a whole system. This centralizes every aspect of the organization on the products and services that are being offered. High-performance marketing also helps the organization to meet the environmental turbulence and diversity by allowing the organization to better understand its market segment. This helps the organization to look at the entire situation instead of just a small portion of it. It also helps the organization to better understand market growth and what the customers are expecting to achieve from a product. High-performance marketing helps organizations to market to the needs of the customer instead of just trying to control the needs of the customer. This is done by harnessing all the necessary market information and viewing each customer differently.

Planning for new products involves aligning an organization's capabilities with its value opportunities. This situation involves an organization to understand what innovations it can achieve. The driving forces behind an organization finding successful innovations are creating an innovative culture, selecting the right strategy, developing and implementing effective new product processes, making resource commitments, and leveraging its capabilities. Each of these steps plays an important role in organizations creating new products that identify with their target market segment. Product and process innovation is an ongoing procedure for an organization. The needs and wants of market segments are constantly changing. Organizations must do continuous market research to keep up with current trends. Companies also need to go through internal and external developments to stay competitive. All of this becomes part of the company's business analysis. This helps an organization to better project its revenue and profits, perform more relevant research and development, and positively test more conclusive marketing decisions. This, in turn, helps a company to build a marketing plan. The marketing plan helps the organization determine when to pull products from the market, when to push the use of new technology, when to build a new product around new technology, when to focus on the production process of a product or service, and when to customize a product or service for improved customer satisfaction.

High-performance marketing plays an important role in planning new products. Each product that is created should be based around the original mission and goals of the organization. High-performance marketing is used to communicate the goals of the organization. It helps to bring the entire organization together. The organization must learn to embrace technology and to incorporate it into its customer relationship management system. This means providing quality products that the market wants with the use of new marketing techniques. These new techniques include using the Internet, email, and business-to-consumer e-commerce. Today's world is considered highly technical, so it is important for organizations to incorporate this trend in their strategic marketing plan. This helps the organization to become more customer-centric. Organizations will be able to effectively retain the right customers with the development of the right products. The right customer is based on the small business understanding the Pareto Rule, where 80 percent of your business comes from 20 percent of your customer, so selecting the right target market or niche is critical to the sustainability of the company.

Next, high-performance marketing is necessary in planning for new products because it helps the organization to become more investment-oriented. By taking the time to understand the market and each customer's needs, the organization can spend money more wisely. This will help the organization to save money on illogical business ventures. Next, high-performance marketing encourages systems thinking. This provides an integrated approach that shows the cause-and-effect relationship of an organization's actions. The organization can receive feedback based on the dynamics of its product or service. Incentives are also important in new product development. People must be motivated to be creative. It is important for an organization to create a framework that allows its employees to move toward higher personal performance.

When small businesses plan for new products or services, it is important for them to avoid incremental thinking. This occurs when an organization creates a product that the customer does not need. The organization tries to use insignificant tactics to control the market instead of listening to each of its customers. When this happens, an organization does not understand its market growth. It is important that high-performance marketing be used to help avoid this mistake. Finally, high-performance marketing needs to be used to help senior executives prepare for a new role within their organization. This will help them to better lead their corporation. This will help the leaders and managers to make more informed marketing decisions. Instead of just looking at the figures of a static budget, the leader or manager will be able to better understand the dynamic value that high-performance marketing can add to the organization. This will help the senior executives to have a better understanding of where the market is going. It will also show the senior executives what it will take to get there with the newly planned products.

High-performance marketing is important in filling the void within organizations. Over the years, marketing has become too marginalized. Marketing will need to change from being placed in a "doer" role to a "leadership" role. Marketing needs to be seen as a leader for change within an organization. This will help an organization to become more effective and efficient. This will add value throughout the entire organization. It will help to "inspire" the organization's employees to work harder, and it will also allow them to work smarter. This will then create more value for the organization and cause it to create a change across the entire organization. Small business survival is improving but still has a long way to go before the percentage of successes outnumbers the number of ones that fail within the first 10 years. With the use of technology and human resources, small businesses have become more effective competitors and have even begun to equally compete with larger corporations that once dominated the business markets. The reason for this improved success is due to leaders, managers, and employees working together to overcome financing issues and risk avoidance, inadequate management practices, stress, improved time commitments, and ineffective business planning. Next, small businesses have transitioned their thinking and core competencies to employee retention by improving their quality of life, financial reward, and independence using human resources. This situation has given proof that with inclusive organizational behavior and through the value of voice, small businesses have developed a Responsibility of Reason to support both individual and business needs to increase their productivity and sustainability in the dynamic business environment that must be taken to reach Responsibility of Reason.

In Figure 12, there are different steps. A stepping stone is a raised stone that is used as a place to step when crossing a path. The first stepping stone for organizations is learning. The goal of learning is to gain knowledge to lead change. Next, learning is the result of individual and unique experiences by the leaders and followers that will use their knowledge to improve overall performance and ensure that future learning occurs for the individual and the business. The second stepping stone is implementing a process. Implementation is a design or method that is used to model a new policy or process when trying to accomplish a task. As a result, implementation is the action that occurs

FIGURE 12 The stepping stones to the responsibility of reason.

after learning has taken place. The third stepping stone is directing. Directing involves the ability of a leader to guide or instruct followers, or for managers and followers to control the flow of a process. Next, directing is used to help provide continuous improvement throughout the organizational hierarchy. The final stepping stone is executing. During this phase, leaders will regularly engage with the followers to communicate the goals and to join all individuals with its strategy. As a result, each stepping stone provides a path for both the individual and the organization to support the Responsibility of Reason.

Simpleton Solution

Whether you are a small business owner, work for a small business, or are a consumer of small businesses, it is important to know the issues that they face. As a small business owner, you want to make sure you can provide goods and services to increase profits and ROI. As a consumer, you want your favorite small business to remain in the marketplace so you can get the products and services you have come to rely on from friendly, family-owned companies. As a result, the success of small businesses has improved since their induction into the competitive market but requires strong organizational behavior, a shared value of voice, and a Responsibility of Reason for remaining in business. As small business owners ourselves, we appreciate your loyalty and support. Here are the key takeaways from the chapter to remember:

- Historically, there has been a 95 percent failure rate of small businesses before the 10-year mark.
- Small businesses have reduced their failure rate to 65 percent in the last decade.
- Small businesses must continue to increase their financing through different methods to improve their investment in resources and transnational competition.
- Small businesses must correct ineffective business planning to change their focus from "here and now" to the "future."
- Small businesses will need to invest in the right marketing choices to promote their products and services to their target markets using the 80/20 rule.
- Small businesses will need to reduce financial and unnecessary risks and only make decisions that support the mission and vision through the responsibility of reason.

- Small businesses will need to create and use a balanced scorecard to "balance" functions that promote the mission and vision with equity and equality in decision-making and actions.
- Small businesses must incorporate a HR function to support the company and the employees in lifestyle, independence, and satisfaction.
- Small businesses require a large time commitment, and leaders must remember to appreciate each employee and support a "work hard/play hard" reward system.

The main takeaway from this chapter is that small businesses are improving their sustainability and making better use of their resources. The main way to do this is to get out from being lost in the "weeds" that can cause distractions from the main mission and vision of the leadership team. It is important to remain content with your mission statement and vision of the leader. Establishing a responsibility of reason will keep businesses focused, create a shared value of voice, improve organizational behavior, and continue to enhance new opportunities for sustainability to succeed in the target market.

CHAPTER 8

RESPONSIBILITY OF ENLIGHTENED LEADERSHIP REASONING

The Situation: I'm Rubber and You Are Glue

It was a typical day at school. Jessica, who was one of the original teachers at the school, was coming in for another day of servitude. She was one of the school's two art teachers. During her time there, she had a history of complaining about things that she did not like at school and had caused a lot of issues with the administration. Jessica felt that, over the years, the administration had failed to provide any form of governance or structure to the school, so she constantly asked for it to be implemented. In the morning, Jessica walked through the hallways and greeted each student she saw until she reached her classroom. Jessica opened the door and began to prepare for the lesson for the day. The students would be working on building a city out of paper. Once she was prepared, Jessica sat at her desk as the bell rang. She watched the students come in and sit in their assigned seats. Once the morning announcements ended, Jessica stood up and began going over the day's lesson.

"Good morning, students," she said. "Today, each of you will be drawing a city building. Then we will put them all together and build our own city."

While she was giving the directions, most of the class was paying attention. However, one student who had just returned to class after a long absence and had a history of being problematic was being disruptive. Jessica knew the student had been in juvenile jail for assaulting another student in a fight with a makeshift weapon. "Tommy," said Jessica, "please pay attention. You know the class rules."

He mumbled something under his breath at her. Keeping her professional composure, Jessica kept on giving the directions for the assignment. She then passed out rubber cement, pencils, erasers, scissors, rubber bands, to each student. "Once you have your supplies," she said, "you may begin working."

Jessica was happy to see all the students working hard on their city-building project. Even Tommy had begun working on something. He was busy making balls of rubber cement with paper clips sticking out of them that she assumed would be used for his project. While the class was working hard on their projects, Jessica took the opportunity to get some of her own work done. She had several art drawings to grade from the previous week. As she looked at the drawings, she looked up and saw Tommy holding one of the rubber cement balls with the paper clips sticking out of it in one hand and a rubber band in the other. Thinking nothing of it at the time, she lowered her head and went back to work.

As her head was lowered, she felt something hit her on the shoulder. Then another one hit her on the head. When she looked up, she saw that it was a rubber cement ball with paperclips. "Who hit me with this?" asked Jessica from behind her desk.

She scanned the room and saw that Tommy was holding a big rubber band in his hand while everyone else was holding a pencil and drawing on a piece of paper. She could only assume that he was the one who fired the projectiles at her but wanted to be fair without accusing anyone unfairly. "Tommy," asked Jessica politely, "did you launch these at me?"

Tommy smirked back and refused to answer. He then held the rubber band in his hand in a threatening manner to insinuate that he wanted to launch something else at her. He simply replied, "I'm rubber, and you are glue." Then he put his head down on his desk and slept until the bell rang. When the class ended, Tommy and the other students left. Jessica walked down to the main office to see her administrator. She told them all about what happened in class and what Tommy had done and said to her. "I feel threatened by Tommy," said Jessica. "He assaulted me in class using school supplies as weapons."

Her administrator knew all about Tommy and the trouble he caused in school. However, she was applying to be a principal at another school and did not want any issues. "Now, Miss Jessica," said the administrator, "are you sure this was flung at you on purpose, and it was not an accident? I mean, did you really see it happen? It sounds like you need help and that the stresses of teaching are getting to you. After all, it was just a rubber ball made of rubber cement and paperclips."

Jessica was shocked by the administrator's response. If they would not provide or support educational governance, how could the teacher be expected to maintain order and discipline in the classroom environment that was designed to facilitate learning? "So, you are not going to do anything?" asked Jessica. "I do not feel safe in my own classroom."

"It sounds like you need mental health counseling if you ask me," replied the administrator.

Crushed and humiliated, Jessica went home at the end of the day and cried. She felt unsupported and devalued. Not only were her concerns not heard, but her feelings and needs were also ignored. The administration felt that she was the problem and not the student who had just returned from juvenile hall. The next day, she went into the office to speak to the principal. He was not there, so Jessica made small talk with his assistant. In the background of the main office, Jessica heard two people horsing around. "Stop it," said one, "don't ASSAULT me!"

"I'm rubber and you are glue," replied the second person. "Don't make me use my rubber cement and paperclip weaponry to hurt you again, you big crybaby," replied the other one.

Jessica turned around to tell the two people to stop making fun of her situation. She thought it was two students who had found out and were making fun of her. As Jessica turned, she saw the two individuals who were making fun of her. One was an administrative assistant in the office. The other was her administrator. Everyone in the office was silent but thinking the same thing: *AWKWARD.*

The administrator put her hand out and asked Jessica and the administrative assistant to join her. When their hands touched on top of each other, the administrator shouted, "Go team!" Then, without anything else being said, the administrator went back to her office, and Jessica returned to her room. Nothing else needed to be said. It was clear that there was no educational governance, and it was an environment of "me" instead of "us." One was rubber, the other was glue. What bounced off one stuck to another, causing everyone to work against each other instead of finding a reason to work together.

The Educational Responsibility of Enlightened Leadership Reasoning

There is a critical need for the success of educational governance in its various responsibilities to students, the community, staff, and administration. When discussing the importance of reasons for education, it is important to rely on philosophy and the mutual understanding of shared voice in developing reason. When there is a new reason or a clearly defined shared responsibility, then an educational leadership model can be created for the Responsibility of Reason. To begin this process, it is important to first analyze and improve teaching and learning through effective educational governance and administration.

It is important to understand and define the behavior of educational governance. The governance of educational administration has a large effect on the teachers and students within their schools. It helps to regulate and define the relationships between administration, teachers, and students within the school. Next, educational governance is responsible for creating positive relationships and a direct connection with communication and outside agencies to gain additional support. When there is good governance, positive behavior will be shared between the group members or stakeholders. Educational governance will seek to increase participation. Participation is important to enable everyone to have an equal opportunity or voice in sharing their thoughts and opinions throughout the various levels of hierarchy in the school system. This situation enables everyone to become freely associated and supportive of each other to help build stronger governance within each level of the school-wide system.

Educational governance works to create a rule of law for everyone to follow. The framework of the school will be shared, enforced, and implemented by the administration, teachers, students, and other stakeholders to help bring everyone under the same guiding principles through social and organizational justice in an equal and equitable manner. The third behavior of successful educational governance is transparency. Transparency allows the administration to share what is going on and why something is occurring through policies, procedures, and regulations. Since the policies will apply to all stakeholders, they must be communicated internally and externally to the organization to ensure accountability.

When there is strong educational governance, the stakeholders can respond to any given situation quickly and efficiently. This behavior is important since decisions will need to be made within a reasonable amount of time in an ever-changing and dynamic environment. The fifth behavior is to be consensus-oriented. The goal of educational governance is to use the Leadership-Member Exchange (LMX) model to create a large group of followers and to decrease the number of outsiders to the organization. When a consensus approach is used, the decision-making process is more inclusive. This situation causes changes to be more widely accepted and adopted into practice since everyone has been able to participate in the process equally and equitably. Effectiveness and efficiency are important since they help to share information among various groups that are subject to restrictions and time constraints. Budget factors will also play an important part in educational governance, requiring the stakeholders to make the best use of their resources for the greater good instead of only one area. Finally, accountability is an important component of educational governance. Through accountability, everyone is responsible for their contributions, choices, and decisions that impact the organization. Next, having accountability enforces strong ethical principles, a code of conduct, and supports future development and changes to the company.

As a result, educational governance is not separately divided between administration, teachers, students, and other stakeholders. Instead, it is an inclusive collaborative process for each group of people. Collaboration is important when working together to achieve set objectives and goals. Next, collaboration through educational governance promotes vertical implementation so each level becomes dependent on and supportive of the others within the given hierarchical structure. Through vertical integration, there will be a greater positive impact on achievement, an increased level of sustainability, and resiliency in overcoming change or obstacles in the future. Educational governance will support teachers to help students learn. The students will then support themselves, the community, and outside organizations through what they have learned for future generations. As a result, educational governance is important in having a positive impact on the Responsibility of Reason in leadership, management, and lifelong learning.

There are different styles of educational governance based on the philosophy of the leader or leadership team members. These styles include centralized, decentralized, external or internal, autocratic or democratic, and creative education management. Centralized educational governance is a hierarchical system used by the administration to ensure that all decisions are conducted and made within the governing body of the leader. This situation forms a top-down approach to leadership. As a result, centralized educational governance will create a streamlined process and standardized approach to policies and procedures for everyone involved. Finally, centralized governance will help to create an effective and efficient organization where resources will be allocated without a competitive political climate. However, centralized educational governance can create inflexibility within the structure of the organization and cause a lack of understanding or support in the decision-making process or when adapting to change.

When governance is decentralized, each local stakeholder is responsible for making decisions. The local stakeholder can be the administrator, teacher, student, or members of the community. With this approach, the goal of educational governance is to encourage and enforce collaboration, diversity, flexibility, and innovation through autonomy. With autonomy, policies can be customized to meet the local objectives and goals, given the diverse needs of the various populations. Finally, decentralized governance will promote and empower each stakeholder within the hierarchy to become more engaged in the governing process. Decentralized educational governance can lead to inconsistency in coordination, policies, and procedures since each locality will be focused on different objectives and goals instead of being controlled by a central location.

Internal governance focuses on the use of its own people and resources as the source of making decisions and acting. The given area has more control to implement change or make decisions within its business operations using its own resources. This situation makes it possible for customized curricula, teaching methodologies, and instructional strategies to be implemented based on the vision and values of the leader. When internal governance is used, it must make sure to remain diverse by avoiding bias or personal preferences that could lead to a decrease in quality or organizational success.

External educational governance relies on outside entities to help lead and guide it. Local, state, and federal entities are relied upon to make decisions and set rules and boundaries to be followed. This situation makes privatized or governmental agencies overseers of the educational process. External governance will increase accountability; it will set the standards and policies required for the entity to operate and function. External governance will be responsible for making sure that everyone is compliant with the expectations and directives. External governance can create several layers of bureaucracy, causing changes to be made slowly instead of when they are needed. External governance can also lead to a lack of diversity, creativity, and low autonomy within the organizational body.

Autocratic governance is based on one leader or authority who is seen as the head of the entity. The authoritarian leader is solely responsible for making unilateral decisions without getting insight or input from the other stakeholders. This situation can promote effectiveness and efficiency since there is no "red tape" to go through to make changes within the policies, procedures, or daily business operations. Moreover, autocratic governance will create a culture of strong discipline and uniformity among all members. Autocratic governance can lead to the isolation of employees and limit collaboration in the decision-making process. It can eliminate the development of critical thinking skills among its followers since they are never given the opportunity to gain knowledge or share their skills and abilities beyond what the leader permits.

When democratic educational governance is used, the decision-making process is a group or team effort. Instead of everything being done by one authoritarian, the emphasis is shifted to enabling everyone to participate and to become accountable for their actions. With this method of educational governance, there is an increased level of ownership and participation among administration, teachers, and students. There is a structure of inclusion and support for one another through collaboration. The increased amount of collaboration and shared leadership can cause slow implementation of new policies, procedures, or changes because of the requirement for everyone to agree and come to a shared point of view. Democratic governance can potentially slow down the administrative governing process since more people are involved in the decision-making process and action plan.

The final governing methodology is creative education governance. Creative education governance is used to create an environment of learning and support for innovation and experimentation of new ideas. Administration, teachers, and students will be given the opportunity to use their vision and thoughts in teaching and learning outcomes. Instead of being administration or teacher-led, the primary focus is on the student. With student or learner-centered education, there is active engagement and diverse learning methodologies that support the strengths of everyone. The main strengths of creative educational governance are adaptability, flexibility, and lifelong learning. For educational governance to be successful, it must have supportive leadership by administration, teachers, students, and all other stakeholders so it can remain effective and continue to implement change through creative practices.

With each method of administrative governance, there are key principles that must be achieved. The first principle is the equal division of tasks among all individuals or groups of stakeholders. Tasks must be divided to help focus on the shared objective and goal of the administrative team. Each individual or group of stakeholders will need to be accountable and responsible for their actions and decisions to create inclusion, shared leadership, and collaboration that lead to achieving objectives and goals. When there is an equal division of tasks among stakeholders, each person is directly tied to the process and will work toward a common goal. Authority and structure are important to educational administration and governance since they will help to make each person follow and adhere to the rules and regulations that were established. When there is respect for leadership, the followers will be more willing to follow directions and enact all guidelines, rules, and regulations. For this structure to work, each person must be accountable for their own actions and decisions. Failure to take responsibility or to adhere to the rules will cause a breakdown in structure and inequity between members. Prioritization will need to be given to the goals of the organization instead of the goals of the individual. If individuals only make decisions for themselves, then there will be competing interests and demands on resources. This situation can cause a breakdown in authority, structure, and governance. As a result, it is important to have shared objectives and goals that become the priority of each individual throughout the hierarchy of the organization.

The fourth key principle is human capital. Human capital is the most important resource to any organization. Administrators, teachers, students, and other stakeholders must be valued for their unique knowledge, skills, and abilities. This situation will help to reduce disengagement or turnover within the system. As a result, valuing human capital and giving them a voice will lead to a supportive environment instead of one that can lead to opposition or dissent. The final key principle of educational governance and administration is resources. There will always be limited resources, causing a competition for who should get what. To avoid this situation, resources must be allocated by the business based on a utilitarian need of the overall governance instead of on an individual, group, or unit. When resources are appropriately allocated, everyone will experience a mutual benefit or win-win scenario instead of a win-lose situation.

For educational governance to succeed, there must be clear and effective verbal communication. Verbal communication is the transactional process between two people that involves the exchange of ideas, information, and thoughts from one to another using dialogue. With verbal communication, people share ideas and thoughts using words and sounds. However, verbal communication can also be achieved through mobile devices and the use of other technology. Technology helps to easily share information throughout the hierarchy in an effective and efficient manner in business and education through talking, the telephone, videos, and lectures. Verbal communication is necessary for educational governance to help create a community of learners and supporters.

In educational governance, verbal communication will lead to different teaching cycles. Within the communication cycle and administrative govern-ance, there are various aspects between the sender and the receiver. There is an interplay between the sender and the message. The sender must take great time and consideration in developing a message. The message is then encoded and sent through a chosen channel for the information to be transmitted to the receiver. Once the message has been transmitted, the receiver will then decode the message that was sent by the sender. The receiver will then com-municate feedback through another channel for the original sender—now the receiver—to hear.

If there is a problem, or noise, the communication process can become invalid. This situation will lead to problems for leaders, learners, and followers to structure their methods, solicit new opportunities, be unable to respond to situations, and not be able to react to situations in a timely manner. Educational governance relies heavily on verbal communication to help each stakeholder interact with one another and to provide a support structure to the situation. Nonverbal communication can also be used to help influence the business process. While verbal communication is important, most of the communication is nonverbal. Actions, gestures, facial expressions, mannerisms, and body posture will be used to communicate a message without the use of words. The actions of the person or group will clearly show what is expected instead of relying on words. To be successful, the administrative governance will need to ensure that the "actions" match the "words" so there is clear communication and interactions between all stakeholders. Both verbal and nonverbal communication are used to influence behavior. If communication is misused or complicated by "noise," administrative governance will become subject to false expectations and undue influence on teachers, students, and other stakeholders. Self-fulfilling expectations can also develop based on the method and mode of communication. It is extremely important to remember to control what you say, how you say it, and how you act when interacting with other stakeholders. These interactions will influence the learning process and impact the Responsibility of Reason in decision-making and when acting in each situation.

Educational governance is supported by 10 important qualities. The first quality is to be strong communicators. Strong communicators are necessary to help give instruction and to support the objectives and goals of the leadership to other stakeholders. Strong communication also helps to support and improve the learning process that helps learners and workers enjoy the learning process instead of seeing it as an obligation.

The second quality of effective educational governance is listening. While it is important to use verbal and nonverbal communication, the transmission of information does not stop when someone stops speaking. The ability to listen helps to observe and understand what is not being said. When individuals become skilled at listening, they reduce anxiety, improve confidence, and further their skills. The third quality of educational governance is to focus on collaboration. Collaboration means that no individual, group, or stakeholder is ever alone. It is important to work effectively and efficiently in a group. Next, it is important for educational governance to keep an open mind to make sure that everyone is included in the process. Third, collaboration places different people in the appropriate roles to eliminate redundancy in tasks and to promote creative critical thinking skills.

The fourth quality is to be adaptable. Adaptability is required to promote constant adjustments in the current and future environments. It is important to be able to continually evolve over time. Change is something that no one easily accepts but is a constant in learning and the workplace. Educational governance will need to include the ability to change in its process to foster new methods of learning, decision-making, and acting. Fifth, educational governance must be engaging. When people are engaged, they will be more involved in the process to avoid being part of the "out" crowd. Effective educational governance will keep individuals moving forward through direct engagement. Instead of being teacher- or leadership-focused, the approach is worker- or learner-focused.

The sixth quality of educational governance is to show empathy. Empathy is the desire and ability to understand the feelings of another person. To become empathic, the person will need to demonstrate an emotional and cognitive response based on the observations of another's experience. When there is empathy, educational governance will help everyone show care, compassion, and concern to help others through the learning and implementation process. The seventh quality is patience. Patience is important when dealing with change and handling issues that arise throughout the planned process. Since there are many factors that cannot be accounted for, patience is required to help accept the things we cannot change, like delays, complaints, and other problems.

The eighth quality of strong educational governance is to promote real-world learning. Instead of using books and materials only found in a classroom, individuals can gain greater knowledge when there is a structure that brings them into the "real" world. This situation can help to engage the person more directly since their learning will come from "real" life examples and experiences. Leaders, managers, educators, and learners will all need to experience real-world learning so they can become prepared for the next step or phase in their process or career. When real-world learning is applied in the process, individuals are more likely to hone their knowledge, skills, and abilities when making decisions or solving practical problems in new situations.

The ninth quality of educational governance is to establish best practices. Best practices are a set of rules or guidelines that work to produce the best possible outcomes in each situation or environment. Next, best practices will guide the stakeholders on how to carry out a task to complete an objective or goal. Third, best practices are ongoing that allow for changes to be made so the person can adapt to the current situation. The advantage of best practices is that they do not set firm rules or regulations that can restrict decision-making or actions based on company policy or bureaucracy. As a result, best practices help to govern the process that educational governance relies on to be successful.

The final quality of educational governance is to be lifelong learners. A lifelong learner is someone who continually learns new things after they have completed their formal education. New knowledge is gained because they enjoy learning and want to improve their skills and abilities. Next, lifelong learning leads to a more positive mindset to meet the changes and challenges in the environment. As a result, lifelong learning will be gained by each new experience, which will lead to additional opportunities, social inclusion, and individual development. When educational governance implements lifelong learning, individuals can improve their knowledge and abilities through formal, informal, career, and self-directed methods of learning.

As a master teacher, educational governance will rely on five primary qualities. The first quality is to focus on learning. Learning provides the ability to discover and understand new things. Once new things are understood, the individual will gain a higher sense of success and accomplishment. As a result, the new level of learning will increase the amount of belief and confidence the person feels when relying on their own abilities and capabilities. The second quality is to be an expert in their practice of pedagogy. Pedagogy is required for the teacher to understand the needs of their learners and to provide the best practices to promote successful learning in the classroom or work environment.

The third quality is to become a content expert. A content expert can take complex lessons, material, or content and transform it into something useful for their learners. The goal of a content expert is to communicate and share information that is suitable and appropriate for their intended audience of learners. Next, the information or content will be delivered in a format that the learners or followers will want to accept. This situation helps to positively impact the learning process to promote learning instead of making it seem like additional or unnecessary work. Content experts can also perform learning through the classroom or using on-the-job training to increase the competency level and experience within a field of study.

The fourth quality of a master teacher is to become a lifelong learner. A lifelong learner is someone who seeks knowledge for their own benefit beyond the required learning objectives and goals. The advantage of a lifelong learner is that they never stop growing or advancing their knowledge, skills, or abilities. This situation makes it possible to focus on individual personal growth and development, which will then be used to increase human capital within the organization. As a result, lifelong learning will lead to developing a positive mindset, advanced cognitive abilities, and the ability to adapt to change instead of becoming complacent in the learning or work process. The final quality is to serve as a leader. Leadership is the combination of behaviors, skills, and beliefs that are used to help align their followers under a shared vision or goal. Instead of operating with individual goals and objectives, leadership will develop a collective or collaborative focus to execute the mission and vision of the leader. This situation will help the learning process as well as the organization to continually develop and grow instead of becoming stagnant. As a result, educational governance must use leadership to unite the workplace, education, and learner in a shared process that benefits each group individually as well as collectively.

Another important aspect of educational governance is to establish the culture and paradigm of leadership, management, and lifelong learning. Culture is used to pass down historical traditions, knowledge, expectations, beliefs, norms, and values to future generations. Next, culture determines the behavior, dress, manners, and rituals that are accepted by a specific society. When one identifies with and embraces the culture, there is a high level of inclusion and support. These traditions can be shared and passed down through stories and authentic leaders of the past who embraced the culture and instilled its importance in future generations.

Within educational governance, it must develop shared norms, belief systems, and values that connect the learner to the teacher, the teacher to administration, and educational governance to organizations in the workplace through shared symbols, beliefs, and frameworks that connect everyone together. When there is a strong culture, there is an increase in engagement, productivity, and individual development. If there is a lack of culture, then educational governance will experience a high amount of turnover, dissent, disbelief, and a decrease in performance, and will become filled with more "out-group" than "in-group" members.

Once everyone has become indoctrinated in the culture, a shared voice will become prominent. A shared voice provides an agreed-upon frame of reference or lens that is used to understand and address key issues, problems, or opportunities. Next, a shared voice is used to market, promote, and express the awareness of achieving a universal objective or goal. First, sharing this voice respects the value and worth of the person. Once the person is heard, their ideas are combined and linked to those around them. Once everyone has shared their voice, collaboration takes place to help everyone listen and then act to make the necessary changes based on what they have said and what they value. Whether it is administration, teachers, students, community members, or other stakeholders, there is a shared paradigm or perspective that is communicated through a shared voice. The value of voice in educational governance is an important component of the Responsibility of Reason in leadership, management, and lifelong learning.

For educational governance to remain effective, it must constantly reconceptualize the role of teaching. In today's world, it is important to recognize that the way learning occurs is different from how it was in the past. Instead of relying on classroom learning with teacher-led instruction, it is now more important to focus on the learning strengths and abilities of the learner. Changing from teacher-focused to student-focused will help to better support the desire and engagement of the learner. Student-focused learning focuses on developing a direct connection between the interests of the learner and what they will learn.

In schools, this can be achieved by making the learning process more meaningful by creating a connection through projects and real-life examples that directly impact the learner. In the workplace, this can be achieved by providing mentorship through on-the-job training and encouraging employees to become involved in projects or teams that they are most interested in. When this occurs, the learning process becomes more meaningful and impactful to the learner, which will ultimately lead to a higher level of knowledge and success.

Finally, educational governance should be reconceptualized to become more humanistic. Humanistic theory focuses on human beings instead of a one-size-fits-all approach to learning and management. This belief supports McGregor's Theory X and Theory Y as they apply to individuals. Theory X believes that people do not want to do something unless they are told. However, Theory Y believes that individuals want to learn for their own benefit. This group of individuals wants to be involved in the process, so they feel respected, valued, and included within the established society.

When using the humanistic approach in educational governance, the self-esteem and achievement of each stakeholder are directly correlated to the unique teaching style that is applied to each learner. This situation leads to improved methods of teaching and support throughout the learning process and the organizational hierarchy. When there is humanistic oversight, there will be humanistic teaching that enables the information to be communicated in such a way that students become motivated to continue to learn. As a result, the goal of educational governance is to promote lifelong learning and to foster the desire of each person to learn so they will want to continue the process.

The humanistic approach to educational governance will lead to new civic and moral virtues. Moral virtues include honesty, integrity, compassion, and fairness in the learning process. With the use of civic and moral virtues, people and humanism will continue to be the primary focus of educational governance. When individuals are valued, they will generate a higher amount of human capital. This situation will help to reconceptualize administration, teaching, and learning. As a result, there will be an increase in aptitude and achievement for all stakeholders as they relate to educational governance.

Educational governance will use various methods to help improve the impact that teaching has on the learning process. Educational governance is required to define, manage, and lead all the various relationships between stakeholders. Within the learning process, it must be determined how learning will occur and how decisions are made. There is an institutional dynamic that is responsible for assigning roles and responsibilities. Next, policies and priorities are determined based on the needs of the people rather than the bureaucratic system. The programs that are implemented will be directly related to the needs of the students, teachers, administrators, businesses, and the community. The local school will work with the school district. The school district will then communicate with the state. The state will take its lead from the federal government, which oversees providing the best opportunities for the people it serves. There is a direct connection between the district, state, and federal levels of education and business. As a result, educational governance oversees the success of all stakeholders and ensures that the concerns of the students, community, staff, and administration are properly addressed.

When educational governance is designed to provide success to educational administration in its responsibilities to students, community, staff, and administrators, WEEDU will occur. There is a change from what each group or what "WE DO" can do to what the collaborative "WE" can do in EDUCATION at all levels in learning, management, and leadership. This transformation will be based on the philosophy of aligning the systematic process and design that allow top-down and bottom-up communication. This situation will help to provide shared leadership and the value of voice to any institution, helping them become a lifelong learning organization. As a result, WEEDU is an important philosophical and practical component in Responsibility of Reason of reason of leadership, management, and lifelong learning for education, business, and the individual.

Figure 13 clearly shows what happens: design minus action creates no WEEDU. A system within an organization occurs when it uses its abilities and skill sets to enable a process change throughout the hierarchy of the company.

FIGURE 13 Non-systematic: No WEEDU.

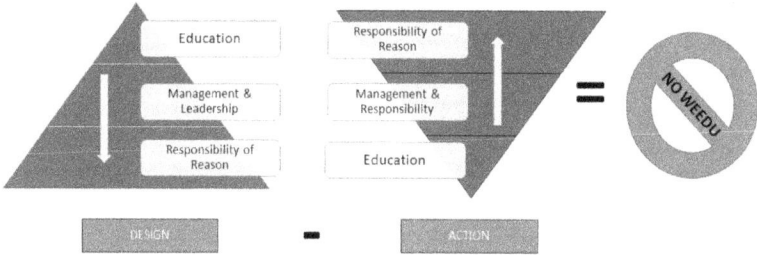

FIGURE 14 Systematic: WEEDU.

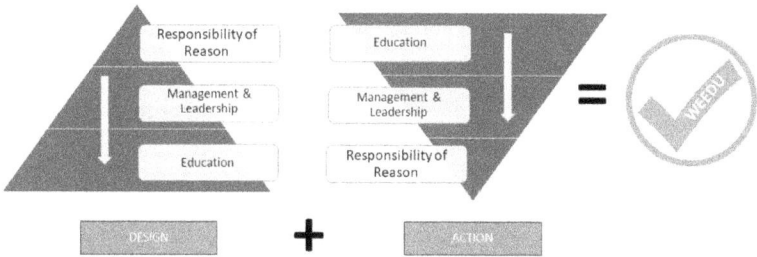

The model uses a pyramid to show the connection and flow of a systematic process to create design and action. At the top of the pyramid, education is required to gain knowledge and philosophy to understand the situation. Once knowledge is gained through the chosen leadership philosophy, the concept is then implemented in management and leadership through a process. The process or design chosen will create the Responsibility of Reason.

Next, the design will require action. In this figure, we see that there is no action. With education at the bottom of the inverted pyramid, there is no philosophy to base a decision or action on. This situation causes management and leadership to guide the organization blindly. This situation causes a lack of Responsibility of Reason. Without Responsibility of Reason, there is no WEEDU in the organization. What will result is a non-systematic process that will cause the organization to suffer from a lack of growth, direction, or shared mission and vision.

Figure 14 supports what happens when design and action are combined to create a sustainable system that leads to WEEDU. For a systematic design to develop correctly, Responsibility of Reason starts the process. When the "who, what, where, when, why," and "how" are clarified, there will be a high level of conceptualization of how to create an efficient and effective design within the organization. Once the Responsibility of Reason has been established, management and leadership can create a unified system or process to follow to create a shared and common goal. Finally, the common goal will drive the education of the followers to implement the design, making everyone part of the design process.

Next, design is combined with action. Once the employee understands the design, they will be able to learn and gain knowledge, skills, and abilities. This situation will make it possible to provide bottom-up communication and knowledge to the managers and leaders. The 360-degree feedback will then help to make improvements to the design process, resulting in further strengthening the Responsibility of Reason. As a result, when design is combined with action, WEEDU will become a part of the organizational culture, shared leadership, and Responsibility of Reason.

Simpleton Solution

Educational governance is a universal need for all institutions. When performing a process to achieve an objective or goal, there must be a logical motive by the leader or institution that leads to the responsibility of reason. This situation will help to create a shared voice and value based on mutual understanding, collaboration, and support of everyone within the stated hierarchy. While it is important to communicate what "we do," it is more important to work collaboratively to understand how we all support one another from the top-down and bottom-up. This situation creates "WE EDUCATION" or WEEDU to help build a learning organization through enlightenment through educational governance. The main points of this chapter are:

- You must clearly define and understand the behavior of educational governance.
- Educational governance establishes the rules and regulations for everyone to follow.
- Educational governance must be responsive to the needs of the leaders and followers.
- Educational governance is not separate between stakeholders; it is a collaborative process.
- You must use both verbal and nonverbal forms of communication in educational governance.

- There must be a combination of top-down and bottom-up communication within the systematic hierarchy.
- It is important to listen to everyone equally to create a shared voice in the decision-making process and when acting.
- Everyone will assist in the role of being a master teacher to communicate knowledge through educational governance.
- Educational governance is responsible for re-conceptualizing how people learn.
- We must change from what WE DO to WE EDUCATION (WEEDU).

Figure 15 shows the benefit of moving from "We Do" to "WEEDU." When this transformation happens, it is like putting the cherry on top of your favorite ice cream sundae. The "cherry" or "WEEDU" is the perfect something that makes something good even better. By achieving success or creating a successful process, that is the cherry on top for any organization. This is the goal of any individual or organization. As a result, getting the cherry on top is a savory treat for the individual or business. However, if the business does not support the transformation from "We Do" to "WEEDU," then the example will take on a negative connotation. The "cherry on top" will represent the negative impact of having an exclusive organizational culture and behavior that leads to a non-systematic process. This failure would not create a shared vision, which would be the "cherry on top" for failure within the company.

The main takeaway from this chapter is that when we have effective and efficient educational governance, everyone and every part of the process will become connected. This situation creates a systemic organizational

FIGURE 15 The cherry on top: WEEDU.

environment where learning can develop and increase for all stakeholders. Next, changing from "we do" to "WEEDU" is like putting the cherry on top of your favorite ice cream sundae. Even if you have a good organizational structure, implementing a systematic structure of support through educational governance will make it even better. The result will be to have educational responsibility of enlightened leadership reasoning.

CHAPTER 9

THE MANY IMPLICATIONS OF RESPONSIBILITY OF REASON AND A COLLECTIVE VOICE

Current and Future Implications of Responsibility of Reason in Shared Leadership and a Collective Voice

The concept of Responsibility of Reason holds significant implications for shared leadership and the cultivation of a collective voice within organizations. In today's rapidly evolving and interconnected world, where organizations operate in complex and dynamic environments, the ability to exercise reason and responsibility in decision-making is essential for promoting collaboration, innovation, and shared ownership of actions. By embracing the Responsibility of Reason, organizations can not only enhance their leadership practices but also empower individuals at all levels to contribute to a culture of shared leadership and a collective voice. The Responsibility of Reason underscores the importance of critical thinking, ethical decision-making, and accountability in leadership roles. Leaders who embody this principle demonstrate a commitment to rationality, integrity, and transparency in their actions, fostering a culture of trust, respect, and open communication within the organization. By encouraging individuals to think critically, weigh alternatives, and consider the broader impact of their decisions, organizations can promote a shared understanding of goals, values, and objectives, leading to more effective collaboration and decision-making processes.

The Responsibility of Reason paves the way for a shift toward shared leadership, where individuals collectively influence and guide the direction of the organization. In a shared leadership model, decision-making is decentralized, and authority is distributed among team members based on expertise, skills, and experiences. By embracing the Responsibility of Reason, organizations can empower individuals to take ownership of their actions, contribute their unique perspectives, and engage in collaborative problem-solving, fostering a sense of shared responsibility and accountability for the organization's success. The Responsibility of Reason will continue to shape the future of shared leadership and the cultivation of a collective voice within organizations. As organizations grapple with complex challenges, rapid changes, and diverse perspectives, the ability to exercise reason and responsibility in decision-making will be critical for fostering a culture of inclusivity, innovation, and high performance. Leaders who prioritize the Responsibility of Reason will be better equipped to navigate uncertainty, drive meaningful change, and inspire a shared vision among team members, promoting unity, collaboration, and a sense of purpose within the organization.

In the context of shared leadership, the Responsibility of Reason offers a framework for promoting inclusive decision-making processes, where individuals participate in shaping strategies, setting priorities, and driving initiatives that align with the organization's values and objectives. By incorporating diverse viewpoints, fostering open dialogue, and valuing input from all team members, organizations can harness the collective intelligence, creativity, and expertise of their workforce, leading to more informed decisions, innovative solutions, and sustainable outcomes that benefit the organization. The Responsibility of Reason can help organizations cultivate a collective voice where individuals feel empowered to express their ideas, concerns, and aspirations. By promoting a culture of openness, respect, and active listening, organizations can create a safe space for dialogue, debate, and collaboration, enabling team members to contribute their perspectives and insights toward common goals. In doing so, organizations can leverage the diversity of thought and experiences within their teams, foster creativity and innovation, and build a strong sense of belonging and engagement among employees, driving organizational performance and success.

The Responsibility of Reason also holds implications for organizational culture, shaping the values, norms, and behaviors that govern interactions and relationships within the organization. By promoting reason, integrity, and accountability as core principles of organizational culture, organizations can establish a foundation of trust, ethics, and transparency that underpins all aspects of their operations. This, in turn, can help mitigate conflicts, build cohesion, and promote a shared sense of purpose and direction among team members, leading to a more resilient, adaptive, and high-performing organizational culture. The Responsibility of Reason will continue to play a pivotal role in shaping leadership practices, organizational dynamics, and the overall success of organizations. By embracing reason and responsibility in decision-making, organizations can foster a culture of shared leadership, collaboration, and a collective voice, enabling individuals to contribute their skills, talents, and perspectives toward achieving common goals and objectives. As organizations navigate an increasingly complex and interconnected business landscape, the Responsibility of Reason will be a guiding principle for promoting unity, innovation, and sustainable growth, empowering organizations to thrive in the face of uncertainty and change.

The Responsibility of Reason holds significant implications for shared leadership and the cultivation of a collective voice within organizations. By prioritizing critical thinking, ethical decision-making, and accountability, organizations can foster a culture of trust, collaboration, and inclusivity that empowers individuals to take ownership of their actions, contribute to decision-making processes, and shape the future direction of the organization. As organizations embrace the Responsibility of Reason, they can build a foundation of shared leadership, unity, and a collective voice that drives innovation, resilience, and sustainable success in today's dynamic and interconnected business environment.

Responsibility of Reason Connects Learning in School

The Responsibility of Reason serves as a guiding principle that connects learning in school, working environments, and the pursuit of individual and community goals, ultimately leading to empowerment and engagement at all levels. By emphasizing critical thinking, ethical decision-making, and accountability, individuals can leverage the Responsibility of Reason to navigate complexities, collaborate effectively, and drive positive change in their personal and professional lives. This interconnected approach can foster a culture of continuous learning, shared leadership, and collective impact that empowers individuals and communities to achieve their goals and aspirations. At the foundation of this connection is the role of education in promoting the Responsibility of Reason. Schools play a crucial role in nurturing critical thinking skills, ethical awareness, and a sense of responsibility in students. By instilling the value of reason and accountability in their educational practices, schools can equip students with the tools and mindset needed to approach challenges, make informed decisions, and contribute positively to society. By integrating the Responsibility of Reason into the curriculum, schools can create a learning environment that cultivates intellectual curiosity, ethical engagement, and a commitment to lifelong learning and growth. As individuals transition from school to the working world, the Responsibility of Reason continues to play a vital role in shaping their behavior, interactions, and contributions within organizations. In a professional setting, the Responsibility of Reason enables individuals to navigate complexities, solve problems, and collaborate with others effectively. By upholding principles of critical thinking, integrity, and accountability, employees can make sound decisions, build trust with colleagues and stakeholders, and drive positive outcomes for their organizations. This approach fosters a culture of ethical leadership, transparency, and shared responsibility that empowers individuals to make meaningful impacts in their workplaces.

The Responsibility of Reason connects individual and community goals by promoting a sense of interconnectedness, shared purpose, and collective impact. At the individual level, individuals can leverage the Responsibility of Reason to set meaningful goals, make informed choices, and take ownership of their actions. By aligning personal aspirations with ethical considerations and community needs, individuals can contribute to the greater good and drive positive change in their communities. This approach fosters a sense of agency, empowerment, and engagement that motivates individuals to pursue their goals and make a difference in the world around them. The Responsibility of Reason serves as a bridge between individual and community goals by fostering collaboration, empathy, and a shared sense of responsibility among community members. By promoting open communication, mutual respect, and a commitment to ethical decision-making, communities can work together toward common objectives, address shared challenges, and build a more inclusive and sustainable future. This collaborative approach empowers community members to leverage their collective skills, resources, and experiences toward achieving shared goals, fostering a sense of unity, belonging, and empowerment at all levels.

Empowerment and engagement at all levels are key outcomes of embracing the Responsibility of Reason in schools, working environments, and individual and community settings. By emphasizing critical thinking, ethical decision-making, and accountability, individuals can take control of their learning, work, and personal development, leading to a sense of self-efficacy, confidence, and agency. This sense of empowerment enables individuals to navigate challenges, seize opportunities, and make meaningful contributions to their organizations and communities, fostering a culture of innovation, resilience, and growth. Engagement at all levels is a natural byproduct of promoting the Responsibility of Reason in education, work, and community settings. When individuals are encouraged to think critically, act ethically, and take ownership of their actions, they become more invested in their learning, work, and community involvement. This heightened engagement leads to increased productivity, creativity, and collaboration, as individuals are motivated to contribute their skills, expertise, and insights toward achieving common goals and making a positive impact on society. This shared commitment to reason and responsibility fosters a culture of trust, camaraderie, and shared success that enhances individual and collective well-being and fulfillment.

The Responsibility of Reason serves as a unifying principle that connects learning in school, working environments, and individual and community goals, leading to empowerment and engagement at all levels. By emphasizing critical thinking, ethical decision-making, and accountability, individuals can navigate complexities, collaborate effectively, and drive positive change in their personal and professional lives. This interconnected approach fosters a culture of continuous learning, shared leadership, and collective impact that empowers individuals and communities to achieve their goals and aspirations, creating a thriving ecosystem of reason, responsibility, and shared success.

Educational and Business Organizations Are Very Similar

While traditionally seen as separate industries, education and work are intricately interconnected and are not distinct entities but rather components of a larger, continuous learning and development ecosystem. The boundaries between education and work are becoming increasingly blurred, as the skills, knowledge, and experiences gained in one setting often directly impact performance and success in the other. By recognizing the inherent synergy between education and work, individuals, organizations, and society can leverage this integrated approach to enhance learning outcomes, drive innovation, and foster a culture of lifelong learning and growth. Education and work share a common goal: the cultivation of skills, competencies, and capabilities that enable individuals to thrive in an ever-evolving and competitive landscape. While education traditionally focuses on imparting theoretical knowledge, foundational concepts, and critical thinking skills, work provides practical experience, hands-on application, and real-world challenges that complement and reinforce what is learned in educational settings. The intersection of education and work allows individuals to bridge the gap between theory and practice, academia and industry, by applying their knowledge and skills in a professional context, gaining valuable insights, and honing their abilities through hands-on experience.

The dynamic nature of the modern workforce requires individuals to engage in continuous learning and upskilling throughout their careers to remain competitive and adaptable in a rapidly changing environment. Education and work are not static but rather dynamic and interconnected processes that inform and enrich one another. Individuals must actively seek opportunities to learn, grow, and develop their skills, both in educational and work settings, to navigate complexities, embrace innovation, and drive positive outcomes in their personal and professional lives. This continuous learning and development approach blurs the lines between education and work, highlighting their symbiotic relationship and mutual influence on individual success and organizational performance. The interconnectedness of education and work is underscored by the growing demand for skilled talent in the global economy. Employers are increasingly seeking candidates with a blend of academic qualifications, practical experience, and soft skills that can only be acquired through a combination of formal education and work experience. This convergence of academic and professional requirements highlights the importance of aligning educational curricula with industry needs, fostering collaborative partnerships between educational institutions and employers, and equipping individuals with the diverse skill sets and competencies needed to succeed in the workplace. By bridging the gap between education and work, individuals can better prepare themselves for the demands of the modern workforce and enhance their employability, job performance, and career prospects.

The rise of technology and digitalization has accelerated the integration of education and work, enabling individuals to access learning resources, skills training, and professional development opportunities remotely and on-demand. Online learning platforms, virtual internships, and digital skills training programs have democratized access to education and work opportunities, breaking down geographical barriers and connecting learners and professionals from diverse backgrounds and locations. This digital transformation has blurred the boundaries between traditional education and work settings, offering individuals greater flexibility, autonomy, and scalability in pursuing learning and career advancement goals. This convergence of technology, education, and work has revolutionized the way individuals learn, work, and collaborate, creating new pathways for lifelong learning, skill development, and career growth. The alignment of education and work is essential for driving innovation, creativity, and sustainable growth in today's knowledge-based economy. By integrating theoretical knowledge with practical experience, individuals can apply their learning in real-world contexts, experiment with new ideas, and develop innovative solutions to complex challenges. Collaboration between educators, researchers, industry professionals, and policymakers is crucial for fostering a culture of innovation, entrepreneurship, and problem-solving that transcends the traditional boundaries of education and work. By creating interdisciplinary learning environments, experiential learning opportunities, and collaboration platforms, organizations can harness the collective expertise, creativity, and diversity of talent to drive technological advancements, economic development, and societal progress.

The interconnectedness of education and work extends beyond individual development to encompass societal and economic well-being. A skilled and educated workforce is the foundation of a thriving economy, driving productivity, competitiveness, and innovation in the global marketplace. By investing in education, training, and workforce development initiatives, governments, businesses, and educational institutions can enhance human capital, create economic opportunities, and promote social mobility and inclusive growth. The integration of education and work enables individuals to acquire the skills, knowledge, and capabilities needed to contribute meaningfully to society, drive economic prosperity, and address pressing social and environmental challenges. This holistic approach to education and work fosters a culture of lifelong learning, innovation, and collaboration that benefits individuals, organizations, and communities across diverse sectors and industries.

Education and work are not separate industries but interconnected components of a larger, continuous learning and development ecosystem. The boundaries between education and work are becoming increasingly blurred, as individuals, organizations, and society recognize the inherent synergy between academic learning and professional experience. By embracing this integrated approach, individuals can leverage their educational and work experiences to enhance their skills, expand their horizons, and drive positive change in their personal and professional lives. This interconnectedness of education and work not only benefits individuals but also promotes innovation, collaboration, and sustainable growth in organizations, industries, and communities. By bridging the gap between education and work, individuals can cultivate a mindset of lifelong learning, adaptability, and resilience that empowers them to navigate complexities, embrace diversity, and drive positive outcomes in a rapidly changing and interconnected world. This holistic approach to education and work highlights the transformative power of continuous learning, collaboration, and shared knowledge in shaping the future of individuals, organizations, and society.

Education, leadership, and management must all be seen as one with the Responsibility of Reason process model to create demand, worker voice and empowerment, and successful organizations that will continue to grow and flourish in a diverse and global environment. Education, leadership, and management are interconnected components of a cohesive process model that, when integrated with the Responsibility of Reason, can drive demand, worker voice, empowerment, and organizational success in a diverse and global environment. By recognizing the symbiotic relationship between these elements and embracing a shared commitment to reason, integrity, and accountability, organizations can create a culture of continuous learning, inclusive leadership, and strategic management that fosters innovation, collaboration, and sustainable growth. This integrated approach harnesses the collective potential of individuals, teams, and organizations to navigate complexities, drive positive change, and thrive in an increasingly dynamic and interconnected world. By providing individuals with the knowledge, skills, and competencies needed to succeed in the workplace, education equips workers with the tools to navigate challenges, seize opportunities, and contribute to organizational success. Education also fosters a culture of curiosity, critical thinking, and continuous improvement that empowers individuals to adapt to changing environments, embrace new technologies, and drive innovation within their organizations. By integrating education into leadership and management practices, organizations can cultivate a skilled and motivated workforce that is well equipped to meet the evolving demands of a diverse and global marketplace.

Leadership plays a pivotal role in driving demand, worker voice, empowerment, and success within organizations. Effective leadership inspires individuals to share their ideas, concerns, and aspirations, fostering a culture of open communication, collaboration, and shared ownership of goals. Leaders who embody the Responsibility of Reason demonstrate integrity, empathy, and transparency in their interactions, building trust, respect, and engagement among team members. By empowering employees to voice their opinions, contribute their expertise, and participate in decision-making processes, leaders create a sense of agency, belonging, and purpose that drives motivation, productivity, and organizational performance. This inclusive leadership approach promotes a culture of shared responsibility, innovation, and resilience that enables organizations to adapt to change, seize opportunities, and achieve sustainable growth in a diverse and global environment.

Management practices play a critical role in translating education and leadership into tangible outcomes that drive demand, worker voice, empowerment, and organizational success. Strategic management aligns education and leadership initiatives with organizational goals, priorities, and performance metrics, ensuring that resources are allocated effectively, risks are managed proactively, and strategies are implemented efficiently. By integrating education and leadership principles into management processes, organizations can leverage their human capital, innovation capacity, and competitive advantage to drive demand, customer satisfaction, and business growth. Strategic management also promotes accountability, transparency, and data-driven decision-making, enabling organizations to monitor progress, evaluate outcomes, and adapt their strategies in response to changing market conditions, technological advancements, and stakeholder expectations. By aligning education, leadership, and management practices, organizations can create a culture of continuous improvement, strategic alignment, and performance excellence that drives demand, worker voice, and empowerment while fostering sustainable growth and success in a diverse and global business environment.

The Responsibility of Reason process model serves as a unifying framework that connects education, leadership, and management to create demand, worker voice, empowerment, and successful organizations in a diverse and global context. This model emphasizes critical thinking, ethical decision-making, and accountability as core principles that guide individual and organizational behavior, foster collaboration, and drive positive outcomes. By integrating the Responsibility of Reason into education, leadership, and management practices, organizations can cultivate a culture of reason, integrity, and transparency that empowers employees, promotes inclusive leadership, and fosters strategic management, leading to improved performance, competitiveness, and sustainability in today's fast-paced and interconnected business environment.

The integration of education, leadership, and management within the Responsibility of Reason process model enables organizations to leverage the collective strengths of their people, processes, and systems to drive demand, worker voice, empowerment, and success. Education equips individuals with the knowledge, skills, and capabilities needed to excel in the workplace, while leadership inspires and empowers employees to contribute their unique talents, ideas, and perspectives toward achieving common goals. Management ensures that organizational resources are aligned with strategic priorities, performance metrics are monitored and evaluated, and decision-making processes are informed by data and analysis, fostering a culture of accountability, transparency, and continuous improvement. By fostering a holistic and interconnected approach to education, leadership, and management, organizations can create a thriving ecosystem of learning, collaboration, and innovation that enables them to navigate challenges, seize opportunities, and achieve sustainable growth in a diverse and global business environment.

The synergy between education, leadership, and management within the Responsibility of Reason process model is essential for driving demand, worker voice, empowerment, and success in organizations. Education equips individuals with the knowledge, skills, and competencies needed to excel in their roles, adapt to changing environments, and drive innovation within their organizations. Leadership inspires and empowers employees to voice their opinions, share their expertise, and contribute to decision-making processes, fostering a culture of collaboration, inclusion, and shared ownership of goals. Management aligns organizational resources with strategic priorities, monitors performance outcomes, and adapts to changing market conditions and stakeholder expectations, ensuring that organizations remain competitive, resilient, and responsive to evolving trends and opportunities. By integrating education, leadership, and management within the Responsibility of Reason process model, organizations can create a framework for sustainable growth, strategic alignment, and performance excellence that enables them to thrive in an increasingly diverse and global business environment.

Education, leadership, and management must be seen as interconnected components of a cohesive process model that, when integrated with the Responsibility of Reason, can drive demand, worker voice, empowerment, and success in organizations operating in a diverse and global context. By leveraging the collective strengths of education, leadership, and management, organizations can cultivate a culture of reason, integrity, and accountability that empowers employees, fosters inclusive leadership, and drives strategic management practices. This integrated approach enables organizations to navigate complexities, seize opportunities, and achieve sustainable growth in today's fast-paced and interconnected business environment. By embracing the interconnectedness of education, leadership, and management within the Responsibility of Reason process model, organizations can position themselves for success by promoting continuous learning, collaboration, and innovation that enhances performance, competitiveness, and resilience in a diverse and global marketplace.

Responsibility of Reason in Leadership, Management, and Lifelong Learning

The Responsibility of Reason plays a pivotal role in shaping leadership, management, and lifelong learning by promoting critical thinking, ethical decision-making, and accountability in individuals and organizations. As leaders, managers, and lifelong learners navigate complexities, embrace innovation, and drive positive change, the Responsibility of Reason serves as a guiding principle that informs their behavior, interactions, and strategic choices. By upholding the principles of reason, integrity, and transparency in their leadership, management, and learning practices, individuals can create a culture of excellence, inclusivity, and continuous improvement that empowers themselves and others to achieve personal, professional, and organizational success. In leadership, the Responsibility of Reason is essential for inspiring trust, fostering collaboration, and driving positive outcomes within teams and organizations. Leaders who embody the Responsibility of Reason demonstrate integrity, empathy, and fairness in their decision-making processes, building credibility, respect, and engagement among their followers. By promoting critical thinking, open communication, and ethical behavior, leaders create a culture of transparency, accountability, and shared responsibility that empowers employees to voice their opinions, contribute their expertise, and participate in decision-making processes. This inclusive leadership approach fosters an environment of mutual respect, trust, and shared ownership of goals, enabling teams to work cohesively, innovate creatively, and achieve sustainable outcomes. The Responsibility of Reason in leadership promotes a culture of integrity, empowerment, and collaboration that inspires individuals to align their actions with ethical principles, demonstrate accountability for their decisions, and lead by example in upholding the values of reason and responsibility within their organizations.

Responsibility of Reason is integral to effective management practices that drive performance, productivity, and success within organizations. Managers who embrace the principles of reason, critical thinking, and accountability can make informed decisions, manage risks proactively, and optimize resources to achieve strategic goals and objectives. By aligning management practices with the Responsibility of Reason, organizations can promote data-driven decision-making, strategic planning, and performance measurement that ensure sustainable growth, competitive advantage, and operational excellence. This responsible management approach fosters a culture of transparency, responsiveness, and continuous improvement that enables organizations to adapt to change, seize opportunities, and mitigate risks in a rapidly evolving and dynamic business environment. The Responsibility of Reason in management promotes a culture of efficiency, innovation, and resilience that drives organizational performance, fosters employee engagement, and enhances stakeholder trust and confidence in the organization's ability to achieve its mission and strategic priorities.

The Responsibility of Reason is fundamental to lifelong learning, as it empowers individuals to acquire, apply, and reflect on knowledge, skills, and experiences that drive personal and professional growth and development. Lifelong learners who embrace the Responsibility of Reason seek opportunities to expand their horizons, challenge their assumptions, and engage in critical reflection to enhance their understanding of themselves, others, and the world around them. By promoting a culture of curiosity, intellectual rigor, and ethical awareness, the Responsibility of Reason encourages individuals to approach learning as a transformative and empowering journey that enriches their lives, inspires innovation, and fosters a commitment to continuous self-improvement and growth.

In leadership, the Responsibility of Reason guides individuals to make ethical decisions, demonstrate integrity, and act in the best interests of their teams and organizations. Leaders who uphold the Responsibility of Reason are guided by a sense of purpose, empathy, and accountability that drives their actions and decisions, fostering trust, respect, and engagement among their followers. By promoting critical thinking, ethical awareness, and transparency in their leadership practices, individuals can create a culture of openness, collaboration, and shared ownership of goals that empowers employees to contribute their talents, ideas, and perspectives toward achieving common objectives. This inclusive leadership approach fosters a sense of trust, loyalty, and commitment among team members, enabling them to work cohesively, innovate creatively, and achieve sustainable success together. The Responsibility of Reason in leadership encourages individuals to lead with integrity, inspire trust, and cultivate a culture of excellence that supports personal and professional growth, organizational success, and positive social impact.

Responsibility of Reason guides individuals to make informed decisions, manage resources effectively, and drive results that align with organizational goals and values. Managers who embrace the Responsibility of Reason demonstrate accountability, transparency, and strategic thinking in their management practices, ensuring that decisions are grounded in reason, data, and ethical considerations. By promoting a culture of performance, efficiency, and continuous improvement, individuals can optimize processes, mitigate risks, and drive innovation within their organizations, fostering a culture of excellence, resilience, and adaptability that enables sustainable growth, operational excellence, and competitive advantage. The Responsibility of Reason in management encourages individuals to lead with integrity, implement best practices, and align organizational strategies with ethical principles, legal requirements, and stakeholder expectations, driving organizational performance, employee engagement, and stakeholder trust and confidence in the organization's capacity to achieve its mission and strategic objectives.

Responsibility of Reason empowers individuals to pursue knowledge, skills, and experiences that support personal and professional development, growth, and fulfillment. Lifelong learners who embrace the Responsibility of Reason, a fundamental responsibility in leadership, management, and lifelong learning, guide individuals to make informed decisions, act ethically, and drive positive outcomes in their personal and professional endeavors. At the core of the Responsibility of Reason is a commitment to critical thinking, integrity, and accountability that shapes behavior, interactions, and decision-making processes across diverse contexts and settings. By upholding the principles of reason in their leadership, management, and learning practices, individuals can create a culture of excellence, inclusivity, and continuous improvement that empowers themselves and others to achieve success, overcome challenges, and drive positive change in a rapidly evolving and interconnected world.

In leadership, the Responsibility of Reason is essential for inspiring trust, fostering collaboration, and cultivating a shared vision of success within teams and organizations. Leaders who embody the Responsibility of Reason demonstrate integrity, empathy, and fairness in their interactions, building credibility, respect, and engagement among their followers. By promoting critical thinking, ethical behavior, and open communication, leaders create a culture of transparency, accountability, and shared responsibility that empowers employees to voice their opinions, contribute their expertise, and participate in decision-making processes. This inclusive leadership approach fosters an environment of mutual respect, trust, and shared ownership of goals that enables teams to work cohesively, innovate creatively, and achieve sustainable outcomes. The Responsibility of Reason in leadership promotes a culture of integrity, empowerment, and collaboration that inspires individuals to align their actions with ethical principles, demonstrate accountability for their decisions, and lead by example in upholding the values of reason and responsibility within their organizations.

Similarly, in management, the Responsibility of Reason plays a critical role in driving performance, productivity, and success within organizations. Managers who embrace the principles of reason, critical thinking, and accountability can make strategic decisions, manage resources efficiently, and optimize processes to achieve organizational goals and objectives. By aligning management practices with the Responsibility of Reason, organizations can promote data-driven decision-making, operational excellence, and performance measurement that ensure sustainable growth, competitive advantage, and stakeholder satisfaction. This responsible management approach fosters a culture of transparency, responsiveness, and continuous improvement that enables organizations to navigate challenges, seize opportunities, and drive innovation in a complex and ever-changing business environment. The Responsibility of Reason in management promotes a culture of efficiency, resilience, and ethical leadership that drives organizational performance, fosters employee engagement, and enhances stakeholder trust in the organization's ability to deliver results with integrity, transparency, and accountability.

Responsibility of Reason is a fundamental principle that guides leadership, management, and lifelong learning by promoting critical thinking, ethical decision-making, and accountability in individuals and organizations. By upholding the values of reason, integrity, and transparency, individuals can create a culture of excellence, inclusivity, and continuous improvement that empowers them to achieve personal, professional, and organizational success. The Responsibility of Reason serves as a guiding light that inspires individuals to act with purpose, lead with integrity, and learn with curiosity, driving positive outcomes, innovation, and sustainable growth in a diverse and interconnected world. Embracing the Responsibility of Reason in leadership, management, and lifelong learning is essential for individuals and organizations to navigate challenges, seize opportunities, and cultivate a culture of excellence, empowerment, and positive impact that drives success, resilience, and social progress in today's fast-paced and ever-changing business environment.

Simpleton Solution

Figure 16 is a model that shows the reciprocity of the linkage between the circle of education, management, leadership, and the Responsibility of Reason. First, education is a personal experience for the leader and follower to gain unique knowledge, skills, and abilities that can be used to support the common goal. Next, education will support questioning and asking the "why" question to gain a better understanding and develop a philosophy. Third, education will require reflection and growth to help the leader and follower based on the new knowledge they have gained to make positive changes and improvements. Finally, education will cultivate the desire to gain more knowledge and further their desire to learn for a mutually shared benefit between the individual, leader, and organization.

The next component of the circle is management. Within management, there is an analysis that takes place. From the knowledge that was gained during the learning process, management then creates a design based on the data, information, and input. The analysis of the situation or process will rely

FIGURE 16 Coming full circle.

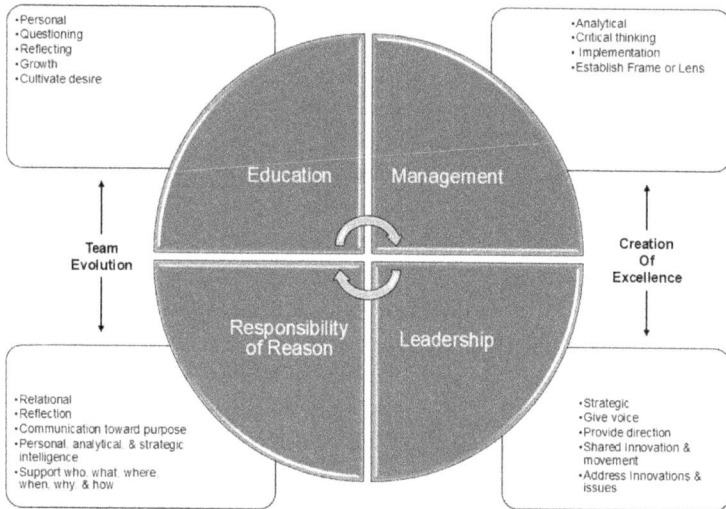

on critical thinking and the open exchange of ideas between the leader and follower. Once the situation is understood, management will implement the design and put it into action. This creation of a system is based on the frame or lens of the leader's mission and vision to achieve a common goal.

The third piece of the wheel is leadership. During the leadership phase, strategic goals are established and communicated through the use of the mission or vision that was created from the philosophy of the leader. The leader will use their mission and vision to give voice to the entire organization, which is comprised of a membership exchange between the leader and followers. Next, leadership will provide guidance and direction to support positive change and sustainable processes in the internal and external environments of the organization. This situation will create shared innovation and movement. Any issues in innovation will be addressed through mutual understanding between the leader and followers in the creation of excellence.

The fourth quarter of the wheel is Responsibility of Reason. The Responsibility of Reason is relational between individuals, knowledge, leadership, and management. All components will work together to create WEEDU for a successful and sustainable process. Next, the Responsibility of Reason will provide reflection to better understand the situation, enabling the organization to become an organic and living entity that can adjust to change and maintain positive organizational behavior. Third, the Responsibility of Reason will create effective communication toward a common goal using personal, analytical, and strategic intelligence that was developed through education, implemented through management, and supported by the leader's vision. Finally, the Responsibility of Reason supports the "who, what, where, when, why," and "how" of what the education portion of the circle originally established. This situation creates team evolution and helps both the individual and organization to come full circle.

This the culmination of leadership, management, and lifelong learning. The process starts with education and philosophy. Philosophy is the foundation of knowledge, existence, and reality for the individual and the organization. Next, philosophy is used by management to create a supportive and sustainable work structure that promotes effectiveness and efficiency for the individual and organization. Third is leadership. Leadership is the ability to influence and guide followers to success throughout all levels of the hierarchy in the institution. Finally, the Responsibility of Reason provides the justification, rationale, and purpose for the decision or action. With Responsibility of Reason, the leader and follower take ownership of the process and, through their actions, strengthen organizational behavior and bring success to the shared vision of the institution. As a result, management, leadership, and lifelong learning are all required to form the Responsibility of Reason.

CHAPTER 10

THE FABLED CASE STUDIES AND RESOURCE GUIDE

Introduction

Welcome to our fabled case studies and resource guide. In this chapter, it is our goal to entertain you with a fun, and too often relatable, parable that explains each complex business concept in a simple and straightforward way. We hope that you find these fabled case studies enjoyable, entertaining, and informative. Once you have finished the stories, please continue to dig deeper into the importance of these topics within your organization so you too can become an agent of Responsibility of Reason in leadership, management, and lifelong learning.

In Figure 17, we can see the coaction of education, management and leadership, and Responsibility of Reason. Synergy is the combined power of the different groups performing together that provide a higher benefit and product than when each area works individually from one another. When there is education, it must be used and applied to a decision or action. If this does not happen, then the knowledge that is gained by the individual is not shared with the organization, causing the focus to be on the person and not the community. Next, management and leadership should support the process, followers, and shared vision. When management and leadership act independently without philosophy or understanding, they will become isolated, and non-synergy will develop throughout the hierarchy of the company.

Finally, the Responsibility of Reason cannot be achieved if education, management, and leadership are not combined in conjunction with a common goal or vision. As a result, it is important to have each of these three components work together to form a symbiotic relationship that provides the transfer of information and support back and forth from each area. When this situation occurs, education will support management and leadership by providing them

FIGURE 17 The synergy of responsibility of reason.

with the knowledge to create a sustainable process. Management and leadership will then be able to create a common goal and shared vision based on sound decision-making and action plans. As a result, there will be an increase in understanding, support, and inclusion of ownership so that each person will become more aware and involved to create the synergy of Responsibility of Reason.

THE ANTHOLOGY OF
OBJECTIVES AND GOALS

It was another day in PleasANTville. PleasANTville was in the middle of a beautiful landscape that was surrounded by trees, mountains, rivers, and dirt roads. As the sun came up, the day began like any other. Ants woke up early and got ready for work. Like all ant colonies, they lived in a structured community and social environment. The red and black ants worked for Queen ANT. Within the ant colony, Queen ANT was the leader of hundreds of thousands of ants. All the ants loved her since she cared about each one of them and wanted the best for them. In return, the ants worked hard for her to expand her Antdom as far as they could see. Ants, after all, were ANTsy to move and explore to new areas.

> ## LEADERSHIP IS IMPORTANT TO ACHIEVING
> ## OBJECTIVES AND GOALS

Within PleasANTville, there were different divisions of labor. Each ant had the responsibility of taking care of themselves while also helping to support the ant community. The job of each ant was to provide a benefit to the ants of PleasANTville so they could live in peace and harmony. While the queen was in charge, each ant learned to work together and communicate what they were doing. The ants were expert communicators and listeners, which helped to make them a tight-knit group. They could pass information back and forth to share useful and important knowledge between the different generations of ants. Ants, young and old, alerted each other when they found food or when danger was present. Ants have been using their secret communication methods to help them expand their colony and safely travel across the world. In fact, there was only one place left for the ants to go where they would always live in peace and harmony. It was a tall mountain they called Mount PleasANT. It was there that Queen ANT wanted to make their new home. This was the big goal of Queen ANT for her and all her ant followers.

> ## COMMUNICATION IS IMPORTANT TO
> ## ACHIEVING OBJECTIVES AND GOALS

Each day, the ants worked hard in their assigned jobs, growing and expanding PleasANTville. The resident carpenter ants were skilled at building things. One group of carpenter ants built underground tunnels for the ants to travel back and forth. The second group of carpenter ants built mounds on the ground to help protect PleasANTville from any unpredictable disasters, while others built mounds in trees to help look out and survey the area. Their main job was to build and expand PleasANTville for Queen ANT and to keep her loyal subjects safe and protected so they could do their jobs successfully.

The next group of ants were the gatherANTS. The gatherAnts' job was to bring back food for the other ants to eat. Since ants worked all day long, they were always hungry. These ants foraged for food. Each day, the gaterhANTS brought back food to PleasANTville. The gatherANTS carried nectar, fungus, insects, and fruits on their backs that had all the nutrients that made ants strong and able to carry fifty times more than their original body weight. The gatherANTs used the tunnels and mounds to travel back and forth when hunting and gathering for food.

When the food was brought back to PleasANTville, it was stored in the ant farm. The ant farm was run by the farmANTs. The farmANTS worked on the ant farm, storing the food and preparing meals for all the ants to eat. Their job was especially important to the ant colony. Without the farmANTS, there would be no food reserve for the ants to stay strong and perform their jobs each day. Without food, the ant followers would not want to work, and there would be unhappiness all throughout PleasANTville.

The final group of ants were the army ants. Army ants were the main line of defense for Queen ANT and her ant colony. The army ants traveled in large squadrons above and below the ground. When they came across dangerous prey, the army ants worked together to form tall columns by working together and using teamwork. They could also link their legs together to form bridges for the other army ants to travel over unsafe terrain. Teamwork helps the army ants overcome any obstacle in their way so they can continue to make the area around them safe so PleasANTville can continue to grow.

> ## TEAMWORK IS IMPORTANT TO ACHIEVING OBJECTIVES AND GOALS

While each ant was happy to do their job for the greater good, every ant wanted to become an army ant. Each year, the best ants from each group were chosen to be new recruits for the army ants. Ants spent all year working hard to distinguish themselves from all the other hundreds of thousands of ants that lived in PleasANTville. To stand out, their record of service, dedication, and attention to detail would be judged against every other ant. Only the top ants would be chosen to become part of the elite force of the army ants. Each ant knew that on the morrow, the list of ants that would be chosen.

One of the farmANTS was most excited about becoming an army ant. Her name was Clare. Clare had been working on the ant farm since she was little. She was very dedicated to her job. She was the first ant to show up to work and the last one to leave at the end of the day. The other ants joked that even though she was an above-ground ant, she never saw daylight since she spent each and every day working. Clare took this as a compliment. She took pride in her work and always made sure that each ant had enough food each day. She always had new ideas and clarity of how things should change to improve or how things could be accomplished. It made her happy knowing that her job helped others to do their jobs. Without her, none of it would be possible. She knew this was the same as all the other ants, so it would be an honor to be chosen as a new army ant recruit.

"Tomorrow cannot come soon enough," said Clare. "I hope they choose me to be an army ant."

"You are too much," said another farmANT. "Who would want to do all that extra work?"

"Are you kidding?" replied Clare. "This is a great chance to go out and see the country and to help make some bigger changes."

"What could be more important than food?" replied the farmANT.

> ## VISION IS NECESSARY TO ACHIEVING OBJECTIVES
> ## AND GOALS

"I agree that every job that we do has a shared benefit," replied Clare. "I am just ready for a change and to help out in a new way."

"Well, be careful," said the farmANT. "Even if you are chosen, those ants all think and work the same. They will make you into a regular G.I. Ant."

"We shall see what tomorrow brings," replied Clare. "Now go home and get some sleep. Tomorrow will be another long day in the life of an ant."

"Good night," said the farmANT.

"Good night," replied Clare.

She waited for the farmANT to leave and then closed the ant farm for the night. She walked home and then crawled into her dirt mound to try and fall asleep. As she curled up, she lay there dreaming about being an army ant. It had been a goal of hers since she had been a tiny Antlet. Before she knew it, Clare had closed her eyes and had finally fallen asleep. It would not be long now before morning came, and she would see if her dream would come true.

> ## BELIEF IS IMPORTANT TO ACHIEVING
> ## OBJECTIVES AND GOALS

The next morning had come. Before the sun rose, Clare was already up and climbing out of her dirt mound, making her way to the center of PleasANTville. When she got there, she saw that she was the first on there.

"Early to bed," she said, "and early to rise. Like the early bird gets the worm, the ant gets the arthropod."

Eventually more ants began to gather with Clare until they all had arrived. She looked around and saw that every red and black ant had come out to hear the announcements of who would be the next army ant recruits. Then from below, Queen ANT appeared from the ground. She stood on top of her mound so she could oversee the entire crowd. With a wave of her hand, the crowd split in two, leaving a pathway down the middle of the crowd. Clare turned and saw the leader of the army ants leading his troops with him before the Queen. Claire and the other ants saluted them as they passed by.

The troops stopped and formed a line in front of the group of onlooking ants. The LieutenANT and SergeANT approached the queen. "Have you made your decision of who the next army ant recruits will be this year?" asked Queen ANT.

"We have indeed," replied LieutenANT.

"What do you say?" asked the Queen.

"SergeANT," said LieutenANT, "you may do the honors."

"With pleasure," replied SergeANT. "The new recruits will be ANTsy and PuritANT."

Everyone cheered for them as they were selected and walked to the front of the crowd. Clare could not believe that her name was not called. She began to doubt all her hard work and dedication that she had put in all year long without any reward or recognition. When the crowd quieted down, SergeANT continued. "And we have one more special ant to recognize [...]"

After a long pause, SergeANT read the name off the list. "[...] the final ant recruit is Clare."

Clare could not believe what she was told. All her hard work had paid off after all, and she was rewarded by her efforts. She was finally recognized by all her peers.

A LITTLE HARD WORK GOES A LONG WAY TO ACHIEVING OBJECTIVES AND GOALS

Clare walked up to join ANTsy and PuritANT in front of the Queen. The three of them were saluted by LieutenANT and SergeANT. "Welcome aboard," said LieutenANT. "You are in good hands with SergeANT."

After SergeANT congratulated them, his face became serious. "Haste makes waste," said SergeANT. "Come with me. We have work to do."

"Yes sir," replied Clare and the other ant recruits.

The other ants dispersed and went back to their daily duties while Clare, ANTsy, and PuritANT followed SergeANT back to the barracks. There, the new ant recruits trained and learned what it was like to take orders and to follow their leader. With each new training activity, Clare grew bigger and stronger. She developed an even better work ethic, and with each new accomplishment, she renewed her motivation. Clare continued to improve her skills, which led to increased self-esteem. Finally, Clare appreciated SergeANT as he coached her to help her improve herself to be the best army ant she could be.

MOTIVATION WILL LEAD TO COMPLETING NEW OBJECTIVES

After two weeks, Clare and the other new recruits had learned everything their job would entail of being an army ant. They learned to take orders, work hard, and never give up. They would have small obstacles that must be completed that would lead to big success. This elite group of army ants would work until their duty was done. "Good job ant recruits," said SergeANT. "Tomorrow you will get your first mission as part of my ant platoon. Remember, without you, success is not possible."

Clare was very excited for her first assignment. "With all of this training," said Clare, "I feel like I can accomplish anything."

"Yeah," replied Antsty, "I am ready to find out what our mission is. You know I can't stand being in one place too long."

"That's true," replied Clare, "but sometimes it's important to stay in one place to learn what you can before moving on to the next thing."

"Truer words have never been spoken," said PuritANT." "As a rule follower, I do not question where I am or what I am doing. I live to follow orders. Change is not always a good thing."

"But sometimes change is needed," said Clare. "Without change, nothing new would ever happen."

"That does not sound like the army ant way," said ANTsy. "I would be too nervous to ever do something I am not told to do."

"I agree," replied PuritANT. "The purest things in life do not change."

I am not sure about that, thought Clare. *If change did not exist, there would be no reason for us to do anything. Time will tell.*

> ## CHANGE IS IMPORTANT TO CREATING NEW OBJECTIVES

It was getting late, and Clare knew that tomorrow they would get their first mission. She joined ANTsy and PuritANT in their barracks and called it a night. She had a feeling it would be her last good night sleep for a while. She did not know what the objective would be, but Clare knew that it would require all her dedication and hard work. After all, the work of an army ant was never-ending.

It was not long before morning came. As usual, Clare woke up before SergeANT blew the horn that signaled the wakeup call to his ant platoon. Clare ran to get in formation, and the other ants soon followed her. Antsy stood on one side of her while PuritANT stood on the other. The other ants also stood there perfectly in uniformed rows, and they were all in synch with one another. "ANT-hut!" shouted SergeANT.

The ants snapped their legs together and stood at attention. "As you know," said SergeANT, "Queen ANT wants to move PleasANTville to a better location. Now you might be asking where that location will be. Instead of telling you, let me show you," he said as he pointed past their heads. "About face!"

Clare and the other ants turned. When they did, they saw a large mountain in the distance past the forest and the trees. "It is up there on the top of the mountain," shouted SergeANT.

"All the way up there?" said ANTSY nervously. "How will we ever do that?"

"We do not question how," replied PuritANT. "We only follow orders."

"Anything is possible with a little clarity," said Clare. "We can do this."

"We will march up to the mountaintop and build our new home inside and on top of the mountain. We will call our new home Mount PleasANT."

"Hoorah!" shouted Clare.

"I like your enthusiasm," replied SergeANT. "Now let's put that to work so we can all be rewarded through your hard work."

> ## YOU MUST HAVE A GOAL BEFORE YOU CAN HAVE AN OBJECTIVE

"The only thing standing in our way," continued SergeANT, "is a molehill blocking our path. Our job will be to remove the molehill so the other ants can follow us up to the mountain."

"That does not seem so hard," said PuritANT, "as long as we are told how to move the molehill."

"I can see that you are loyal, and I like your style," replied SergeANT. "Army ants do not believe in taking unnecessary chances. When we see the hill, we take the hill."

"See the molehill," replied Clare, "take the molehill."

"Hoorah!" shouted SergeANT.

"Hoorah," shouted the other ants in unison.

"We will have two teams working day and night. SquadrANT 1 will be made up of the red ants on the right path. They will be led by Corporal ANTicipant. They will work during the day to move the molehill one grain of sand at a time. SquadrANT 2 will be led by Corporal ANTiquated who will march on the left path. He will continue moving the molehill from the path until this obstacle has been dismANTled and is removed from our path.

"It seems like a good plan," said PuritANT.

"I hope so," replied ANTsy, "because I get nervous being stuck in one place too long. I start to think I will never get any further than I already am."

"We have a good objective," said Clare. "With teamwork and leadership, we can move this molehill in no time."

"SquadrANTS," said SergeANT, "follow Corporal ANTicipant and Corporal ANTiquated so we can begin working immediately."

Clare watched the red ants follow Corporal ANTicipant while she and her friends went with Corporal ANTiquated. "I ANTicipate no problems," said Corporal ANTicipant.

The red ants that followed him in single file and went right to work. They marched down the path and headed for the molehill. The red squadrANT worked together with such effectiveness and efficiency. The head ant took the piece of sand and passed it back to the ant behind them. The next red ant then passed it backward to the ant behind them. They did this until it reached the very last ant in line. The last ant then placed the grain of sand on the ground behind him. When the last ant in line then gave the signal that he was ready for more.

The red ants repeated this process over and over again. They worked from sunrise to sunset. At the end of the day, the red ants had made a large pile of sand and were removing the molehill in front of them a little bit at a time. When their shift was done, the red ants followed Corporal ANTicipant and returned to their camp. "It was a hard day's work," said Corporal ANTicipant as he saluted Corporal ANTiquated.

"And we will have a long night ahead of us," replied Corporal ANTiquated with a salute. "Army ants, it is time to march. To arms!"

The black ants got in line. Since Clare and her friends were the new recruits, they were placed at the back of the line. They raised their front two arms in the air to be prepared to carry away the heavy sandy granules of the molehill. As they marched, they began to sing together.

"March along, sing our song, with the Army Ants of the free.
Count the brave, count the true, who have fought to victory.
We're the Army Ants and proud of our name!
We're the Army Ants and proudly proclaim:
Then it's hi! hi! hey!
The Army Ants are on its way.
Count off the cadence loud and strong;
For where'er we go,
You will always know
That the Army Ants go rolling along."

They marched under the moonlight and sang until they reached the big mound in front of them that blocked their path. "That is a big mound," said Antsy. "We will be stuck here forever."

HARD WORK WILL LEAD TO ACHIEVING AN
OBJECTIVE OR GOAL

"Nonsense," replied PuritANT. "We will not deviate or change from our plan."

"We got this," said Clare. "Teamwork will see us through."

"Now ants," said Corporal ANTiquated, "we will do today what we have always done before.

"We are off to a good start," said PuritANT since he did not like change.

"We will line up and move this molehill one grain of sand," shouted Corporal ANTiquated. "We will not stop until the job is done!"

Every ant got into a single file line. ANTsy and PuritANT were at the end of the line, followed by Clare. When Corporal ANTiquated blew his whistle, the black ants went to work. The black ant in the front of the line grabbed a large granule of sand and passed it back. Just like the red ants, the black ants passed it back to each ant until it reached the end of the line. When Clare received the granule of sand, she neatly stacked it behind her since that is what she was instructed to do. There was already a pile there that she assumed was from the black ants moving their part of the molehill, so she added to it. "That's one down," Clare signaled to the front of the line.

When word reached the front of the line, the lead black ant sent another granule of sand down through the line. Clare placed it on the ground next to the other one. She did this repeatedly all night long. By the end of the night, Clare and her squadrANT of black ants had made a large pile.

When the sun began to rise, it was time for the black ants to return to their ant camp. They walked back along their path and then made their way into their bunks to get some sleep for their next long night ahead of them. As they slept, Corporal ANTicpant marched his red ants back along the left path. However, when they got there, they were shocked. The molehill that had spent all day moving was now back and was as tall as when they first started. This did not phase Corporal ANTicipant in the slightest. He knew that there would always be setbacks but did not let him stop him. "There are always obstacles to overcome," said Corporal ANTicipant. "We will just have to work twice as hard."

His speech motivated his squadrANT of ants. The black ants went back to work just like they had done the day before. They moved one grain of sand at a time and placed it in a pile behind the last ant in line. They did this all day long. When the ants had finished their work, they worked twice as hard as before. The molehill was now small in front of them, while the pile that was moved was stacked tall behind them. "Good work, ants!" said Corporal ANTicipant. "The red ants should be able to finish this up tonight. Then we can move up to Mount PleasANT and live happily ever after under the rule of Queen ANT."

Then Corporal ANTicipant marched his troops back down the path to their camp. At the same time, Corporal ANTiquated marched his squadrANT of red ants down the path to the molehill. When they arrived this time, he saw the same thing as the red ants. The pile was higher than ever. It was so high that even Clare could see it from the very back of the line. While he was perplexed at the situation, Corporal ANTiquated did not believe in giving up. He believed that what he had always done before would always work. "Back to work troops," said Corporal ANTiquated. "It looks like we have another long day ahead of us. Double time it!"

The black ants lined up under the command of their leader. They went right to work. They worked twice as hard as the night before. With each hour that passed by, the pile of sand from the molehill they were trying to move had grown significantly higher behind them. "Good work," said Corporal ANTiquated. "We have made excellent progress tonight. I knew our old trusted and true way of doing things would pay off."

Clare looked at the pile and began to have her doubts. "Something seems wrong," said Clare to PuritANT. "It is strange how the pile returned when we spent so much time clearing it the night before. Plus, the red ants worked hard all day. This molehill should be gone."

"You are thinking nonsense," replied PuritANT. "We have followed the orders of Corporal ANTiquated. "He would not lead us wrong."

"I hope not," replied ANTsy. "You know I get nervous when things do not go as planned."

The black ants returned the same way they had come until they too hard returned to camp. ANTsy and PuritANT went right to sleep while Clare laid awake. She could not stop thinking about what was going on with the molehill. *How can the molehill return in day and night?* wondered Clare. *That seems impossible. There must be a clear and logical explanation.*

REPEATING THE SAME PROCESS DOES NOT
ALWAYS LEAD TO SUCCESS IN OBJECTIVES
OR GOALS

The next day, the same thing happened. Corporal ANTicipant led his red ants up, and they found the same thing had happened. The squadrANT worked even harder, and Corporal ANTicipant never gave up hope of achieving his objective so they could reach their goal. Corporal ANTiquated also returned to find the same thing. No matter what they had done before, it had been undone when they returned. While believing that no change in process was needed to achieve the goal, Corporal ANTiquated continued using his same approach. He refused to make any changes.

This process went on and on for weeks. Both squandrANTs had not made any more progress than they had when they started. The molehill kept reappearing and was as tall as ever. At the end of a long night's work, Clare decided to take the initiative and see what might be causing the problem. She wanted to watch the red ants and see how they were working to move the molehill. "Something must be done about this lack of progress," said Clare. "I will observe the red ants in the morning."

The next morning, Clare quietly got up and snuck out of her bunk. From the camp, Clare could see Corporal ANTicipant lead his squadrANT back toward the molehill. She tiptoed on all her legs so she would not be heard following behind them or sneaking out of camp without permission from Corporal ANTiquated. She knew he would not approve since this action was not part of his original process and he did not like to change how he did things. Clare followed the ants through the forest and saw Corporal ANTicipant give the order to stop when they reached the pile in front of them. "I need to get a better look so I can see clearly what they are doing," said Clare.

OVERCOMING FEAR OF CHANGE CAN LEAD
TO ACHIEVING OBJECTIVES OR GOALS

She found a nearby tree and began to climb up until she came to a long branch. She made her way to the end of the branch and then sat on a big green leaf. From there, Clare could see everything. She saw the red ants forming a line to begin their work. Clare watched as the red ants moved the grains of sand from the front of the line to the back. "I don't see anything different here yet," she said. "I better keep watching."

Clare watched as the last red ant in line was given the grain of sand. The red ant then took it and placed it on an existing pile that was on the other side of the path. That is when Clare realized what was happening. "Hey," said Clare, "they are placing their grains of sand on the pile we had moved."

They continued to do this all night long until the pile the black ants had cleared was restored to its original size. She could not believe what she was seeing. She knew that both squadrANTS of ants were doing the same thing during the day and night. "Ants are normally great communicators," she said. "We were all given the same directions to move the molehill. How could this miscommunication have happened? Instead of working together to achieve our objective and goal, we are working against one another."

Clare knew that she must do something about this if they were ever going to be able to move the molehill and make it to the top of Mount PleasANT. She climbed down the tree and ran back to the camp. As she did, she saw the Corporal ANTicipate coming back down the path. She also saw Corporal ANTiquated getting ready to get his squadrANT ready to go back to the molehill and start their work. Clare knew she must do something. She saw SergeANT and LieutenANT talking about the lack of progress.

"I have never had an objective I could not achieve," said SergeANT.

"I agree with you," said LieutenANT. "I never had not met a goal."

"I know how we can achieve both your objectives and goals," Clare said as she ran over to them.

**PAST SUCCESS DOES NOT ALWAYS LEAD TO
ACHIEVING AN OBJECTIVE OR GOAL**

SergeAnt and LieutenANT both looked at her. "Isn't she one of the new ant recruits?" asked LieutenANT.

"Yes, sir," replied SergeANT, "but she was the top candidate for becoming an army ant. I think we should listen to what she has to say. The one thing ants do best is communicate with one another."

"You may proceed, Private Clare," said LieutenANT. "How can you help us achieve our objective and goal?"

"Ants are good communicators," said Clare, "but sometimes it's better to see things with your own eyes to find clarity."

"I agree," said LieutenANT, "we all could use a new perspective on the situation."

SergeANT then signaled to both corporals to stop their squadrANTS that were both coming and going. When he gave the signal, all the ants stopped.

"Army ants," said SergeANT, "Clare has something to show us all. It is time we listen to her. After all, she is a valuable member of ant team."

"Thank you," said Clare. "Being appreciated helps us all to work hard to achieve our objectives and goals. We can all share the leadership to support one another to be successful. Follow me."

Clare led LieutenANT, SergeANT, ANTsy, PuritANT, and all the others to the molehill.

"Why is Clare leading us here?" asked ANTSy. "We all have been coming to the same spot for weeks."

"I agree," said PuritANT. "I do not like change, but I am ready to move on from being stuck in the same spot."

"I am glad to hear you say that," replied Clare. "So am I. I am sure that we all are tired of repeating the same process every day and night and not making any progress. Earlier today, I climbed up this tall tree and saw what the problem was. Each squandrANT of ants was given a clear order to move the molehill out of the way. While each group of ants did their job," continued Clare, "they were actually working against one another."

"What do you mean?" asked SergeANT.

"Come with me," said Clare.

Clare then led SergeANT and LieutenANT up the tree and to the leaf she sat on earlier that day. "Now look down below," said Clare.

CHANGING YOUR POINT-OF-VIEW CAN LEAD TO ACHIEVING AN OBJECTIVE OR GOAL

"By golly," said LieutenANT, "you are right! We have been our own worst enemy."

SergeANT looked down and knew what was happening and causing them to not achieve their objective. "Both squadrANTs were following orders. Corporal ANTicipant and his red ants worked hard during the day, moving the molehill from one pile to another. However, Corporal ANTiquated also moved their pile of the molehill back to the other pile. Without knowing it, both groups were working hard to move the molehill back and forth from the piles of each squadrANT."

"We have been making a mountain out of a molehill," said LieutenANT.

"I'm afraid so," replied Clare. "We all have been responsible for making the mountain out of the molehill."

"Thank you, Clare," said LieutenANT, "you have given us CLARITY."

"I thought my communication was clear," said SergeANT. "I now see that it is important to work together and to not just rely on just using ANTiquated ways or with ANTicipation to be successful. It also takes clarity to work together to achieve results in objectives and goals. This would not have been possible with Clare."

CLARITY WILL ELIMINATE MAKING A MOUNTAIN OUT OF A MOLEHILL

"It would not be possible without us all," replied Clare. "Each one of us is a part of the mission, strategy, objectives, goals, and results for Queen ANT and PleasANTville."

"You will make an excellent leader one day," said LietuenANT.

"She already is a leader," replied PuritANT and ANTsy.

"I could not agree more," replied SergeANT. "Would you lead us in our new mission, Project CLARITY? The objective is to remove our mountain of a molehill so we can obtain our goal of reaching Mount PleasANT."

"Absolutely," said Clare, "as long as we all work together."

"What do you say, army ants?" asked both Corporal ANTicipant and Corporal ANTiquated."

"Hoo-rah!" shouted the red and black army ants.

Clare then led the way to the molehill. Instead of the red and black ants traveling on separate paths, they went together, lined up next to one another, until they reached the molehill together. "Now," said Clare, "both teams will work TOGETHER until the molehill is no longer standing in our path."

When she gave the signal, the red and black ants worked side by side, removing the molehill. With their teamwork and shared objective, this process did not take long at all. When the molehill was cleared, the ants cheered when they saw the clear path ahead of them.

"We have achieved our objective," said SergeANT.

"Thanks to Clare and her CLARITY," said LieutenANT, "and for bringing us all together."

"Thanks to our TEAMWORK," replied Clare. "This success could not have been possible without everyone here or those back in PleasANTville who did their jobs so we could do ours. We cannot only rely on ANTiquated processes or anticipation of success. Instead, we must work together and reliANT on one another."

> **YOU MUST BE RELIANT ON EACH OTHER TO ACHIEVE OBJECTIVES AND GOALS**

"Now that we have achieved our objective," said LieutenANT, "we can report back to Queen ANT that it is time for us to move up the mountain."

They all marched back together from the molehill, past their camp, and then into PleasANTville. When they arrived, LieutenANT and SergeANT told Queen ANT about what they learned and achieved with the help of Clare."

"You are a very special ant," said Queen ANT. "We can all learn a lot from you. I am promoting you to Sergeant Major of ANT CLARITY to make sure we always understand and think things through so we can be successful as a team."

PuritANT and ANTsy cheered for their friend. All the other ants cheered too. They knew that with Clare in charge of CLARITY they would be in good hands. Queen ANT and her loyal followers would be able to achieve any objective and goal with CLARITY.

Queen ANT then gave the order to move out of PleasANTville and to the large mountain ahead that would be the spot of their new home. Clare and the other ants walked along the past and past the spot where the molehill used to be. It felt good to pass this spot and to move on to achieving their goal after completing their objective.

> **GOALS CANNOT BE ACHIEVED WITHOUT CLEAR OBJECTIVES**

Epilogue

Clare, ANTsy, PuritANT, and the rest of the ants made it to the top of the mountain. Together, they worked hard to make Mount PleasANT their new home. The ants divided up their work, and each had an individual job that would help to support the rest of the ants under Queen ANT. Clare remained busy working with LieutenANT, SergeANT, Corporal ANTicpant, and Corporal ANTiquated to create simple objectives that would lead to achieving long-term goals. Through teamwork, shared leadership, and clarity, Clare and the ants lived in peace and harmony atop Mount PleasANT. Each morning, Clare would sit on top of the mountaintop with her ANTsy and PuritANT looking out to see everything in all directions. "Now this is a beautiful sight," ANTsy and PuritANT. "You can see everything from here."

"It certainly is," replied Clare. "Things have never been so clear as they are now."

> **CLARITY WILL ALWAYS LEAD TO ACHIEVING OBJECTIVES AND GOALS**

Dig Deeper: The Ant Farm of Clarity

You have just completed reading the parable about the Anthology of Clarity of Objectives and Goals. As you traveled along with your guide Clare, you learned that clarity is a very important component of setting goals and objectives. While the story touched on many of the main principles, we must now dig deeper into understanding clarity and how it directly impacts leadership and management roles within an organization. No matter what good or service industry your business is in, it will follow a systematic process that relies on simple communication, easy-to-follow directions, and for every individual to be responsible for their actions based on well-thought-out decision-making.

We will pretend that your organization is like an ant farm. While the farm appears to function seamlessly on the surface, there are many different tunnels that travel in different directions to help support the entire structure of the ant farm. Each ant has an objective to perform a single task, while each of the ant's jobs supports the larger goal of creating a successful ant farm. What makes this possible? The answer is clarity. Ants are natural when it comes to following orders and working toward objectives and goals. With their "see the hill—take the hill" mantra, they never stop working together until they have reached their ultimate target as shown in FIgure C1.

FIGURE C1 Dig deeper: The ant farm of clarity.

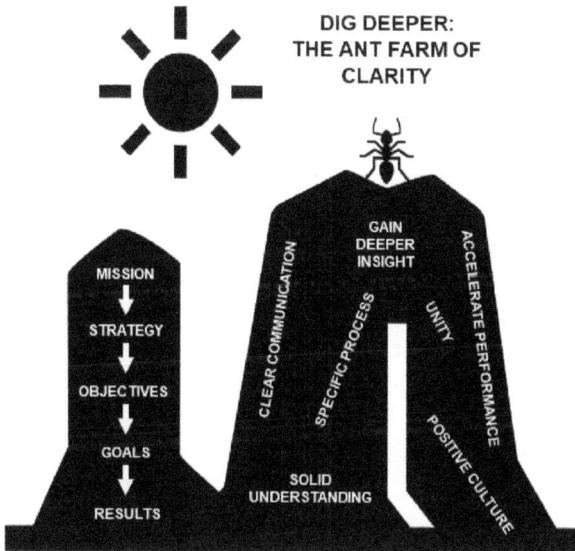

When we talk about clarity, the first thing we must do is to define the steps within the process. First, clarity is centered around the mission. A mission is something that the leader decides needs to be accomplished, and it will take everyone working together to achieve this result. This mission provides the overall goal of what the individual or company is working to achieve. How we decide to achieve this goal is called the strategy. Strategy encompasses how the individual or business sets objectives, goals, and priorities. Next, the strategy will determine what steps or actions will be taken to physically achieve the desired outcome based on politics and the use of resources. While the resources are a means to an end, the action taken determines exactly how those resources are executed to successfully complete the mission.

Next, objectives are used as milestones of smaller steps that need to be completed that will lead to the completion of the goal. An objective enables a person or business to move forward in their actions based on their chosen direction or strategy. With the use of objective, a strategic advantage will be gained to help move forward in a singular direction that is focused on the mission. Once the objectives have been determined, the goal becomes the result that guides the entire process. A goal must be SMART, meaning it should be specific, measurable, attainable, relevant, and time-bound. Each step, or objective, is based on achieving your goal. As you complete each objective, you become one step closer to reaching your goal through strategy and guided actions.

Within goal setting, there are three different types of goals to consider. The first type is performance goals. Performance goals are based on a set standard that is dictated or controlled by the individual or organization. The second type is a process goal. Process goals are based on specific processes, actions, or activities related to performance and outcomes. This type of goal is also directly controlled by the individual or business. The third type of goal is an outcome goal. Outcome goals are focused on the result and if the process led to a successful outcome. Support of the successful goal is based on the evidence where the result took place based on the strategy and objectives to support the outcome.

Finally, clarity is responsible for the key results of the success of the endeavor. Key results are achieved when there is collaboration toward a common or shared outcome that uses goal-setting techniques to overcome a challenge or achieve a new opportunity for the individual or business. One cannot have key results without an objective to first achieve. To have key results, the objectives will need to be simple and achievable. Second, they must be specific and measurable. Finally, key results should not only focus on results but should also be used to recognize and celebrate success within the strategic and systematic process.

Now let us discuss the principles of clarity. First, clarity revolves around priorities being organized and determined to be achieved within a certain time frame. To help achieve these priorities, a mantra or idea can be repeated that is used to keep everyone focused on the outcome. In the example of the ants, "see the hill—take the hill" was the mantra used to keep everyone working. However, Clare pointed out that to be successful and to achieve the goal, the new mantra had to become "see 'our' hill—take 'our' hill" based on restructured priorities that were more in line with the mission to one day reach Mount PleasANT.

The second principle of clarity is to lead by example. When creating a system, the leader is both responsible for creating the mission and helping their troops (ants) follow along so they can be successful. The leader must dedicate the necessary time and effort to achieving the set priorities along with everyone else to help build unity and to create a shared leadership model for everyone to participate in. The third principle is to eliminate the less important tasks. When the process becomes simplified, it becomes "clear" what needs to be done to achieve success. When you spend more time on smaller or insignificant tasks, critical time is taken away from the important tasks using the path-goal theory. The path-goal theory is used by the leader to find the right motivating factors that will guide individuals toward success based on their own unique style and ability to motivate workers by understanding their unique characteristics.

The fourth principle of clarity is to keep it simple and avoid mixed messages. While a leader may think their directions are clear, they may, in fact, be contradictory and can cause confusion and become counterproductive to the mission. Leaders will need to avoid mixed messages that create competing priorities and create an obscure focus or viewpoint of the mission. Like the LieutenANT, he thought his orders were clear. However, by having two different groups conduct the same function both groups of army ants were competing with one another, causing the mission to not be achieved. With any company, clarity of direction and making sure that thing is communicated as simply as possible is necessary to achieving objectives, goals, and success.

The result of clarity is to know exactly what you specifically want to accomplish or achieve. Clarity also helps the leader to determine with whom or with what will be needed to focus on the successful outcome of the mission. The first step in this process is to ensure clear communication to understand the purpose or "why" of the mission. Second, a clear and specific process is needed to help achieve small objectives and to move down the path toward the overall goal. The third step is to prevent "stalling out" during the process. Clarity should always be used to help move forward and to accelerate the performance level of everyone.

Fourth, clarity requires the ability to not just follow along but to ask courageous or brave questions. Not asking questions causes everyone to remain complacent, resulting in a lack of growth and success. However, being fearless and questioning the current paradigm will lead to a deeper understanding of insight and enable every individual to develop a responsibility of purpose and reason. The fifth step in the process of clarity is to create new positive organizational behavior and culture. When everyone works together around a shared idea or belief, the team (army of ants) will work in unison and achieve a higher level of success than they would if they were to work alone or in a silo.

The final principle is to lead with clarity of a purpose, plan, and responsibility. The purpose within clarity establishes the "why" and answers the need for the mission. Next, a plan is important to help leadership mobilize their army of workers (or ants) to achieve the goal or vision established by the leaders throughout the hierarchy of their organization. Third, responsibility must be shared throughout the entire organization to be successful. While everyone will have a specific role or function, the process is shared responsibly and requires the full support and responsibility of each member of the team. Only when everyone is working together and sharing the same idea can clarity exist within the organization's vision, mission, and organizational culture.

Now that you have dug deeper and fully understand the ANThology of clarity, it is time to go back to your ant farm and dig a new tunnel or path that leads to success. Remove all the mole hills or mountains that remain in your way. Do not be afraid to ask the necessary questions that can only lead you to a clearer understanding of the mission. Remember your mantra and work hard every day to complete your objectives and reach your goals! When you do, you will stand alongside Clare on the top of the anthill with your arms up in victory, shouting along with Clare, "I can see clearly now! Bring on my next mountain to climb!"

The ANThology of Writing an Objective and Goal

Now that you have read this book, you see the importance of having clear objectives and goals. An objective is a short-term action that is measurable and has a tangible outcome. Management relies on objectives to guide or control a process. The purpose of an objective is to achieve greater results called goals. Unlike an objective, a goal is intangible and is not measurable. Next, goals are focused on a larger purpose and the long-term vision of the leader. Third, a goal is the aim, purpose, or intention of what the leader seeks to accomplish through their mission and vision. As a result, both objectives and goals have their unique purposes but work together to help bring success to the individual and the organization.

OBJECTIVES

Purpose-driven	You will need to determine specific decisions and actions that will help move you toward the larger mission and vision.
Concept and Mindset	You will need to be able to develop a process for problem-solving through creativity and conceptual understanding of the process.
Focused and Specific	It must be very specific to include one outcome. Each outcome will be used to continue progress toward a final goal.
Tangible	You will need to create something than be accomplished and witnessed to determine achievement or success.
Measurable	It will be easy to measure and determine success through quantifiable results.
Scope and Sequence	It will be small and narrow in scope to keep the focus simple and on one thing at a time.
Timeline	There will be short-term results and with specific deadlines to achieve success before the next one can begin.
Feasible or Possible	It must be achievable to create benchmarks and milestones within a greater process.
Benefits and Outcomes	They will be used to progress you toward success and centered around the leader's goal and vision.

Key words used in writing objectives include:

- Classify
- Compare or contrast
- Demonstrate

- Describe
- Discuss or explain
- Identify or illustrate
- Locate or outline
- Recognize
- Report or restate
- Review or summarize
- Show

GOALS

Purpose driven	Are necessary to help determine what will be accomplished through a shared process and vision.
Concept and Mindset	Will require the ability to be conceptual and to understand the "bigger picture" of the leader's mission and vision.
Focused and Specific	Will be focused on mission and vision but will be unspecific since they are extensive and encompassing declarations.
Tangible	Can be both tangible and intangible in nature based on the established mission and vision that has been communicated.
Measurable	Will be hard to measure than objectives since they are based on wide-ranging visions and statements.
Scope and Sequence	Will be broad in scope and sequence since it provides the umbrella framework for all an entire decision-making or action process.
Timeline	Will be long-term and will require several steps to be accomplished before it can be completed.
Feasible or Possible	Will be feasible and possible to achieve success to create positive change in organizational behavior and culture.
Benefits and Outcomes	Must provide vision and purpose that can be achieved through the leader and follower within the organization.

Key words used in writing goals include:

- Become
- Deliver
- Diversify
- Effectively

- Efficiently
- Enhance
- Foster
- Improve
- involve
- Increase
- Keep up-to-date
- Maximize
- Reduce

The ANThology Reference

"The Army Goes Rolling Along" lyrics modified and provided by https://www.army.mil/values/song.html

A VAMPIRE IN A ZOMBIE APOCALYPSE: ENACTING CHANGE IN A COMPLACENT WORKPLACE

The Past

Vampires! During the Middle Ages, everyone in Romania was afraid of them. While there were good vampires in other cities and towns around Europe, the ones in Romania were not the same. Rumors spread to Transylvania that vampires were evil creatures that only came out at night to hunt human beings. Vampires were believed to have one objective and goal. Their objective was simple: to suck the blood from the living so they could remain part of the undead. Why, you may ask? Simply put, their goal was to live for eternity. This seemed simple enough to a vampire. However, if you were one of the living, you did not support the culture or behavior of vampires. In fact, you saw them as being represented by the dark side of leadership. They took what they wanted for themselves and gave nothing back to others.

Led by one leader or matriarch, the other vampires had to follow their command. The strategy, objectives, goals, and decision-making were all determined by the self-serving leader. The matriarch's name was Fangiella Vam Press. While she grew stronger, the rest became weaker. This was otherwise known as vampire leadership. To make matters worse, each coven or group of vampires was part of a matriarchal culture. The followers of Fangiella Vam Press were subject to her behaviors, which included egoism, individualism, and narcissism. As you can imagine, these were all undesirable behaviors that ultimately led to a poor organizational culture for all vampires in Transylvania.

VAMPIRE LEADERSHIP WILL NOT LEAD TO A POSITIVE CHANGE

The culture and behavior of vampires were so horrible that the undead decided to strike back. While a few were part of the in-group with the patriarch, most who were unwittingly turned into vampires saw themselves as part of the out-group of the vampire leadership. They knew that the matriarchal vampire could only come out at night under the light of the moon. That is when she would give the order to hunt and suck the blood of unwilling participants, making them one of them against their will. Fangiella Vam Press called her strategy "Management by Moonlight."

MANAGEMENT BY MOONLIGHT WILL NOT ALLOW THE LIGHT TO SHINE ON CHANGE

The out-group of vampires was tired of getting a bad rap based on the actions of their leader. They believed that vampires could be more than what Fangiella Vam Press allowed them to be. They knew they could be better creatures. They wanted to enact change. To stop her evil wrath and to attempt to change their behavior and culture, the out-group of vampires wanted to change their environment. One vampire, Count Alacardo, had the idea of giving the vampires in Romania a new purpose. He thought that since they would be around for eternity, they might as well have a job. Before he was turned into a vampire, Count Alacardo had graduated from Transylvania University with degrees in business management and entrepreneurship. He had always dreamed of owning and operating his own business one day. He was very reliable in school, and he was given the name "Count" since he could always be counted on.

Count Alacardo decided he would open a business and give the vampires who no longer wanted to follow the vampire leadership style of Fangiella Vam Press a better purpose in their life […] errr […] afterlife.

"What type of business would be best for vampires?" asked Count Alacardo. He thought long and hard. While he thought, he polished his fangs until they were nice and shiny. Then it hit him like a silver bullet to a werewolf.

"I've got the perfect business idea," said Count Alacardo, "that will be good for all vampires. I will build a bank. It will be called *The Blood Bank*."

Count Alacardo was very happy with himself for coming up with this idea. He had good intentions of building a business that would give vampires a great place to work. *The Blood Bank* would give the vampires a purpose that was focused on positive organizational behavior and culture. He went to work right away. While Fangiella Vam Press was busy sinking her fangs into feeding her habit, Count Alacardo was hard at work building his bank until it was built and ready for business.

The Blood Bank stood on the corner of Witches and Brew. The name "Blood Bank" was lit up in red letters. The slogan beneath it read "Where We Vant to Suck Your Blood for You." Count Alacardo opened *The Blood Bank* as a place for vampires to store their own blood so they could feast on it later and no longer had to feed on other humans and prey. He wanted to change the image of vampires so they were seen as contributors to society and had a place to call their own.

Those that worked and did business in *The Blood Bank* experienced a change in culture from Fangiella Vam Press. The employees were happy, and many of the customers wanted to work there as well. Count Alacardo was very happy to see that *The Blood Bank* had made a positive change in the lives […] or afterlives […] of the vampires. Before long, the people and vampires in Transylvania had turned on Fangiella Vam Press. The other covens of vampires around Romania had decided that Fangiella Vam Press and her vampire leadership style were no longer necessary, so they retired her. The board of vampire stakeholders called an emergency meeting and summoned Fangiella Vam Press to join them.

> **A DISENGAGED LEADER WILL LEAD TO A BAD CULTURE OR BEHAVIOR**

When she arrived, they thanked her for her service and wished her the best wishes in her future endeavors. Then they offered her a nice gift and severance package for her retirement. She was given a nice stake […] through the heart. Her job was now done. Her vampire leadership style and management by moonlight would no longer be tolerated. The vampire stakeholders did not want Fangiella Vam Press' contributions to be in vain. After all, there was a time when her methods were necessary, but those times had long since passed. The stakeholders took the remains of Fangiella Vam Press and made a generous deposit to Count Alacardo's blood bank. He kept her "contribution" to *The Blood Bank* in a special safe so he would always remember the importance of being a good leader and creating a positive organizational culture and behavior for their followers.

"We expect good things from you," said the vampire stakeholders. "We would hate to have to 'retire' you like Fangiella Vam Press if you fail to succeed. Keep up the good work."

"If not," said another one of the stakeholders, "we will raise the stakes […]"

"[…] and lower them in your heart so you can have a nice rest forever!" The sentence was finished by another one of the stakeholders.

Count Alacardo took their words to heart, literally! "I will do my best not to fail you," he said. "But more importantly, I do not want to fail my fellow vampires. Their success and well-being are very important to me. You can count on me to make a difference."

Count Alacardo bowed as they left and went back to their secret headquarters in Western Romania since they avoided anything in the East where the sun rises. "It's back to business," he said. "Chop Chop! We must work long and hard to make the stakeholders happy."

By all accounts, Count Alacardo had good intentions when he established *The Blood Bank*. He wanted to change the culture and behavior of his fellow vampires. Now that Fangiella Vam Press was gone, vampires no longer had to suffer the shameful reputation of being blood-sucking leeches and a literal "drain" on society. As time went on, Count Alacardo was able to make *The Blood Bank* successful. He had expanded its location to take over the entire block. It was filled to the brim, and every vampire was given a job to work at in the company.

IT TAKES MORE THAN GOOD INTENTIONS TO ENACT A POSITIVE CHANGE

They worked during the night and the day with Count Alacardo's special invention of sunproof shades on the windows so no sunlight would get in to burn them into vampire crisps. While his intentions were good and he thought the vampires would enjoy being surrounded by one another, he noticed a change in their behavior that altered the culture of *The Blood Bank*. Instead of the vampires being happy, they were becoming disengaged in their work. They no longer hung their fangs out at the water cooler. Instead, they drudged around the office and seemed to lose interest in their work. The purpose they once had could no longer be seen in their eyes.

WHEN THERE IS HIGH DISENGAGMENT THERE EMPLOYEES WILL BECOME ZOMBIES

The vampires spent their days and nights absentmindedly walked around the office. They constantly knocked things over and left trash and debris everywhere. Instead of keeping up the neat appearance that vampires were known for, they now dressed in tattered rags that hung from their bodies. What little color they had in their faces had drained, and they had turned white as ghosts. The vampire followers also lost any ability to have a thought or opinion. When Count Alacardo tried to have a meeting, they only replied with mindless moans and grunts. "This is hopeless," he said as he was met with even louder groans. "Meeting adjourned."

Count Alacardo looked at the clock and saw that it was midnight. He stepped outside to get a breath of fresh air. Let's face it. When vampires do not take care of themselves and are in a confined area for an extended period of time, it can start to smell pretty ripe. Count Alacardo looked up at the moon and remembered Fangiella Vam Press and feared that he had inadvertently turned into her. While he was not forcing the other vampire to go around sucking the life source out of innocent people, they were just as lost in the same type of monotony and had become deader than a doornail. The followers stopped doing their daily work or taking part in anything related to the daily routine at *The Blood bank*.

Over time, the followers of Count Alacardo became part of the out-group from the leadership team. They had been worked to death. Count Alacardo took his slogan of "We Vant to Suck Your Blood for You" too seriously and drained the lifeblood out of his own fellow vampires. Because of this, they no longer seemed to have a purpose or seemed to want to share the same positive culture and behavior he had worked to create at *The Blood Bank*.

He looked through the window and saw the vampires aimlessly wandering around, no longer willing to think or be productive. They had been reduced to rotting shambles with no mission or purpose. "The stakeholders are going to kill me," said Count Alacardo. While he knew, in most cases, that people would say that and not mean it. However, vampires meant it.

"I must do something to change things for the better. I only wanted something better for my fellow vampires. This cannot be how it ends."

Then Count Alacardo looked back through the window. He saw the vampires had gotten out of hand. They were worse than ever. There were too many of them to control. They had become like the living dead. Were they vambies? Or were they zompires? No, they had, in fact, become zombies. Count Alacardo did not know what would happen, but he knew they must not be allowed to escape until they had been returned to normal. "I hope it is not too late," said Count Alacardo with great fear and trepidation. "All I can say is…

HERE LIES YOUR

COMPANY FROM

NO CULTURE OR BEHAVIOR

The Present[...] Zombie Apocalypse!"

When things could not seem worse, they were. As Count Alacardo boarded up the door so the zombies could not escape and wreak havoc on Transylvania, a bat carrying a message arrived at *The Blood Bank*. When the bat landed on the ground, in the blink of an eye it transformed into a vampire. "Greetings from the VEOs," said the vampire. "The vampire executive officers are doing their annual check-in with your area. They have heard that things at *The Blood Bank* are not going as planned. You will have time until the next full moon to make improvements, or they will be coming here to [...]"

"Let me guess," replied Count Alacardo, "Fangiella Vam Press me."

"Yes," replied the vampire. "You will receive the golden stake to the heart of retirement."

"Vonderful news," said Count Alacardo sarcastically.

"But do not worry," said the vampire. "The VEOs sent me to help you out. They seem to think that between the two of us, we can fix things."

"That is all I wanted to do," said Count Alacardo. "My intentions were good, to help vampires have a purpose and to belong in a shared culture. To have the same positive behaviors and experiences."

"Well, you know what they say about good intentions," replied the vampire. "Believe it or not," he continued, "Fangiella Vam Press also felt as you did."

Count Alacardo and the vampire looked inside the window and saw the chaos ensuing. Zombies were everywhere, destroying everything in sight. "However," said the vampire, "if we do not pay attention to the warning signs, the culture can change, and things can get out of hand."

Count Alacardo could not disagree. It was clear that he needed help. Unlike Fangiella Vam Press, he recognized that he could not do it alone. After all, it was not about him. It was about each vampire at *The Blood Bank*.

"I could use some help," said Count Alacardo.

"The VEOs are glad to hear that," said the vampire. "They want you to succeed. They sent me to help. As a great vampire once said, 'You can COUNT on me to help make a difference.'"

"That sounds familiar," replied Count Alacardo. "I hope that I still can."

"Everyone makes a difference," replied the vampire. "It is only a matter of whether the difference is positive or negative. That is what makes great leadership different from vampire leadership in terms of culture and behavior."

"So, let's get to work," said the vampire, "but first let me introduce myself. I am Dr. Acula Vam Pyre. I graduated first in my class from Transylvania University, where I earned my VhD and studied how to create a strong V(ampire)ision and mission to help any business succeed. While we live for eternity, most businesses do not. Now, let's work together to help raise your business from the dead."

"I vant the blood bank to succeed again," replied Count Alacardo, "and for my v(ampire)employees to return to their old happy selves."

"Then we have already begun the first stage of the process," replied Dr. Acula Vam Pyre.

"What is the first stage?" asked Count Alacardo.

"It is simple," replied Dr. Acula Vam Pyre, "to be willing to enact change within your business to improve culture and behavior for the good of your vemployees."

"I think I understand," said Count Alacardo. "Change is important since it can lead to new positive situations. If I am willing to enact change, then we can have a competitive advantage and improve the knowledge, skills, and abilities of the zombies [...] errr [...] I mean vampires. It is my job to motivate them, so they continue to grow and not become dead inside."

> ## YOU MUST BE WILLING TO CHANGE IF YOU ARE TO CHANGE THE CULTURE AND BEHAVIOR

"You hit the nail on the head," replied Dr. Acula Vam Pyre.

"Thank you for the clarity," said Count Alacardo, "but could we not say nail on the head? You know how vampires feel about those."

"Fair point," replied Dr. Acula Vam Pyre. "I will enact change and listen to what you need. I value your voice."

"So now that we know that we have to enact change," asked Count Alacardo, "how do we start the process of improving the culture and behavior at *The Blood Bank*?"

"It is going to take hard work," replied Dr. Acula Vam Pyre. "Let's begin by unlocking those doors and getting our hands dirty alongside the zombies [...] errr [...] vampires."

"Are you sure you want to do that?" asked Count Alacardo.

"Absolutely," replied Dr. Acula Vam Pyre. "To enact change, the leader must share their vision and mission with those who follow them. Followers want to make their leader proud and work hard for them. If they do not, it might be because they do not know what the objectives and goals of the leader are. When is the last time you let your employees know your vision and mission?"

> LEADERS MUST SHARE THEIR VISION AND MISSION IF THEY HOPE TO ENACT A POSITIVE CHANGE

"I told them the first day we opened *The Blood Bank*," replied Count Alacardo. "Since then, I just assumed they knew."

"Since vampires live forever," said Dr. Acula Vam Pyre, "it can be easy to forget. Also, objectives and goals will change over time."

"I see your point," replied Count Alacardo. "I need to let my followers know what they are working toward so they can remain motivated. I am ready to sink my teeth into this problem."

Count Alacardo then took the lock off the door and went inside with Dr. Acula Vam Pyre. "Attention," said Count Alacardo, "I would like to thank you for working at *The Blood Bank* and making it a success. It could not have been possible without your hard work and dedication. Let's remember that our objective is to keep the business open and to help our fellow vampires. Our goal is to always have a great place to work that provides a service to our community members for eternity. I want to share this vision and mission with you so we can work together to succeed and improve ourselves as well as those around us."

When Count Alacardo had stopped speaking, he noticed that the door was left open behind him. He thought the zombies would walk out and escape. To his surprise, none of them did. While most continued to move about aimlessly, some of them seemed to listen to what he was saying. They still acted like zombies, but Count Alacardo began to see a small change in them.

"What's the next step?" asked Count Alacardo.

"Next," replied Dr. Acula Vam Pyre, "is accountability."

Count Alacardo thought back to when he hired each of his vemployees. He had given them all a job description but did not really explain what it meant or why each one of them was important. "I think I understand," said Count Alacardo. "Leaders and followers must share equal responsibility in decision-making, performance, and behaviors. As the leader, it is my job to set an example. Let me see if I can remove this nail from the coffin and rectify this situation, if you will."

"Attention," continued Count Alacardo, "I would like you to know that I rely on each one of you. Each of you is an important part of *The Blood Bank*. I want you to know that I am committed to being a good leader to you and know you all are good vemployees to me. I give you my word that from now on there will be shared leadership and responsibility in each action of *The Blood Bank*. After all, it cannot be possible without you. If we are all committed to each other, *The Blood Bank* will remain for eternity, and we will have success."

> **BOTH THE LEADER AND FOLLOWER MUST BE**
> **ACCOUNTABLE IN THE CHANGE PROCESS**

"Good speech," replied Dr. Acula Vam Pyre. He watched as more of the followers began to listen once again to Count Alacardo. They stopped destroying things and trying to eat each other's brains (since that is what zombies do). Some of the followers began doing small tasks around *The Blood Bank* like they used to do. All it took was a little reminding, encouraging, and accountability.

"We are on a roll," said Count Alacardo. "What is the next step?"

"This one is a difficult one," replied D. Acula Vam Pyre, "but not impossible. You must now become a visible advocate of the organizational culture and behavior that you want them to follow."

"You mean they must see me in action so they will know what they should do?" asked Count Alacardo.

"Exactly," replied Dr. Acula Vam Pyre.

Count Alacardo knew he had to be brave. He walked in between the zombified vampires and did not let their behavior bother him. He remained calm and confident. He could feel his followers watching him. He knew it was important for them to see him dressed neatly in his cape and to focus on his job. He did not get distracted by the chaos around him. When some of the zombies saw this, they knew they could do the same. They did not have to be like everyone else. They began to remember their human [...] err [...] vampire worth and capital. Count Alacardo and Dr. Acula Vam Pyre watched as more of the zombies began to clean up their appearance. Some slicked back their hair so it was no longer unruly, and they tucked in their torn clothes and put their capes back on while the rest still seemed lost in Zombieland.

REMEMBER THAT HUMAN CAPITAL IS AN IMPORTANT PART OF CULTURE AND BEHAVIOR

While not every follower was changing, Count Alacardo was happy to see the positive changes in some of them. He knew if they could change, the rest could too. He would not give up hope. If they could not count on him, then who could they turn to? "Let's keep going," said Count Alacardo. "We only have until the next full moon, and it will be here before we know it."

"You must figure out what parts of the culture and behavior can remain as part of *The Blood Bank* and what must absolutely be changed," said Dr. Acula Vam Pyre.

Count Alacardo thought about what he had just learned. "When changing the current culture," said Count Alacardo, "it must be made clear what must absolutely be changed by the leader while having the followers help determine what else might be included in the change process."

Count Alacardo knew that it was his job to provide the structure and guidance for the others to follow. "Fellow Blood Bankers," he said, "I need your help. We need to change the culture and behavior of our beloved *Blood Bank*. As the leader, I expect us all to support *The Blood Bank* in our decision-making and actions. If one of us does not do our job, none of us can do our job. From now on, we will all respect one another and share in the responsibility of being successful. We will show up to work on time and help one another out so we never turn on one another."

"Lyle," shouted Count Alacardo, "this means you too!"

Lyle was trying to eat Gwendolyn's brain out of the back of her head when she was not looking but instantly stopped. Lyle saw the other zombies looking at him, and he did not want to let them down. He grunted, which Count Alacardo took to be an apology.

Lyle patted Gwendolyn on the head and stood still. "That's better, Lyle," said Count Alacardo.

"As I was saying," continued Count Alacardo, "you are here to work for me, and I am here to work for you. Together we are *The Blood Bank*. If you have any suggestions or ideas you think would help make us successful, please share them in this suggestion box. I value your feedback."

Count Alacardo placed the box in the center of the room. He saw a zombie grab something to write with. They ripped off part of their tattered shirts to write a suggestion on and stuck it in the box. When the zombie placed it in the box, Count Alacardo was glad to see others doing the same thing. However, he would have preferred if the zombies used paper instead of their old, smelly rags, but it was a start. He decided to celebrate the small steps that would lead to improvement. The important thing was that his followers were becoming motivated to make a positive change at *The Blood Bank*. Count Alacardo would make sure to value their feedback and to read each of their suggestions and try to make them possible if it did not interfere with the new shared vision.

> **FEEDBACK IS NECESSARY IN ENACTING POSITIVE CHANGE AND CREATING CULTURE AND BEHAVIOR**

"Excellent," said Dr. Acula Vam Pyre. "You are becoming a natural at enacting change in your company."

"I am excited," replied Count Alacardo. "What else can we do to make a more positive change?"

"Next," replied Dr. Acula Vam Pyre, "you can align your culture with your brand name and image."

Count Alacardo looked around *The Blood Bank*. He noticed that the image of *The Blood Bank* did not look much like a bank. It did not look like much of anything besides a playpen for zombies. He went over to the wall and plugged in a cord that lit up the sign that said *The Blood Bank* and the slogan beneath it that said "Where We Vant to Suck Your Blood for You." When the red lights came on, the zombies stopped dead in their tracks. They were awestruck by the bright sign. Some began to remember what it meant and what it stood for.

Count Alacardo went around and gave everyone a new name tag with the company logo on it. The name tags were in the shape of blood drops with their names in the middle of them. He even put one on himself. "When you wear these," said Count Alacardo, "you are part of *The Blood Bank*. You are part of the brand image."

The zombies liked their new name tags. They pointed and grunted at each other as they tried to say each other's name. When they all wore the name tags, all the zombies began to feel like they were part of a team and began to work together again. They smiled as much as a zombie could smile and began to feel proud to be part of the team.

> ## ALWAYS CONNECT YOUR BRAND NAME OR IMAGE TO YOUR CULTURE AND BEHAVIOR

"The name tags were a hit," replied Dr. Acula Vam Pyre. "It amazes me what even a small thing such as that can do to help motivate and improve performance in a workplace."

"I agree," replied Count Alacardo. "The name tags bring everyone together while also making each person unique by showing their individual name. This works to help the person and the company be recognized at the same time!"

With each change that was made, the zombies began to act more like their vampire selves. However, there was still some work to be done, and the next full moon was in a few days, leaving not much time. "What do I do next?" asked Count Alacardo.

"You mean what do *WE* do next?" replied Dr. Acula Vam Pyre.

"Yes," responded Count Alacardo, "I mean we. This is a shared effort to make positive changes."

"What *WE* must do next is to measure the efforts of the team to see how effective and efficient they are in their performance." Since they had been zombies, the followers did not get any work done. In fact, they had done more work for Count Alacardo, causing the business to undisputedly fall into disrepair. "You will need to develop targets and metrics for each follower so they will know how they are doing."

> ## IT TAKES "WE" TO BE EFFECTIVE EAND EFFICENT IN ENACTING A POSITIVECHANGE

At first, Count Alacardo thought about painting targets on the backs of the zombies that were still not responding to the changes. *One good silver arrow will solve this problem*, he thought. Then he remembered that he was also responsible for the mess they were in. He wanted a second chance to fix things, so all his followers also deserved one. Count Alacardo quickly dismissed the notion of using his zombified followers as target practice and went about making target metrics for each person. He went around and gave each person their metric and then observed their behavior. Those who completed the task got a Bloody Nose cherry soda to drink. "That hits the spot," said one of the zombies, using more words than grunts.

When the other zombies saw it, they wanted one too. Each zombie worked hard until everyone was drinking their Bloody Nose sodas. Count Alacardo was happy to see that everyone was happy and was able to be rewarded for their hard work and contributions to *The Blood Bank*. He wanted to keep the success going. When a target was met, he continued to reward them with different treats that motivated them internally and externally to continue not only working hard for their own success but to help support the mission and vision of *The Blood Bank*. Count Alacardo was careful not to rush the change process in each follower. Instead, he got to know each one and worked with them so they could learn at their own pace or help one another. Short-term objectives would lead to the completion of long-term goals. Dr. Acula Vam Pyre was tickled red to see this since he knew this strategy would help bring everyone together to enact change in their culture and behavior.

> **YOU CANNOT RUSH CHANGE. IT WILL TAKE TIME TO GET EVERYONE ON BOARD**

"There are only two more steps to go," stated Dr. Acula Vam Pyre.

"That is good news," replied Count Alacardo. "There are only two more nights until the full moon."

"Haste makes waste," said Dr. Acula Vam Pyre. "What we must do now is what we can now instead of putting things off for the future."

At first, Count Alacardo was confused by this. Being a vampire meant he could live forever. They literally had all the time in the world. But then he understood what Dr. Acula Vam Pyre was saying. "Even though we have an infinite amount of time, we should always be productive," said Count Alacardo. "The more we get done today, the more changes we can make in the future. I may never have everything I wish to have right now, but if I do not do things now, I will definitely not have the extra resources later."

> ## THERE WILL NEVER BE A "PERFECT" TIME TO ENACT ORGTANIZATIONAL CHANGE

Count Alacardo went over to the wall and wrote a list of things to get done for the night on his red board. He wrote down goals that they could do to help ensure that positive change would happen in the future. The zombies read the list and knew that each one could help them. The list was for the leader and followers to:

- Be specific in their decisions and actions.
- Be measurable in its level of impact or success.
- Be achievable in their individual and shared work.
- Be realistic in getting done what they can each day.
- Be timely with results and feedback to make new changes.

By having this belief, Count Alacardo provided simple changes to make each day that would lead to new changes in the future. As a result, the zombies were able to determine what goals they felt they could achieve and had the flexibility to work on the areas that they needed most. Not only did this help them to grow individually, but they also became a stronger team. With the use of these change processes, most of the zombies had already begun to change back to their old vampire selves, and without a moment to spare. There was still one more change to make, and only one night left to do it before the VEOs would arrive to evaluate his leadership and success of *The Blood Bank*.

"We have made excellent progress," said Dr. Acula Vam Pyre. "There is only one last thing to do to enact an everlasting positive change in the behavior and culture of *The Blood Bank*.

"Please do tell me what I have to do," replied Count Alacardo.

"The final step," replied Dr. Acula Vam Pyre, "is to be bold and lead the change process. Leaders are responsible for leading the change process. It is not good enough to only 'say' something. Instead, you must also 'do' something."

Count Alacardo thought back to Fangiella Vam Press and her management by moonlight vampire leadership style. She said what she wanted done and expected everyone else to do the work for her. He did not want to be like that. Count Alacardo wanted to be the person they "counted" on the most.

"While it is important for me to both 'say' and 'do' to set an example," said Count Alacardo, "real change happens from all levels within *The Blood Bank*. Each follower is an agent of change. Each follower is an extremely valuable resource to the company based on their knowledge, skills, and abilities. All the followers must share the responsibility of enacting change to improve the organizational behavior and culture."

"Getting the followers to do that is the blood-red cherry on top," replied Dr. Acula Vam Pyre. "How will you do this?"

"I will give them something to sink their teeth into," replied Count Alacardo. "I will start by not making my employees work non-stop around the clock. We can both work hard and play hard. I will celebrate each employee and give each workday a theme that will make working fun again at *The Blood Bank*. First, the followers will get time off so they can recharge their blood batteries and will want to work hard. I will also create a break room called *Coffin Corner* for everyone to use. Next, we will have a theme for every day of the week based on the feedback from the followers. Looking at the suggestion box, we have great ideas that include Maniacal Mondays, Terrifying Tuesdays, Wicked Wednesdays, Long in the Tooth Thursdays, and Fangtastic Fridays."

> **LEADERS MUST BE BOLD AND BE THE CHANGE CHAMPION FOR THEIR FOLLOWERS**

"Those are all excellent ideas," replied Dr. Acula Vam Pyre. "I think you should share them with your followers and see how they react."

"There is no time like the present to make changes," said Count Alacardo. He shared his ideas with the zombies, and they all began to grunt and cheer. Then he noticed something amazing. The zombies began to change. They became zompires, to vambies, and then back to full-fledged vampires. The positive change had been enacted and it showed. They were a team once again. "I am glad to have everyone back," said Count Alacardo. "I see that change is not an easy process to undertake. It is important that we continue to make changes to help us all move forward."

The crowd of vampire followers agreed. "Tomorrow night is a new beginning," said Count Alacardo. "Take the day off so we can start fresh."

The vampires went home for the first time in a long time, where they got their much-needed rest. When the sun went down, the vampires then returned proudly wearing their blood drop name tags to *The Blood Bank*, where they saw Count Alacardo and Dr. Acula Vam Pyre waiting for them.

"Welcome to the new *Blood Bank*," shouted Count Alacardo, "where we bank on you making a difference! To show you how much you are appreciated, we have gone to *Stake and Bake* to get all of you your favorite food and dessert. Steak tartare and blood pudding for each of you."

The vemployees were happy and enjoyed the new changes in behavior and culture at *The Blood Bank*. After devouring their food, they went right to work singing the song "I'm a Vampire."

> *"I never age and I'll never die*
> *Unlike all the stars in the sky*
> *I'll be young forever*
> *But why?*
> *Cause I'm a vampire"*

Count Alacardo and the other vampires were all working so hard that he did not realize that the full moon had appeared in the sky or that the VEOs had come into *The Blood Bank*. When he saw them, Count Alacardo put his finger inside his shirt collar, which was feeling tighter by the minute. Dr. Acula Vam Pyre introduced the VEOs to him.

"So, this is the infamous *Blood Bank*," said one of the VEOs. "It definitely lives up to its expectations."

Count Alacardo was not sure if that was a good thing or a bad thing. Was she referring to the zombie apocalypse or something else? *Would this be where I get my retirement stake through the heart?* he wondered.

"We always try to meet and exceed expectations," replied a nervous Count Alacadro, "by changing with the times."

"I like what I hear," replied the VEO, "and more importantly, I like what I see. You have very happy workers and *The Blood Bank*. I am very happy with your progress here. Would you mind helping us open more *Blood Banks* across Romania?"

"As long as I can take Dr. Acula Vam Pyre with me," replied Count Alacardo. "WE make a great team."

"That sounds like a great idea," replied the VEOs. "Vampires can all learn a lot about change from you both. We must get back to Romania to discuss some other business. Time flies."

With that, the VEOs turned into bats and flew off into the moonlight. "Well, it looks like we did it," said Count Alacardo. "It would not have been possible without you."

"Or without them," replied Dr. Acula Vam Pyre as he gestured to all of the vampires who worked with them.

"Nothing would be possible without them," admitted Count Alacardo. "WE all make a good team and will be responsible for enacting change in behavior and culture wherever life […] or the afterlife […] takes us."

ENACTING CHANGE IN CULTURE AND BEHAVIOR CANNOT BE ACCOMPLISHED WITHOUT TEAMWORK

The Future

Count Alacardo and Dr. Acula Vam Pyre went all around Romania and Europe. Together, they opened many different branches of blood banks for vampires. With their efforts, they enacted positive changes in culture and behavior wherever they went. Through their hard work, Count Alacardo and Dr. Acula Vam Pyre transformed Romania into one of the major change agents of the world. Instead of being considered an old, decrepit haunted town, it was now a popular tourist attraction. People from all over the world came to hear them give inspirational seminars on enacting the change process within any organization to develop positive behavior and culture. Today, Count Alacardo and Dr. Acula Vam Pyre have written the best seller, *The Positive Vampire in Me: The True Story of Changing Myself for You*. Their book is currently used as a professional development tool for organizations everywhere around the world. They currently reside on the beach, soaking up the sun since they learned to enact change and adapt to their new environment, enjoying positive behavior and culture with all those around them.

> ## ENACTING CHANGE IS AN ONGOING PROCESS. THE POSSIBLIITIES ARE ENDLESS IN THE FUTURE WITH A SHARED POSITIVE CULTURE AND BEHAVIOR

SINKING YOUR FANGS INTO ENACTING CHANGE AND IMPROVING ORGANIZATIONAL CULTURE AND BEHAVIOR

You have just completed reading the parable about *A Vampire in a Zombie Apocalypse: Enacting Change in a Complacent Workplace.* As you followed along with Dr. Acula Vam Pyre, you learned that enacting change is a very important component of a leader within the workplace. While the story touched on many of the main principles, we must now dig our fangs deeper into understanding how enacting change and improving organizational culture and behavior will improve the workplace. No matter what goods or service industry your business is in, it will follow a systematic process that relies on energetic and dedicated leaders and followers that fully embrace the organizational behavior and culture.

We will pretend that your organization is like The Blood Bank. While the Blood Bank was successful in the beginning, over time it fell into ruin and decay. Employees became zombies from a lack of energy and motivation. This situation caused them to no longer be embraced by the organizational culture and behavior. Each employee must be appreciated and valued for their strengths. Next, each employee must be challenged in their work. Third, leaders must invest in their employees to enact change and to strengthen organizational behavior and culture. If you can successfully enact change, your zombies will become living employees again, leading to an improved shared culture that will help make your organization relevant in the future.

The most difficult objective an organization will face is enacting change. Change is important within any business since it can lead to new positive situations. The second advantage of enacting change is that it helps retain a competitive advantage or edge in your industry market. Third, change will help to improve the knowledge, skills, and abilities of both leadership and employees so they can continue to grow and experience personal and professional advantages that would otherwise not be available to them. Fourth, change will help the individual and the company remain relevant in their respective business environment so they can continue to experience success instead of failure.

Change will encourage innovation. Innovation is necessary in adjusting policies, procedures, culture, and behavior. Change will lead to the development of skills. Improved skills of each leader and employee will be used to strengthen their support and to get them to become part of the "in group" of the organizational behavior and culture. Third, change will develop leaders and employees to work together to share responsibility and voice in new business opportunities. Finally, change will improve the morale of the organization. When enacting a positive change, the company will adopt new and diverse ideas that will commit everyone in the organization to working together to adopt an inclusive culture and behavior that supports their objectives, goals, and success.

When improving organizational behavior and culture, there are several steps that can be taken to strengthen the buy-in and support of everyone. The first step is to define the values and behaviors that are required or desired to be shared throughout the organization. Organizational values are the principles created by the leadership that guide the purpose and mission of the company. The values will help to manage and gauge the interactions between the leader and follower in both the internal and external environments. Next, the values will be used to help people understand the daily interactions between one another and how those interactions are translated into specific actions throughout the hierarchy. As a result, values are shared at the low, middle, and top levels of a company and are expressed in the organizational culture and behavior.

Next, organizational behavior and culture must be directly aligned with the processes and strategy of the company. The mission, vision, and values will need to be communicated and understood so that each person knows what is expected of them. With a shared vision, the leader and followers will be more closely connected and inspired to achieve a common purpose or goal. With an effective vision, clarity in decision-making and actions will guide each person in their daily duties within the organization. As a result, the vision of the leader will define how people should behave and will form the basis of the culture within the company.

Third, organizational culture and behavior must instill accountability. Accountability means that both the leadership and employees share equal responsibility for their decision-making, performance, and behaviors. When there is shared responsibility, each person is accountable for what they did or did not do. As a result, there will be an increase in employee commitment to the organizational culture, which will cause an increase in performance levels throughout the hierarchy of the business.

The fourth step is to have accessible and visible advocates of the organizational culture and behavior. For change to be enacted through culture, it must start from the top. The leadership team will need to make their vision and expectations a priority for everyone, including themselves, to follow. Next, the leadership will also need to recognize their human capital as its greatest asset to ensure that they are included in any changes for the future. The leader will need to provide a structure or framework that will help to share their vision and provide a structure so everyone will have the opportunity achieve success.

The fifth step is to define what is negotiable to remain and what must be changed. When changing the current culture, it must be made clear what must absolutely be changed along with what might be able to be included. While it is hard to make this type of decision, the leader is required to provide guidance and a structure for employees to follow. By stating these guidelines, it becomes clear what can be expected. However, it also enables employees to have a say in other areas of the culture. This situation helps the employees to become part of the change process through trust and shared leadership.

The sixth step is to align your culture with your company brand or image. Whether or not your company sells a product or service, it is built on strong brand recognition and an easily memorable brand name or image. When culture is changed to be structured around brand recognition, the target audience or niche market will become more loyal. Brand recognition and organizational culture will create a shared relationship that fosters diversity and cultural innovation in both internal and external customer experiences.

The seventh step is to measure your efforts effectively and efficiently. Metrics will need to be determined and implemented to see the success of everyone within the organization. When implementing change, the greatest source of information and perceived success is received through employee feedback. Feedback will enable the leadership team to hear from their followers about what is going right, along with what needs to be improved. When employees can use their voice, it enables them to be heard. This situation will increase employee engagement and make them feel more valued. As a result, feedback will help the business to determine what gaps there are between actual and desired results, creating a positive change in organizational behavior.

The eighth step is to not rush the change process. Most people fear change and will be slow to want to deviate from what they are currently doing. This situation will cause the process of enacting change to take time and become a long-term goal instead of a short-term objective. Organizational culture and behavior will not change immediately since it was not created in one day. The initial belief and buy-in will take time to establish and create. When change happens, you must repeat this process. It is important to remember to give individuals time to adjust. You do not want to rush change and create chaos and inconsistency within your organization. When change is intentional, the leader should set benchmarks and milestones that create achievable objectives that will lead to the completion of the overall goal. As a result, enacting change is a process that should provide a direct and logical rationale about why the company must enact the change process, and how it will improve the organizational culture and behavior.

The ninth step is to invest in the change process today instead of putting it off until the future. Most companies will suffer from a lack of resources or staff. This situation can cause a company to want to make changes but to hold off doing anything about it by saying, "One day I will have the necessary resources and people to make this change." With this belief, the leader will never make a change since they may never get what they are hoping to have. This situation makes it important to make the change now with the resources and staff you currently have, so it will lead to future changes within the organization. As a result, the changes made now will be used to enact future positive changes in organizational behavior and culture.

The final step is to be bold and lead the change process. Leaders establish the vision and mission of the company. Through the vision and mission, leaders will be able to encourage and motivate by putting their decision-making into action. By not only "saying" but also "doing," leaders will provide an example for the employees to follow. However, change does not have to come only from people who hold high positions of power within the organizational hierarchy. Instead, change can be enacted by any agent within the company. Since individuals are the company's most valuable resource, each can influence others based on their knowledge, skills, and abilities. As a result, each person within the organizational hierarchy shares the responsibility of enacting change and improving organizational behavior and culture.

SINKING YOUR FANGS INTO THE ENACTING CHANGE PROCESS

Now that you have read this book, you see the importance of enacting change and improving organizational culture and behavior. Change is the catalyst for future opportunities and success. The purpose of enacting change is to improve and strengthen organizational behavior and culture through shared leadership and voice. When there is shared leadership, there will be an increase in trust and responsibility between the leader and the followers. This situation will cause everyone to work together to have a stronger bond and connection when enacting change to experience shared success. Enacting the change process will keep both the individual and organization accountable in their decision-making and actions. As a result, enacting change will make both the individual and the company invest in themselves to increase the value in their behavior and culture.

STEPS FOR ENACTING POSITIVE CHANGE

- Encourage and invite each person within the organization to be an active participant in the cultural and behavioral change process.
  - People need and want to be heard.
  - Their voices drive their behavior and attitudes.
  - Provide methods of feedback to share their thoughts, opinions, and feelings.
- Develop a trusting environment and process for individuals to share their thoughts through.
  - Surveys.
  - Comments.
  - Open forums.
  - Open-door policies.
  - 360-degree feedback.
- Verify that thoughts and feelings are heard.
  - Qualitative data.
  - Quantitative data.
  - Eliminate bias.
  - Facilitate communication.
  - Feedback and follow-up.
- Explain the "who, what, where, when, why, and how" of the need for change.
  - Address the reason behind change.
  - Answer the "What's in it for me?" question.
  - Analyze different outcomes and needs of diverse populations.
- Share your leadership vision and mission.
  - Visualize your objectives and goals.
  - Explain importance of shared leadership.
  - Encourage support and commitment.
- Involve everyone with how they can help support and lead change.
  - Explain it's a long journey and everyone will reach the destination together.
  - Explain importance of performing normal duties but also consider how to direct new change.
  - Share progress reports and status updates.
  - Get collective feedback for the team.
  - Continually engage all individuals to work collaboratively to support positive organizational culture and behavior.

**STEPS TO CHANGE CULTURE
AND BEHAVIOR**

- Develop a sense of motivation and purpose for both the individual and organization.
- Embrace the diversity of everyone in the workplace
- Use societal values and critical thinking skills that support future growth.
- Promote the psychological safety and well-being of everyone.
- Create a sense of belonging for the leadership and followers.
- Set clear rules and define expectations.
- Praise the positive results of decision-making and actions.
- Provide challenge, rigor, and support to individuals to ensure success.
- Adjust or change perspectives to support future needs.
- Revamp or modify expectations for objectives and goals.
- Intercede only to only support positive behavior and culture.
- Implement restorative disciplinary actions based on vision and mission.

A VAMPIRE IN A ZOMBIE
APOCALYPSE REFERENCE

INDEX

www.ingramcontent.com/pod-product-compliance
Lightning Source LLC
Chambersburg PA
CBHW031416180326
41458CB00002B/394